SHELTERING THE JEWS

SHELTERING THE JEWS

Stories of Holocaust Rescuers

Mordecai Paldiel

Foreword by Franklin H. Littell

Fortress Press
Minneapolis

To Rachel–
affectionately

SHELTERING THE JEWS
Stories of Holocaust Rescuers

Cover and text designed by Joseph Bonyata.

Cover and text photos courtesy of Yad Vashem, Jerusalem. Used by permission. Photo of Varian Fry courtesy of United States Holocaust Memorial Museum Archives; Cynthia Jaffe McCabe Papers. Used by permission.

Cover photos (clockwise from top left): Anna Bogdanowicz, Oskar Schindler, Sarah Melezin, Sempo Sugihara, Hetty Voute, Cornelia Blaauw, Giorgio Perlasca, Raoul Wallenberg, Paul Grüninger, Arnold Douwes, Adelaide Hautval, Max Liedtke, Rev. Bruno Reynders with children.

Library of Congress Cataloging-in-Publication Data

Paldiel, Mordecai
Sheltering the Jews : stories of Holocaust rescuers / Mordecai Paldiel
p. cm.
Includes bibliographical references and index.
ISBN 0-8006-2897-7 (alk. paper)
1. Holocaust, Jewish (1939–1945) 2. Righteous Gentiles in the Holocaust. 3. World War, 1939–1945–Jews–Rescue. I. Title.
D804.3.p36 1995 95-44541
940.53'18–dc20 CIP

The paper used in this publication meets the minimum requirements of American National Standard for Information Sciences–Permanence of Paper for Printed Library Materials. ANSI Z329.4-1984.

Manufactured in the U.S.A. AF 1-2897

00 99 98 97 96 1 2 3 4 5 6 7 8 9 10

Contents

Foreword Franklin H. Littell	*vii*
1. Introduction	1
2. Hiding and Sheltering Conditions	11
3. The Art of Passing	49
4. Movement from Place to Place	61
5. Children on the Run	103
6. Special Rescue Stories	125
7. Dangers of Detection	159
8. The Significance of the "Righteous" Deeds	186
Appendix: The Righteous among the Nations at Yad Vashem	*203*
Notes	*207*
Bibliography	*212*
Index	*217*

Foreword

Franklin H. Littell

Mordecai Paldiel has held for more than a decade the best listening post in the world for identifying and honoring rescuers of Jews during the Holocaust: he has been director of the office at Yad Vashem in Jerusalem dealing with "the Righteous among the Nations." In that office he has heard and/or read all of the records, prepared the analyses and rejections or recommendations for the final decision of the public committee, and himself led many of the services in which the rescued and rescuers celebrate their reunion in Jerusalem.

Himself a "hidden child," although he holds a doctorate in Holocaust Studies from Temple University he has never let his scientific interest drown out his human compassion and sensibility.

No one is in a better position than Dr. Paldiel to select the tales that need to be told about sacrifice and heroism among the gentiles (including some Christians) who—in the belly of the beast—defied the killing machines of the Nazi Third Reich. In addition to moving stories about persons, his keen analysis of the factors that made rescue dangerous, difficult, and heroic contributes substantially to our understanding of life and death in Hitler's Europe.

When Dr. Paldiel was doing his graduate work in Holocaust Studies at Temple University, he wrote one of his major papers on "Hitlerism and Manichaeism." In it he showed how a strange vision of a cosmos in which the forces of good and evil—of light and dark—are pitted in mortal combat, equal in strength and with the outcome still uncertain, informed the Führer's view of history. The ancient Manichaean religion, rejected as heresy by some church fathers and totally repudiated by others, reappeared in the modern age in the Nazi dictator's ferocity against the Jews. In his view the Jews were an all-pervasive power of evil, to be eradicated by sacrificing if necessary all other political and military goals and even the German nation itself.

Those who risked sheltering the Jews, if they were religiously articulate, believed that in human history the decisive victory of the Good had already been set in place, if they were simply upright human beings and understood their identity in their quality of humanness (*Menschlichkeit*).

A great read for its stories, Mordecai Paldiel's book also displays profound wrestling with human identity in life and death.

For this reason was man created alone;
To teach that whosoever destroys a single soul,
It is as though he had destroyed an entire world.
And whosoever preserves a single soul,
It is as though he had preserved an entire world. . . .
Therefore every single person is obliged to say:
The world was created for my sake.

—*Jerusalem Talmud Sanhedrin:* 23a–b

No man is an island, entire of itself.
Every man is a place of the continent,
A part of the main. . . .
Any man's death diminishes me.
Because I am involved in mankind.
And therefore never send to know
for whom the bell tolls;
It tolls for thee.

—John Donne, *Devotions* 17

Chapter 1

Introduction

For 12 years, during which time the Nazis expanded their rule across Europe, Jews everywhere were subjected to intense persecution and eventually to extermination. Beginning in 1933, with Adolf Hitler's accession to power in Germany, the machinery of destruction was set in motion. It began with the passing of special laws that, in quick succession, disenfranchised the Jews of their civic rights, segregated them from the rest of the population, and robbed them of their economic livelihoods. With the start of World War II in 1939, the Nazis passed to more extreme methods, which eventually took the form of a plan for the murder of all of Europe's Jews. The actual mass killings began in the summer of 1941, with unprecedented shootings of tens of thousands of men, women, and children in front of open pits. Not satisfied with the killing pace, the Nazis quickly came up with a more efficient and "clean" murder method: gas vans and gas chambers. Specially constructed death camps (such as Auschwitz, Treblinka, Sobibor, and Belzec) were built, mostly on Polish soil, where the unsuspecting victims were brought by train. This program of murder of innocent persons, officially approved at the highest level of the German government, culminated in the deaths of six million Jews.

Persons who tried to save Jews from falling into Nazi hands were punished with unprecedented severity. In

Eastern Europe, such "offenders" faced the death penalty; in Western Europe, helpers of Jews were carted off to concentration camps, where many perished. Non-Jews who, in spite of the risks to themselves, helped Jews survive the Holocaust (the term used for the Nazi mass murder of European Jews) are conferred the title of "Righteous among the Nations" by Yad Vashem, the Israel national Holocaust memorial in Jerusalem.

The term "Righteous among the Nations" has deep roots in Jewish tradition. It already appears in the sayings of the rabbis of the talmudic period (first and second centuries C.E.), though its meaning was not precisely defined. In the twelfth century, Maimonides, the great Jewish philosopher, theologian, and codifier of the *halacha* (Jewish religious law), defined this term as referring to non-Jews who followed certain minimal norms of just behavior (also known as the seven precepts of Noah's descendants), which included the prohibition against shedding innocent blood. Another, more popular, interpretation attributed the title of "Righteous among the Nations" to non-Jews who showed exceptional favor to Jews, such as the Persian king Cyrus, who in the sixth century B.C.E. freed the Jews from their Babylonian bondage and allowed them to return to their ancestral home. In general, in both the legalistic and more popular meaning of the term, a certain moral comportment was felt to be binding on the holder of this title, with special emphasis on that person's sensitivity to the needs of others (the Maimonidean view), as well as to the welfare of the Jewish people (the popular view).

When Israel's parliament, the Knesset, called into being a national Holocaust memorial under the name of Yad Vashem, it was meant primarily to commemorate the six million Jews of Europe murdered at the hands of the Nazis and their collaborators. But the 1953 Yad Vashem law also was aimed to highlight the role of individual non-Jews who tried to save Jews from the Nazi-instigated Holocaust, and to express the appreciation of the Jewish people for their humanitarian conduct. The Knesset thereupon chose the ancient Hebrew term *Hassidei Umot Haolam* (Righteous among the Nations) to designate non-Jews who, in the legislation's wording, "risked their lives to save Jews" during the Holocaust, and obliged the newly established Yad Vashem memorial to document and honor them. The linkage between the rescue of Jews from annihilation with the risk to the life and safety of the non-Jewish rescuer has since formed the basic criterion for the attribution of the "righteous" title by Yad Vashem.

To appreciate better the significance of those termed righteous in this study, let us reflect on the setting in which non-Jewish rescuers of Jews operated. We are referring to one of the darkest periods in the annals of humankind; to the rule of a murderous regime, armed with an unprecedented ferocious machine of terror, and unabashedly displaying a total disregard of the most elemental principles of personal conduct and the rights of individual persons. The Jews were singled out for destruction for no other reason than the Nazi decree that anyone with Jewish blood in his or her veins (even a Christian by belief) was a threat to the Germanic "superior race" and had to be eliminated — men, women, and children, the elderly as well as infants. A sophisticated killing machinery was improvised, with tentacles reaching out to the far corners of the European continent, and all Jews in German-occupied countries (which by 1942 comprised almost all of Europe) found themselves trapped and condemned to oblivion. The fact that Germany was involved in a global contest that taxed all of its resources did not dim in the least the murderous intentions of the Nazi hierarchy but, paradoxically, intensified their determination to rid Europe of all Jews.

The mass killing of Jews began in the summer of 1941 in the newly conquered territories in Russia, but the ground had been carefully prepared earlier, beginning with Hitler's rise to power in 1933. By a gradual and well-calculated process, Jews were at first placed in a special category, then denied civic and economic rights. Within a few years Jews found themselves outside the pale of the law—a phenomenon unprecedented in European history for any group of people. The disenfranchising of Jews was copied in other countries overrun by German armies in World War II, at times aided by local collaborators (such as the Vichy regime in France and the pro-fascist Hlinka regime in Slovakia). By the time the killings began, Jews had already lost all civic rights; police protection was denied them and the courts were closed to them; they were at the mercy of anyone wishing them harm. Within a few short years, all Jews had been relegated to the status of a pariah people —and the world stood by, took note, and did nothing.

The Nazis followed no well-defined and comprehensive master plan but improvised and gradually intensified their methods in quick succession, within a relatively short span of years. A general pattern, however, evolved, which may be divided into two principal headings: segregation and expropriation, then deportation and killing. At first, Jews were set apart from the rest of the population through special laws and decrees, and with a few strokes of the pen all civic rights enjoyed by Jews were annulled. This was followed with the physical segregation of Jews from the rest of the population in specially designated areas (usually the least attractive streets, which in the case of Poland were walled off from the rest of the city). At the same time, Jews were deprived of most of their economic pursuits; they were either forced to sell off their holdings at ridiculously low prices, or had their property expropriated by the state.

With all Jews in Nazi-controlled lands (which by 1942 comprised Germany, Poland, the Soviet Union, France, Belgium, the Netherlands, Norway, Bohemia, Slovakia, Yugoslavia, and Greece) deprived of civic rights and livelihoods, and closeted off in specially designated areas, the Nazis were ready for the final move. For a time they equivocated, deferring a final decision. Some proposed removing all European Jews either to a distant island, such as the French-controlled Madagascar, or to a special reserve in Eastern Europe. On the eve of the invasion of the Soviet Union in June 1941, however (some historians place the date a few months later), Hitler made the fatal decision to henceforth "resolve" the Jewish issue by physical liquidation.

At first, the Nazis toyed with the idea of mass shootings, which were carried out in the newly conquered areas of the Soviet Union. When this proved not feasible (not enough Jews were being killed fast enough with the available manpower), the Nazis decided to use gas as the main killing device. New killing facilities were constructed (mainly in occupied Poland), to which Jews from all over Europe would be dispatched. These plans were finalized and synchronized in a top-level government meeting in a Berlin suburb in January 1942, known as the Wannsee conference.

Beginning with the summer of 1942, large-scale deportations moved most of Europe's Jews by cattle trains to specially constructed death camps, where most were put to death by gassing. The elderly, the young, pregnant women, the feeble-bodied, and anyone else considered by the Nazis as unfit for hard labor, hence useless, were immediately killed. The others were assigned hard labor under the most inhumane conditions, where most fell from exhaustion, starvation, disease, or brutal treatment. Only a few survived to tell the world of life in the concentration camps, life on that "other planet," in the words of one survivor.

By the end of 1942 the majority of the ancient Jewish communities in Poland, Holland, and other European countries had been consigned to the gas chambers, and most Jews in countries fully occupied by the Germans had "gone with the wind." Only in Italy and its controlled territories, as well as Hungary (up to 1944), were Jews still free from physical harm. In 1943, the ancient Jewish Greek community was devastated by the Nazis, and an attempt was made to do likewise with the Jews of Denmark. That year, too, with the capitulation of Italy, the Nazis set in motion the machinery of destruction in that country. In 1944, with the German occupation of Hungary, hundreds of thousands of that country's Jews were deported to the Auschwitz death facilities, where most were gassed on arrival. The Nazis left no stone unturned in their mad zeal to murder all of the continent's Jews. Even the ancient Jewish community on the island of Rhodes, off the Turkish coast, was affected. The island's fifteen hundred Jews were taken by boat to the

Greek mainland, thence by train to the Auschwitz gas chambers—altogether a thousand-mile trek. The operation took place in July 1944, at a time when German armies were steadily losing ground and withdrawing on all battlefronts. It is estimated that close to four million Jews met their death in the many notorious concentration camps that dotted the European landscape, but especially in conquered Poland, and some two million Jews were killed in other brutal ways, such as on-the-spot massacres before open ditches, or died as a result of malnutrition and disease. Mass shootings were orchestrated by special mobile killing units, the notorious *Einsatzgruppen,* which operated in Russia, Ukraine, and the Baltic countries. They were aided by other German military and police units as well as by pro-Nazi paramilitary formations from among the native populations.

At the same time, the Nazis made it clear that they would brook no interference with the murder of the Jewish people, an operation euphemistically termed the "Final Solution" of the Jewish question. Any segments of the conquered populations who did not see eye to eye with the Nazi method of solving the supposedly grave "Jewish problem" and, repelled by the gruesome killings, contemplated helping Jews escape the Nazi dragnet, risked severe punitive measures on themselves and their loved ones. In Poland, for instance, public bulletin boards in the major cities warned the population that either helping a Jew to escape from the ghetto or extending shelter and transportation to a Jew outside prescribed areas was a transgression punishable by death, and that no mercy would be shown to offenders. In other countries, the populations were also warned in writing or over the radio of the dire consequences to themselves of helping a Jew elude capture by the Nazis. (For more on the dangers facing rescuers, see chapter 7.)

The outside world, even nations at war with Nazi Germany, showed no exceeding zeal (to put it mildly) to help fleeing Jews reach safe haven. The great democracies maintained their stiff prewar quota systems, which allowed no more than a trickle of Jews to be admitted to their countries (witness the *Saint Louis* affair, where a boatload of more than nine hundred German Jews was refused landing on Cuban and U.S. shores and made to sail back to Europe). U.S. officials, especially in the State Department, used intricate bureaucratic procedures not only to discourage but actually to sabotage rescue operations by private agencies and organizations.[1] Palestine, the future homeland of the Jewish people, was equally shut by the British government to Jews fleeing for their lives, in order to curry favor with the Arabs, most of whom clamored for a Nazi victory. In 1939, on the eve of the war, the British government issued a policy statement that limited the influx of Jewish immigrants to Palestine to 75,000 over the next five years. This policy came at a time when hundreds of thousands who had succeeded fleeing from the Nazis were desperately looking for a safe haven, if only on a temporary basis. Neutral Switzerland, for reasons of its own, also shut its borders to Jewish refugees, and not a few who had managed to outwit the frontier guards and make it across into Switzerland were unceremoniously shoved back into German-occupied France and left to the mercy of the Gestapo and the French police. Inside German-dominated Europe, the churches with few exceptions remained silent, and many even applauded this ferocious onslaught against a people whose religious teachings and scriptures formed the basis for the Christian church's own ethos.

Were a person from another planet to survey the situation of the Jews in mid-1943 in those countries directly occupied by the Germans, he or she would be surprised, if not shocked, to notice that a whole stock of the human species was systematically being decimated in a way not practiced on the most hunted animal. For, whereas laws restrict the hunting of certain animals to prescribed seasons to prevent their extinction, it was open season on Jews every day of the year; the intention was to bring about their elimination, to the last person. Even those who had opted out of Judaism were condemned to death. For example, Sister Bernarda, the former Gertrude Stein, rejected her Jewishness, took a nun's vows, and retired to a Dutch convent; in 1942 she was fetched by the Nazis and dispatched by train to Auschwitz, where she perished.

The frightening uniqueness of the Holocaust also stems from the fact that this murderous operation was devised, supervised, and carried out by government bureaucrats (in Germany and allied countries), who thought nothing of consigning millions of innocent people to their death, and who made sure the victims would not take to their grave (or the crematorium) items of value or of benefit to a country at war. Thus the Jews to be slaughtered were first dispossessed of their valuables, then enslaved. Before they were killed, their hair was shorn and their clothing, shoes, and personal items (such as eyeglasses) shipped back to Germany and recycled for the war effort. Likewise, gold was extracted from the teeth of the corpses. The bodies were then unceremoniously disposed of by burning (some Nazis even speculated about using the ashes to fertilize fields). All this was done by a government that claimed to be at the forefront of European and Christian civilization. Never before in recorded history had a whole stock of the human species been condemned to immediate and total extermination by another human stock — but it happened in the twentieth century, in civilized Europe, before our very eyes.

To survive this terrible onslaught, Jews desperately sought the help of non-Jews, of good-minded persons ready to risk their lives in order to spare one or more Jewish lives. Any Jewish person still alive in a German-occupied country in late 1943 who was neither confined to a ghetto, nor in any Nazi-controlled camp, nor sheltered by friendly partisans, survived only because he or she was being aided (or his or her presence was overlooked) by individual non-Jews to avoid capture by the Nazis and their collaborators.

This help could be of two types: passive or active. Passive assistance meant not informing the authorities of a Jew known to be residing in the vicinity or known to be hiding with someone else—a conspiracy of silence. Active aid meant taking an active role in securing the safety and welfare of the harried Jew, either by sheltering the person in one's home or other safe place, or by providing a new set of credentials to make it possible for the person to pass as a non-Jew. It could also take the form of helping the Jew flee into a less dangerous area. Survival for a Jew in an area under direct Nazi control was impossible without such aid. Some persons exacted payments in return for their aid, which in all cases was a risky undertaking for the helper. In this study we do not deal with those who helped because of a hope of gaining personal tangible benefits.

It should be borne in mind that most of those who helped Jews for strictly financial reasons tired of their commitment at some point and turned out their wards. This was especially likely to happen when the money ran out or the rescuers felt confident they could lay their hands with impunity on the balance of the moneys held by those in their care. There were tragic finales to such instances, recorded especially in Eastern European countries. In this volume we will concern ourselves solely with those who helped for mostly humanitarian reasons.

The outside world was largely silent—even the "good guys" (the Allied nations who were at war with Nazi Germany but did little to help save Jews, or to make it easier for those who tried to help); the civic and religious leaders in most European countries were silent. The deeds of those who helped Jews survive in spite of the dangers to themselves are therefore of special significance. Not a few lost their lives in the process; others accepted economic hardships as a result of sheltering Jews in their homes; and all lived in constant fear (which they learned to master) of betrayal by informers, extortionists, or plain anti-Semitic zealots within the population.

They are heroes of a special kind. Mostly unassuming people who never thought of themselves as anything but ordinary men and women, they suddenly found themselves caught up in a terrible human tragedy affecting another people. Challenged with the call for help, they tried their best to live up to the dictates of their conscience in the worst times imaginable. Most do not consider themselves heroes or their deeds heroic. They claim they were simply fulfilling a basic and common human obligation—of helping others in great need, persons whose lives were unjustly threatened by a criminal regime. Although they knew that by helping Jews they could lose their lives (though most hoped to make it through to see better days), they sought no accolades. Most preferred to remain anonymous in the postwar period; their stories came to light and their deeds were disclosed only because of the initiative of the saved parties, those who benefited from their aid. In a world proliferating with villains and scoundrels, these rescuers remain the true heroes of that dark period. They come from all walks of life and represent all social classes. They are the exception to the rule: when others either participated in the orgy, applauded the perpetrators, or stood by and watched, the righteous were the only non-Jews who tried to save.

To better appreciate the uniqueness of their deeds, we turn to examples of the most common forms of help, beginning with providing shelter in one's home.

Chapter 2

Hiding and Sheltering Conditions

Testimony of Felix Zandman (Poland)

I was born in 1927 in Grodno, Poland. When the Germans occupied our city, my family was moved into a ghetto. On Friday, February 12, 1943, in the morning, I left the ghetto for work as a helper to a bricklayer. That afternoon, while at work, we were told that the ghetto was surrounded by troops and that a deportation was taking place. I decided not to return to the ghetto. I took off my yellow Star of David patches, which were sewn into my coat, and escaped from the workplace into town. I crossed the town, crossed the Niemen Bridge, wandered around until dark, and then went to a person who used to be the nanny of my cousins. She permitted me to sleep in a barn with cows and told me that I must leave in the morning.

Early in the morning, I left and went to Lososno Forest. Our family used to have cottages there where we would spend our summer vacations. The cottages were dismantled by the Russians (or Germans), and only one little house where the innkeeper lived was left intact. The family that lived in that little house, the Puchalskis, for years guarded our cottages. During summers I would play with their children, and I knew that the family had a high respect for our family and liked us. During the deportation of 10,000 Jews from the ghetto in January 1943, my aunt and uncle fled from the transport and spent two days in hiding with the Puchalskis. They came back to the ghetto and told our family that the Puchalskis wanted to help us. I therefore decided to go to them and ask them to hide me for a few days, and then I would go deeper into the countryside to join the partisans. I was then 15 years old.

When I appeared at their house, they received me with great warmth, gave me something to eat, and afterwards asked me to agree to stay with them—not to go to the partisans, as this was a very dangerous and almost impossible task. Anyhow, they didn't know where to find the partisans, nor did I. The Puchalskis offered to hide me until the end of the war. I did not have any money, not even a watch, to offer them. They were extremely poor. Everyone was hungry there, yet they offered to share with me what they had.

I asked Mrs. Puchalski why she was risking her life and the lives of her husband and five children. She said, "God sent you to us. I dreamed for many years to be able to repay your grandmother for her kindness. Whenever I was in trouble, she would help me. One day when she saw I was ready for birth, she put me into a hospital—the only time I had a baby in a hospital—and brought me gifts after my baby was born." She continued, "I prayed that one day I could repay that, and here you are, God sent you."

The same day, Saturday, February 13, in the evening, my uncle arrived at the Puchalskis'. He told me that when he returned to the ghetto from work he escaped from an execution, and that probably our families were already deported. Next evening, four additional people arrived at the Puchalskis'. The Puchalskis put everyone (we were now six people) into a potato cellar some 50 meters from the house. After a few days it was decided that the place was not safe and the men started to dig a hole under the floor of the house to make a new hiding place. The hole was 1.5 by 1.5 meters square and 1 meter high. The entrance was a cutout in the floor under the bed. After a few days two of our persons left. The four of us, and later another person who joined us, stayed in that hole for 17 months. Every day someone from the Puchalskis would bring us food and take out our wastes. Two of the hiders had some money, and that allowed us not to starve, as the Puchalskis were very poor. When the money ran out, the Puchalskis would give us whatever there was to eat, sharing with us the little food they could retain. During the whole period of hiding, we were treated with the highest respect and loved by everyone.

In 1943 the family consisted of Jan Puchalski, who worked in a tobacco factory; Anna; and five children: Irena, 16; Sabina, 13;

Krysia, 11; Wladek, 3; and Wanda, 1 year old. The two small ones did not know that under the floor people were hiding. The Puchalskis knew of the terrible danger–certain death for everyone, including the little children–if the Germans would discover us. Yet at no time did they ever hint that we should leave. In moments of despair, the Puchalskis, even the children, tried to build our morale and prayed for us. During a house search by the Germans, they did not lose their cool and were able to distract the Germans so they would not find our hiding place. Some Christians were hiding Jews for money; not in the case of the Puchalskis. They risked their lives and the lives of their five children out of good heart, belief in humanity, and belief in God. Thanks to them the five Jewish people whom they were hiding, as well as the two who stayed there just a week, survived the war.

Hiding in Private Homes

The Nazis would not limit themselves to repeating the old-time anti-Semitism, spiced with perhaps relatively more outbreaks of controlled violence; their intent was much more far-reaching and destructive. Realization of this did not dawn on the Jews under German domination at first. By the time Jews fully awoke to the fact that they stood to gain nothing by waiting further, it was very late in the game—the Nazis were moving in for the final kill. At this eleventh hour, it was time for some hard decision making.

To avoid immediate arrest and deportation to the death camps, one had to undertake a painful and radical transformation of one's living conditions, something for which none had prepared themselves physically and emotionally. Simply put, one had to disappear from public view for an indefinite period of time. A Jew needed new credentials in order to pass as a non-Jew, or help in fleeing to a safer region, or shelter. Survival meant the art of becoming a "nonperson," of making oneself invisible, and for all intents and purposes ceasing to exist—yet, simultaneously, continuing to live. To make this possible within the shortest time, a secure and secret hiding place had to be found with a non-Jewish person. A rescuer was needed who was prepared not only to shelter the fleeing Jew, but also to feed and care for him or her for an unspecified period of time—for as long as it might take until the country was rid of the Nazis and their collaborators. The fugitive Jew had to be ready to place himself or herself at the mercy of others, often total strangers, for better or worse, while at the same time erasing all traces of his or her person and whereabouts.

To mislead the authorities, two forms of dissimulation were attempted. One might leave behind a garbled note or intimate to friends that one was about to put an end to one's life. Or the person might hint that he or she was planning to cross into a country over which the Germans had no direct (or a less rigorous) control. These steps were meant to mislead the enemy into believing the Jew was no longer alive or was living elsewhere, when actually he or she had gone into hiding, in some cases very close to the former home.

This was anything but a luxurious arrangement. As a "nonexistent" hidden person, the fugitive Jew had to settle for being cooped up in a hiding place. This could be any location believed to keep the fugitive securely hidden and isolated from the rest of the world. Conditions in such shelters, as one may imagine, were uncomfortable to say the least. Generally speaking, however, hiding places in Western European countries were relatively more convenient (if one may use such term in this regard) than in Eastern European countries; that is, fugitive Jews stood a better chance of being offered a small, secluded side room or a section in a room or a corner in an attic as a hiding place. In Eastern Europe, conditions were more primitive, with people hiding in holes underground, beneath rooms, or in fields or forests—anywhere to keep out of sight and try against all odds to survive as the most hunted species on earth.

The ideal hiding place was a shelter so well camouflaged that neither the alert eye of a policeman or inquisitive neighbor, nor the sniffing of dogs, would detect the presence of a living human being. People went to extremes in their rush to survive undetected. Hiding places were in all instances uncomfortable, but degrees of discomfort varied. In some cases persons simply lived in the same apartment with their benefactors and took precautions not to be seen by outsiders. Where the risks of detection seemed greater, others settled for smelly attics, damp cellars, stuffy back rooms, or the inside of double walls. In even more uncongenial circumstances, especially in Eastern Europe, some shelters took the form of a pit under the floor of a living room or kitchen, inside a haystack, or in a bunker beneath crouching cattle and pigs wallowing in their filth (it was felt that the intense stench of the animals would probably keep the police hounds away). A shelter could also be an isolated cave or forest hideout in the open countryside or a dark corner in a condemned and bombed-out building. In many instances, persons scarcely had room to stand up, and in some cases were forced to remain in a sitting or crouching position for many hours a day.

Hiding a fugitive Jew was anything but an easy undertaking. It required more than willingness, courage, and readiness to imperil the lives of one's family. Also needed were an ability to devise and camouflage the hideout, contingency plans in cases of emergency, or contact with like-minded individuals who would risk taking the Jew in the event of an imminent raid. In the Netherlands, for instance, experience taught the hosts as well as the hiders that movement and frequent changes of hiding places were essential for survival. There were blackmailers anxious to inform on a Jew in hiding in return for even a petty reward. The Gestapo (the German political police charged with apprehending opponents of the Nazi regime) routinely paid one quart of brandy, four pounds of sugar, and a carton of cigarettes, or a small amount of money, to anyone turning in a Jew.

The building and arrangement of hiding places became an art. People built double walls and hanging ceilings behind which Jews sometimes lived for as long as two years. Attics and cellars were camouflaged. Annexes in old office buildings were also used, as in the case of the Frank family in Amsterdam (where Anne

Frank wrote her famous diary). Jews were hidden in house garrets, closets, cow sheds, stables, haystacks, graves, or unused zoo cells; in disabled and unused heating stoves, haylofts, holes, caverns in the fields and forests—in short, any conceivable place on the ground, above it, or beneath it where the presence of a living being was considered unlikely.

When the hiding place was located in the host's home, it sometimes took the form of a secreted and unused back room. Such was the case for Lilli Schiff, a theatrical dress designer who was hidden for three and one-half years by her friend and former client, the Viennese stage actress Dorothea Neff, in an unused back room of her centrally located flat. Neff continued her stage performances and entertained friends and colleagues at home after opening nights, while Schiff remained closeted in the secluded room. In a different episode, Zysla Kuperszmid and her daughter hid in an abandoned upper-story apartment in a building in the Warsaw ghetto, which had already been emptied of its Jewish inhabitants. They were cared for by Janina Skowronek, whom Zysla had befriended only a little while earlier. Later, when the Germans permitted the emptied homes to be repopulated by non-Jews, Skowronek and her family quickly moved into that building, and there they remained together with their Jewish wards.

Shelterers also looked after the special needs of persons in hiding. Hiders kept their charges informed of the progress of the war. Stanislaw Jackow, in Stanislawow, Poland, spent many hours playing chess with the persons hiding under his home. Sister Marie-Gonzague Bredoux, in southern France, attended to the religious needs of the two Jewish women she hid: candles to celebrate the advent of the Sabbath on Friday evenings, and special dishes for preparing food during the Passover holiday. In the case of the two youthful Gutgold brothers, who were hidden in the Warsaw flat of Alexander Roslan, their benefactor dug into his meager savings to buy an ultraviolet lamp for the boys' use to compensate for the lack of sunlight in the secluded room.

When conditions allowed, the hidden person enjoyed

unexpected comforts. Eleven-year-old Hetty, who was hidden by Dr. Michal Majercik in his home in Bratislava, Slovakia, moments before she would have been snatched by the police, was given a separate room and provided with books so that her self-education would not suffer during this period of forced confinement. The Zilber family were offered a separate upstairs room in the home of Rev. Gerardus Pontier, a Calvinist pastor in Heerlen, Netherlands, where they were initially sheltered. The rescued family had only recently met their benefactor, when Rev. Mr. Pontier accosted one of the Zilber boys in the street in mid-1942. Noticing the Star of David patch on the boy's jacket, which all Jews in German-occupied Holland were obliged to wear even before the start of the deportations, the pastor offered his help should they ever need it. Responding to the boy's hesitation at this impromptu gesture by a stranger, the churchman said: "Son of Israel, we are happy to give you whatever help.... Don't worry, my child.... God will protect us." In the short interlude that the rescued family was to spend in the reverend's home (they had to leave hurriedly for their own security), they enjoyed the amenities of their own furnished room.

Whatever the living conditions, however, extreme precaution always had to be taken not to inadvertently disclose to outsiders the presence of Jewish persons on the run. The slightest omission, slip of the tongue, or untoward movement could spell disaster for both rescuer and wards. In the Dutch village home of Laurens Mieloo, the hidden Jewish couple were carefully instructed not to approach the window of their upstairs separate room, which was uncurtained, as were most similar windows in this particular village. The Mieloos feared that installing curtains would raise questions in people's minds and attract undue attention to their home, and this of course was to be avoided at all cost.

Lea still remembers with trepidation how, as a five-year-old girl, she briefly stared out of the window of the house where she was hidden in Tarnow, Poland, and saw a woman pointing an accusing finger at her from across the street. Her benefactress, Janina Filozof, quickly stole the girl out in a large suitcase and took her by train to another city, where she tried to find a safe place for the distraught child.

In some instances, the presence of hidden Jews was not even revealed to members of the rescuer's own family, especially when the hiding place was physically separated from the homeowner's dwelling space. In the case of Franciscus Molmans, from Holland, three of his four children were not told that the sealed upstairs annex sheltered a Jewish couple, who remained hidden for two years. The fear of a slip of the tongue by the smaller children could not be discounted.

For better protection, rescuers in some cases added a secluded niche in their apartment home by blocking off a hallway behind which were hidden one or several Jews. In one such case in Strij, Poland, seven persons were hidden in a section of an apartment blocked off by a closet.[1] Zbigniew Kaminski added a wall in a room in his grandmother's home in Przemysl, Poland, where he hid a Jewish family. When that arrangement proved no longer feasible, he rented a house on the outskirts of the city of Zielonka, digging a hole underneath the floor and camouflaging the entrance to it with a wooden toilet seat. To account for the noise during the construction of the shelter, Kaminski added rabbit cages to the basement. The rabbits later provided him with an excuse for purchasing an inordinate amount of food. Eventually 11 persons found refuge in that shelter for different periods of time.

In another similar episode, space inside an uninhabited second home was converted into a hiding place. Antoine Abbeloos, from Brussels, Belgium, hid a Jewish couple in an unfinished section of a home still under construction. Likewise, Jozef Job, in the Tarnow region of Poland, hid a Jewish man and his daughter, who had been found walking aimlessly in a snowstorm after they had escaped a Nazi "action" (a term used in Eastern Europe for a violent roundup and killing raid of Jews) in a nearby city. Father and daughter were sheltered in the attic of a half-finished new home next door to Job's.

A hiding place could be any crevice or cubicle. Ignacy

Kurjanowicz, in Brest-Litovsk, Belarus, hid his former employer in a cubicle inside the wall behind the home's heating oven. This hiding place, which measured 0.8 meter by 1.2 meters, was sealed off with bricks, and the hidden person, who was forced to remain in a crouching position, was told to knock with an ax whenever he felt the heat of the oven was too stifling and he needed to step out. André Donnier, a physician in southern France, was able to secure the release of Jonas Fischbach and his wife from Rivesaltes (a French detention camp for foreign-born Jews), and sheltered them in a unused shed in the back of his garden. At precisely six every morning, the Fischbachs were allowed to use the toilet in the clinic and fetch fresh water in a pitcher and bowl; they remained closeted in their hiding place for the remainder of the day. The Donnier nurse brought them their meals. Mrs. Fischbach passed her time sewing clothes, which Mrs. Donnier then sold privately to help defray the expenses of sheltering the couple.

Hiding places could also be found in secreted sections of business establishments. Probably the best-known such example is that of the Frank family and friends in Amsterdam, who were hidden in the annex of their previous firm's office building. The entrance to the secret annex, to the rear of the building's upper two floors, was sealed off with a bookcase. The eight hidden persons had to avoid making noise during the day's working hours, when the office personnel downstairs went about their business routine.[2] In a related case in the Netherlands, a Jewish couple hid upstairs in a building that served as a shorthand training school. Before the war, one of the hidden persons had taught English commercial correspondence there. Now fearing deportation to a concentration camp, he asked for and was offered a hiding place by his previous employer in an unused upstairs annex, together with his bride.[3]

In Eastern Europe, particularly Poland, such luxuries as separate rooms were the exception to the rule, and many persons hid in the most unlikely places. Thus, up to 22 persons who had escaped from the burning

Warsaw ghetto were hidden in an underground shelter for 16 months in the home of Jerzy Kozminsky in a Warsaw suburb. To help defray the expenses of their benefactors, a watchmaker among the hidden persons was brought watches to repair. To outsiders, the unseen watchmaker was explained as a disabled uncle living with the Kozminskys. In Zborow, southern Poland (now Ukraine), the Ukrainian Anton Suchinski hid six Jews for nine months in a pit measuring 2.5 meters wide by 1.2 meters long and 0.8 meter high. The persons inside could hardly move, except to sit up, and they shared one kerosene lamp. By night, Suchinski let down food through the trapdoor and removed the bucket that served as a chamber pot. Likewise, 14 persons hid under the living room floor of Mykolas Simelis, a forester in Veyvis, Lithuania. He had placed a closet over the trapdoor in his living room leading to the underground bunker. In this case, the rescuer was able to install electricity and a stove for the people's comfort; hay and blankets served as bedding.

The more imaginative among the rescuers devised more intricate hiding places near their homes to afford maximum security to their charges. Jonas Paulavicius, a carpenter in Panemune, Lithuania, placed himself at strategic spots on roadways where fugitive Jews were likely to pass, in order to offer them his aid. To accommodate his wards, he built three independent shelters in the yard of his home, where he hid a total of 14 persons, 12 of them Jews (the two others were Russian prisoners of war who had deserted from a pro-German Russian military unit). At the same time he sheltered a Jewish lad in the attic of his home. He kept each group of fugitives ignorant of the others' presence, so as to minimize the chances of disclosure; in the event of one group's capture, even torture would not make them reveal the presence of others in Paulavicius's home—they simply would not know of it. Luckily for all, the place was never raided.

Other rescuers sometimes went to even greater lengths. Izydor Wolosianski, of Drohobycz, Poland, in one of the few cases of the rescue of a large group of Jews, hid 39 persons in an unfinished, partly underground home, on top of which he had built his own home. The half-constructed rooms were presently transformed into a series of interlocking cellars that were further expanded into the bottom soil to enlarge the living space. A trapdoor led from the rescuer's kitchen. Gas and lavatory facilities in one section of the hiding place provided the only space where the fugitives could stand erect. Similarly, Stanislaw Jackow, from Stanislawow, Poland, hid 31 persons in an underground cellar, which the inhabitants termed the "biggest underground hotel in town." The hidden persons drilled 25 feet below the earth and tapped fresh water; this allowed for the installation of an indoor toilet. These, however, represent the exceptional cases. Most rescued persons did not benefit from such amenities, and most hiding places, especially in Eastern Europe, were not fit for habitation even by house pets.

Not surprisingly, existence under such trying conditions was a day-by-day nerve-wracking and excruciating experience to the hidden persons. Maks Etingin, his brother, and parents were cooped up in a tunnel-like hole in the Vilnius region for almost 10 months. Food was pushed through a narrow opening by their rescuer, Boleslaw Boratynski, and the bodily wastes removed. Boratynski, whose wife was expecting a child, had decided (against his parents' advice) to shelter the fugitive Jews and thus repay a favor by the elderly Etingin years before the war, in spite of the risks to himself and his family.

In another episode, 14 persons were cooped up in total darkness in a tiny shaft under the master bedroom of the home of Maria Szczecinska in Staszow (near Kielce, Poland) for 21 months. A bed was placed above the entrance to the hole, which was large enough for a skinny person to squeeze through. A pail upstairs was available for toilet use, but only between 11 P.M. and 2 A.M. When visitors were present in the home (and this could last for several days), people had to control their bowel movements or relieve themselves in the shaft.

In another similar story, 18 persons were hidden for a year and a half in an underground shaft, divided into three sections, underneath their previous home in Zolkiew, Poland. It was so hot that men and women wore only underclothing even during cold weather, and the extensive perspiration produced skin inflammation on many of the hidden persons.[4] A lucky survivor, who with 12 others had hidden in a narrow hole for 26 months under the home of Szczepan Bradlo, a farmer in the Tarnow region of Poland, relates that after liberation, "we had to teach my mother how to walk all over again. We had to learn to speak properly—we had only spoken in whispers for more than two years. All of us were suffering from malnutrition and rotten teeth—but we were alive."

Jozef Zwonarz, an engineer in Lesko, Poland, decided to shelter four Jewish persons in an underground shaft beneath the workshop shed near his home. The hidden persons stayed in the "tomb" (as they called it) for two years. During that whole period they saw no light and could not stand up, but either sat or lay down. To feed them, Zwonarz stole from his own family; his wife suspected he was providing for a mistress. One evening, the hidden persons overheard Zwonarz's wife berate her husband, after she had followed him into the shed, for his supposed infidelity: "You ought to be ashamed, carrying on like this at such a late age. . ., a father of five children." The several Nazi and collaborating Ukrainian security offices that were located across from the home did not add to Zwonarz's peace of mind. When the hidden persons had to exit the place, they found out they could not use their limbs. In the words of Dr. Wallach: "I fell and could not get up. I could neither walk nor stand, I had to creep up to the house. We exited the shed at nightfall, but the dim light was to us a torching sun, for we had not beheld light for almost two years."

Leon Wells, who had fled the notorious Janowska camp in Lvov, describes the difficult conditions facing the 24 persons, including himself, who hid in a nearby underground shelter. The shaft was located underneath the pigsty, which was considered an ideal place because the breathing noise of the hogs sounded similar to that of human beings; the hiders could, consequently, inhale freely. The place, however, was only about 10 by 13 feet. The stifling heat created by such a large group made it impossible to wear anything but one's underwear in spite of the November cold outside. From the perspiration and forced immobility, persons developed red spots all over their bodies. All kept to strict silence. Some stayed awake to make sure none made inordinate noises in their sleep. At night, the trapdoor was left slightly ajar to allow fresh air to penetrate. In a corner a curtain hid a chamber pot that served the whole group.

Initially, the rescuer Kalwinski was paid by one of the more well-to-do hiders for the upkeep of the others. They all became jittery when that man's funds dwindled, and they feared that they would soon be evicted. Kalwinski had agreed in the beginning to shelter only a few persons, but allowed himself to be talked into adding others. Two couples had first hidden with another Gentile, but that man had taken fright and wanted them out. Fearing that if they were captured and tortured, they would betray him to the authorities, he thought of simply killing them. He relented when, through a third party, contact was made with Kalwinski, who agreed to hide the additional persons in return for their appropriate sharing of the maintenance expenses.[5]

Similar harsh conditions are reported by the Gold family, who were sheltered in a basement hole of an unused garage shack next to the home of their benefactor, Dr. Alexander Mikolajkow, in Debica, Poland. "We lived in darkness," recalls one survivor. "We couldn't even have a candle, because it would consume too much oxygen. When it rained, the water would rise as high as our necks. We would spend one or two days submerged. But the wetness kept out the insects. They could not live there; only we lived there." When they were liberated, the Gold family could not walk or stand the light of day. Their bodies had swollen from hunger. The Russians who examined them predicted that 9 out of the 13 in the group would surely die. "But we did not. All of us rallied save one. He died of TB a few months later. . .. You couldn't imagine you'd get back to normal life. But life is so much stronger."

As one would expect, life under such difficult conditions took its toll of hidden persons' nerves and even lives. Some sought a way out through suicide. Janina Skowronek, in Warsaw, had to dissuade Zysla

Kuperszmid from this thought with words of comfort and encouragement. In the home of Rozalia Paszkiewicz, in Strij, Poland, where seven persons were hidden, a baby was born to one of the hiders; it was feared that its cries would endanger the whole group and their benefactress, so it was strangled by its father. Similar cases of infanticide occurred in other hiding places, where mothers had to decide between the survival of the larger group in hiding versus that of a sole crying infant. Who is to judge?

Lack of food was another serious problem. In the home of Wiktoria Pokrywka in Lvov, there was not enough food for the seven people in hiding. When one person succumbed to starvation, his body had to be removed without the other tenants noticing it. The hiders decided to burn the body in the stove. When an additional person died, his body was carried down to the building's cellar and buried. Then came the death of a third person. After the war, two more persons died from exhaustion and tuberculosis. Such were the harsh realities faced by Jews, determined to survive at whatever cost. Everyone hoped to be one of the lucky ones to make it through. Of the original seven persons in the preceding story, only three survived. They gradually regained their former strength and, repressing psychological scars and searing memories, tried to rebuild new lives.

Hiding on Farms

For those who hid outside the city perimeter, even greater precautions had to be taken, especially against betrayal by informers. In the city it was relatively easier to move around, generally pass unnoticed (the larger the city, the better the chances), and easier to flee and mingle with the crowd at a moment's notice. These advantages did not prevail in a small locality, where all residents knew each other. The slightest change in a person's lifestyle (such as avoiding receiving visitors at the rescuer's home or reducing one's socializing in the local pub) would immediately catch the attention of others and invite questions, which might arouse suspicions.

At the same time, there could be advantages in hiding

in a small town, a village, or an isolated farm. If, for instance, the inhabitants of a particular locality shared the same values and saw each other as an ideologically knit community, as was the case in the Protestant enclave of Le Chambon-sur-Lignon in southeast France, or in the several Baptist communities in the Ukraine, then the chances of survival might be much better than in the city. In addition, in case of emergency, such as the disclosure that a raiding party was on its way toward the village, an alert could be sounded in time for the fugitive Jews to flee to a nearby forest or other locality. These conditions, however, did not generally prevail in most small localities on the conquered continent; the communities indeed fended for themselves but were not ideologically bound, ready to act in unison against an outside threat. And in the villages of Eastern Europe, feelings against Jews ran as high as in the large cities, sometimes even higher.

In the Netherlands, the hiding of Jews in villages, farms, and small localities was quite widespread. The deeds, for instance, of Johannes Bogaard and his family have assumed legendary proportion. A deeply religious Calvinist, he cared for several hundred Jewish fugitives who were hidden in Nieuw Vennep and neighboring farms to the southwest of Amsterdam. Such a large operation could not go on unnoticed for long, and the police staged raids in which several Jews were netted. Bogaard's father and relatives were also deported to a camp.

The two largest recorded cases of the hiding of Jews on farmland areas in Western Europe occurred in Le Chambon and Nieuwlande. In Le Chambon-sur-Lignon, France, perhaps as many as five thousand Jews passed through the town and outlying villages and farmsteads en route to other hiding places inside France or across the border in Switzerland, or for an extended stay in the mountainous region of the Le Chambon region. In Nieuwlande, Netherlands, two enterprising underground operatives, Arnold Douwes and Max Leons (a Jew who posed as a Christian seminarian), together arranged and supervised hiding places among the villagers for several hundred Jews.

Across the border in Germany, a former Jewish cattle merchant (who had been decorated with an Iron Cross for bravery during World War I in the German army) found refuge in a string of farmsteads in the Münsterland region. The man, his wife, and daughter rotated, mostly separately, among a group of friendly farmers who knew of their true identity, and they thus outlived the Nazi regime.[6]

Of particular interest is the role of the German major Eberhard Helmrich, who operated a farm in Drohobycz, Poland, on behalf of the German army. Helmrich made it a point to hire Jewish men and women from a nearby ghetto, treated them kindly, and arranged for them to flee when the farm was closed. He also arranged for close to a dozen Jewish girls, who could pass as Ukrainian country girls, to be sent to Berlin; there, with the help of his wife Donata, they were assigned domestic work in private homes.

It was common practice in Nazi-occupied Europe for able-bodied men and women from the occupied countries to be sent to Germany for various labor assignments—except for Jews, unless they could disguise their identity. Conditions in Germany were bad, but not as bad as those in Poland and other Eastern European countries, where the life of an "inferior" Slav counted for nothing with the Germans.

Whereas most Jews on the run in Poland preferred the better flight opportunities offered by larger localities (it is estimated that more than half of the hidden Jews in Poland circulated in the Warsaw metropolitan region), hiding on farms was the only alternative for those who found themselves fleeing Nazi killing raids in outlying areas. Shelter on a farm could be either in the farmer's home, granary, barn or cowshed, or in the fields. Franciszek Zalwowski, in the Tarnopol region, hid eight Jews in a potato field hole, and four more in the barn. Jan Puchalski, from the Grodno region of Poland, at first hid a group of fugitive Jews in a hole in a field that was used to store potatoes over the winter. He then moved them to an underground shaft in his home, where they lay in a crouching position for more than a year.

Hiding places in barns could be in either an attic or

an underground shaft. The young Morris sneaked into the pigsty garret of Jan Sagan, a farmer in the Janow Lubelski region, Poland, with whom Morris's father had done business before the war. He remained incognito for several days, observing from his hideout Sagan's movements and conversations with others, to get a feel of the man's true character and behavior. When he felt Sagan could be trusted, he disclosed himself to him, and was not disappointed.

Franciszka Halamajowa, in the town of Sokal, Poland, hid 15 persons in a barn loft for 14 months. Hogs and poultry were brought in as a cover for buying additional foodstuff; hence the place was turned into an animal barn in order to mask the presence of the fugitive Jews. This, naturally, had its side effects, such as lice, fleas, and other insects. One woman came down with typhus and died after a three-month illness. But the others survived and thought nothing of the discomforts while in hiding. Staying alive was all that mattered.

In the village of Rytwiany, Andrzej Dajtrowski sheltered the Goldenberg family, from nearby Staszow, in the barn attached to his home. A wall inside the stable (which contained a bin from which the animals were fed) was dismantled and moved forward, creating a space of some six feet. There Dajtrowski placed four bunks for use by six persons. The entrance was through the attic of the house. After all the fugitives had entered, the farmer closed the entrance and covered it with hay. Another hiding place, to be used during emergency, was built in a different section of the stable.

The Ukrainian Pavlo Girasymchuk, in the Tuczyn region, hid a group of Jews between two sacks of wheat in his granary. They had to endure heat, stench from bodily wastes, lack of washing facilities, and the constant fear of being uncovered with each flurry of shots heard in the distance.

There was a distinct advantage in choosing a hiding place as close as possible to farm animals. The animals' stench served as a deterrent to raiders accompanied by sniffing hounds. Needless to say, the hiders had to be prepared to put up with the continuous stench that penetrated their underground shaft. Avigdor and Feiga

Mandelbaum and another Jewish couple were hidden by the Wiejak couple in the Pulawy region, in a hole underneath the pigsty. There they remained for over a year. The Mandelbaums relate that many times they wanted to put an end to their lives, but Alexander Wiejak begged them not to do this, so that there would be witnesses after the war to tell of the crimes of the Nazis.

Ivan Kaczerowski, a Ukrainian farmer in the Tarnopol region of Poland, prepared a bunker in a corner of his stable reserved for pigs; the entrance was via a trough from which the pigs were fed. Wasyl Dzywulski, another Ukrainian farmer in the same region (who belonged to a Baptist church), hid 13 Jews in a pit underneath a stable. The entrance to the hiding place went directly through the cow stalls. When Dzywulski fed the cows, he would place additional food in a bucket beneath the cattle fodder, then slip it through the hidden trapdoor in the floor. When the persons in the pit could no longer defray expenses for their upkeep, Dzywulski's daughter scoured the countryside at night to garner corn from other fields. When liberated, the people suffered from rheumatism and bad eyesight, but they were alive.

The determination of these rescuers to see their charges safely through the war, in spite of the extreme risks to themselves, is sometimes hard to understand. Zofia Piotrowska, the wife of a farmer in the Rava Russka region of Poland, who hid a Jewish couple in a pit under a pigsty for 16 months, kept encouraging her wards and herself with the words: "I want to live and know that I saved two persons from death."

An isolated farmstead close to a forest, where one could escape at a moment's notice in case of emergency, was a distinct advantage. Jan Chodor's house was adjacent to a forest and was far from other houses in the village of Przedborz, near Kolbuszowa, Poland. The back of the barn faced the forest and was left unlocked so that Norman and a group of fellow Jews hiding in the forest could enter unnoticed and at their own volition. "We entered only at night, and left at night," Norman recalls. "We came to the barn during heavy rain, blizzards, and heavy snowfalls"; also, occasionally, when one of the forest dwellers was ill and needed a place to rest and recuperate. Mrs. Chodor and her family fed them graciously.

In the village of Dolny Taran, Slovakia, six persons were hidden by Jan Caraj in a distant field where he prepared for them a large hole in a haystack. The place was so narrow that there was no room to sit up, and they had to fend off marauding rats hunting for food. When the winter rains made it impossible to stay inside the haystack, Caraj brought the fugitive Jews to his home and hid them in a storeroom area that was blocked off by a large closet.

The fears, travails, and sufferings of a large group of persons, huddled together in a cramped pit inside a stable, is well portrayed in Leon Wells's account of hiding conditions in Wojciech Kalwinski's barn on the outskirts of the city Lvov (today in Ukraine). There were 22 persons in that pit. In Wells's words: "Two of us always had to sit on the 'toilet' [pot], since it was impossible for us all to lie down at the same time." The heat was stifling. When the trapdoor was opened at night to allow fresh air to penetrate, "even the smell of the hogs and the urine and other liquids from the stable dripping down on us through the open trapdoor could not make us forego the precious cool air." On top of this, there was constant tension as a result of competition over favorable sleeping positions inside the pit and claims of favoritism in the distribution of the meager food supplied to them by their benefactor. This added fuel to the other irritating factors already present, such as differences based on economic and class backgrounds, the unrequited affections of a man toward a woman inside the shelter, and ongoing fears of betrayal to the Nazis. This had happened to a group of Jews in a nearby home, where both the rescuer and his wards were publicly shot.[7]

In a ceremony at Yad Vashem in 1984, Dr. Prokocimer, on behalf of all survivors, presented to the Kalwinskis' son a scroll with the following inscription: "Presented, as an expression of deep gratitude, to the son of the unforgettable Wojciech and Katarzyna Kalwinski, the noblest and greatest of Poles, people of rare courage who risked their own lives and of their family and saved 24 Jews during the murderous German occupation in Lvov in the years 1942–44."

Hiding in Religious Institutions

Although the Nazi regime signed a Concordat with the Vatican in 1933, in which it guaranteed the inviolability of the Catholic church's institutions, in practice this agreement was no more honored by the Nazis than many other solemn undertakings with various local and foreign organizations and governments. The agreement meant even less when religious institutions opened their doors to shelter Jewish fugitives. This sheltering constituted a flagrant violation of existing laws and governmental regulations, and clerics knew well that they risked retribution in the event of disclosure. All mainline churches in Germany made serious efforts to arrive at a modus vivendi with the Nazi regime, even if it meant abandoning the Jews to their fate and not voicing protests on their behalf before the authorities. But the Nazis would not be satisfied with a silent acquiescence on the Jewish issue and demanded total obedience to the Nazi state and its self-proclaimed Führer. Many (but not most) churches found it hard to stomach this, and on this issue the seeds of dissension were sown.

The churches themselves had, paradoxically, paved the way for Hitler's ruthless treatment of the Jews. For generations, church teachings derided the Jews as a perverse and culpable people who lived under God's wrath for not accepting the Christian faith. In recent times this view was voiced by no less an opponent of Nazism than Pastor Wilhelm Niemoeller, who at his 1938 trial by the Nazi state reiterated his personal dislike of Jews; he noted what a "painful and grievous stumbling block" it was for Christians that God had found it necessary to reveal himself in the form of a Jew.[8] Several years earlier, in 1935, Niemoeller justified the generations-old anti-Jewish bias because "the Jews have caused the crucifixion of God's Christ.... They bear the curse, and because they rejected the forgiveness, they drag about with them as a fearsome burden the unforgiven blood-guilt of their fathers."[9] Niemoeller and his predecessors took pains to cultivate the deicide charge in the minds of many Christians. By a strange historical twist, this facilitated Hitler's implementation of the "Final Solution," which for him was a necessary first step toward the total eradication of the Judeo-Christian religious teaching.

If churchmen of the caliber of Niemoeller could justify God's "curse" on the Jews, much less could be expected from other German clergy (especially those affiliated in the German Christian movement) who hailed Hitler as the incarnation of the true Christian hero, come to deliver the faith from the poisonous encroachment of the Jews. Still other lesser enthusiasts of National Socialism welcomed the anti-Semitic measures of the new regime as a long-hoped-for therapy. The influential evangelical theologian Paul Althaus, for instance, greeted the coming of Hitler as "the German people coming to its sense." In 1934 he helped draft a statement that read: "We as believing Christians thank the Lord God that He has in our need presented us with the Führer as pious and faithful overlord," and pledging to "assist the work of the Führer."[10] Prelates in countries adjoining Germany (especially in Poland, Hungary, Slovakia, and Romania) could be found advocating similar restrictions of the rights of the Jewish populations in their midst, on the German model.

In Germany, most evangelical church pastors swore fidelity to Hitler in 1938 and adopted the Aryan clause in their churches, directed at Jewish converts to Christianity. In flagrant disregard of Christian teachings, "non-Aryan" Christians were either removed or fully segregated in their churches. In a 1941 statement, several church leaders in Germany publicly consented to have abolished all fellowship with Jewish Christians. A few courageous pastors remarked that under the new church regulations, "neither Peter nor Paul, not even the Lord Jesus Christ Himself would be permitted to preach."[11] Bishop Theophil Wurm, the head of the German evangelical churches, agreed that the Jews represented "a dangerous element in the population," and hence voiced no objection to the anti-Semitic measures. He waited until July 1943 before officially protesting in a personal letter addressed to Hitler the extermination of "non-Aryans" (the word "Jews" was not mentioned). By then, few Jews were left in Germany.

The church's record in protecting its own Jewish converts proved dismal. It is estimated that there were some forty thousand Jewish converts to Christianity.[12] After agreeing to the segregation of these Christians within the churches, and to their subjection to restrictive measures affecting all those born Jewish, the churches abandoned them to their fate. Most were dispatched to concentration camps. The lonely protests by a few courageous clergymen against the silence of their elders failed to have an impact.

Julius van Jan, a pastor in the Württemberg region, delivered a ringing sermon in which he denounced the events of Kristallnacht of November 1938 (during which the government staged mass riots against Jews and their property, including houses of worship, across Germany). He asked: "Where is the man who in the name of God and of justice, will cry like Jeremiah, `Maintain righteousness, rescue those deprived of their rights out of the hands of the transgressor'?"[13] Several days later he was manhandled by a Nazi mob and taken to prison. Helmut Hesse, who in June 1943 outrightly condemned the persecution of Jews and called for "resistance to any effort to liquidate Jewry," was hauled off to the Dachau camp, where he died in November of that year.[14] In a postwar statement, Niemoeller admitted: "There was not one single voice to be heard affirming in public that murder is murder."[15]

There is no telling what the effect on the Nazi leadership would have been of a public protest by church dignitaries and theologians. That Hitler was sensitive to public opinion is suggested by his cancellation, in August 1941, of the euthanasia program that had claimed the lives of some seventy thousand mentally handicapped Germans, after Bishop Von Galen in Münster publicly castigated this form of mercy killing. On March 7, 1943, some six thousand Gentile women staged a demonstration in Berlin, demanding the release of their Jewish spouses. The Nazi leadership hesitated at opening fire on German women (they would have acted otherwise against a conquered population), and the Jewish men were promptly released. It was the only public anti-Nazi manifestation during the entire period of Nazi rule, and was spearheaded by women acting on the spur of the moment. German church leaders chose to remain silent. The same can be said of eminent clergymen in other European countries, especially in Eastern Europe. In Germany, as early as 1933, the churches failed to meet the challenge head-on. We shall have occasion in later chapters to mention some church prelates in France and Greece who voiced their protests over the treatment of the Jews.

In light of the traditional theological anti-Semitism, coupled with the silence of church hierarchies at the Nazi anti-Jewish measures, it is indeed miraculous that not a few of the clergy extended help to Jews in various ways. Those offering assistance were to be found in significant numbers in both Catholic and Protestant churches, more so in Western Europe, and relatively less in Eastern Europe. That they could bring themselves to this decision is testimony to the strength of the human spirit in the face of theological and personal biases militating in the opposite direction. We can only guess at how many more lives could have been saved if the church leadership had shown the way.

The Catholic clergy enjoyed certain advantages over other denominations that facilitated their provision of help to Jews. The hierarchical and disciplined structure of the Catholic church, coupled with the requirement of obedience of all clergy to higher church authorities, assured a greater degree of compliance, discretion, and protection for sheltered persons (especially in monasteries and convents) than was possible in other churches, and even more so than in secular organizations and private agencies. This is, of course, a broad, general statement; in practice, ideologically knit Protestant religious communities, such as the Huguenot descendants in France, the Calvinists in the Netherlands, and the

Baptists in Ukraine, were at times much more motivated in their readiness to help Jews in distress than the more structured Roman Catholic Church. In addition, the risks of denouncement and retribution were far too severe for much trust to be placed on the loyalty of too many persons even within a highly structured church. In the case of convents and monasteries where the brothers and sisters faithfully cooperated with their elders in the rescue of Jews, great accomplishments could be performed.

Thus in Assisi—a town of shrines, churches, monasteries, and convents in central Italy, dedicated to the memory of Francis of Assisi—Monsignor Giuseppe Nicolini made the decision to turn the town into a refuge for fleeing Jews after the German invasion of Italy in September 1943. He enlisted several trusted aides, such as Padre Rufino Niccaci and Don Aldo Brunacci, and some two hundred Jews were sheltered in that hilly town. The townspeople kept their silence and none betrayed the presence of Jews in the town's many religious institutions. In the words of Don Brunacci: "In all, about two hundred Jews had been entrusted to us by Divine Providence; with God's help, and through the intercession of Saint Francis, not one of them fell into the hands of their persecutors."

At the Catholic Marist order in Budapest, under the guidance of Brother Albert Pfleger with the assistance of Nina and Valdemar Langlet of the Swedish Red Cross, some sixty to seventy Jews were sheltered in the order's compound. Here too, the fidelity of the brothers stood the test, but they were betrayed by a Gestapo agent who gained entrance in the guise of a refugee. On December 9, 1944, the place was raided, the monks arrested and tortured to make them disclose vital information on the order's rescue activities. Their lives were spared only on the intercession of the Swedish Red Cross and the papal nuncio in Hungary. The hidden Jews were shot.[16]

Also noteworthy are individual nuns in positions of authority who enlisted their subordinates to help Jews on the run. Sister Margit Slachta, of the Benedictine order in Hungary, instructed her sisters to open the order's doors to fleeing Jewish women. In 1943 she traveled to Rome to plead before Cardinal Spellman of the United States (who was on a mission to the Vatican) to help alleviate the condition of Jews in nearby Slovakia, who at the time were persecuted by a regime that swore fidelity to the Catholic faith. Other nuns who displayed valor and loyalty to the human cause include Sister Clotilde Regereau, of the Daughters of Charity in Paris. She admitted the Jewish Muller family into the order's compound after they had been found wandering in the city's Metro during the giant roundup of Parisian Jews in July 1942; a nun they had accosted on a Metro train had directed them to the nearest Daughters of Charity address. After a short rest, Sister Clotilde arranged more permanent hiding places for the family elsewhere.

Sister Zsuzsanna Van, of the Society of the Holy Virgin in Budapest, admitted Jewish children as well as several adult women. Sister Zsuzsanna recalls the day in December 1944 when she had to make a difficult decision on whether to admit the first Jewish woman. "'I'll be killed,' said the lady, but I still objected because of the risk and we had enough work with the children. I said goodbye and we started upstairs. I made two steps or three and was not able to continue. I could not take the next step. I called the lady back. She was the first adult."

Anna Borkowska, the mother superior of a Dominican convent outside Vilnius, Lithuania, admitted a dozen Jewish men and women to the convent, headed by Abba Kovner. Kovner tried to mastermind a rebellion of the Jews in Vilnius ghetto from a cellar in the convent. Years later, he lauded the mother superior in a special poem as "Anna of the Angels."

Mention should also be made of clergymen who helped Jews find sheltering places in their parishes or nearby. Abbé Antoine Dumas, for one, helped disperse fleeing Jews in the village of Saint Just en Doizieu, near Lyon, France. After the war a group of grateful Jews received permission to install in the local church, next to the statue of Mary, a commemorative tablet that reads: "To the most beautiful of Israel's daughters. In gratitude for the protection extended to her coreligionists in this parish during the years of Nazi persecutions of Jews, 1941–44." Don Giovanni De Simione first hid a group of 12 Jews in a Florentine convent, then had them moved to Treviso, near Venice. There he helped a Jewish woman deliver a baby in a hospital, and together with other fellow clergy tried to make life somewhat more tolerable for this group of Jews under the harsh economic and political conditions of German and pro-Nazi fascist rule in northern Italy.

There are no fewer celebrated cases of Protestant clergy helping Jews in their great distress. But since Protestant churches generally possessed neither the solid hierarchical structure nor the rigorous discipline of the Catholic church, the scope and influence of Protestant rescue activities remained mostly the reserve of individual pastors. This could be turned into an asset, however, when ministers whose minds were kindled with a strong altruistic fervor did not have to contend with a cumbersome and bureaucratic church structure in their determination to help Jews. Moreover, a lone minister could at times single-handedly sway a whole congregation and launch a large-scale rescue undertaking. Rev. Leendert Overduin in Enschede, in northern Holland, created a widespread network of aides who helped him save hundreds of Jews in his city. Rev. Sebastiaan Ader scoured the Dutch countryside to find safe refuge for fleeing Jews whom he picked up in various places, but mostly in Amsterdam.

In probably the most celebrated case of Christian charity, the Protestant communities of Le Chambon-sur-Lignon and its environs (descendants of the Huguenots) in southeastern France were led by a group of dedicated pastors (foremost among them André Trocmé) to transform the region into a vast haven for fleeing Jews, numbering into the thousands. Trocmé's inspiration was mainly biblical, although the community's history as a persecuted religious minority also helped cement their determination to aid others in distress. When a government official asked him the names of Jews in the town, Trocmé is reported to have refused with prophetic firmness, insisting that as a religious shepherd he was responsible for all the persons in his community, be they Christians or Jews. He was briefly jailed by the French authorities, then released. Later, especially after the southern part of France came under direct German control, Trocmé thought it best to go underground until the country's liberation.

Pastor Erik Myrgren of the Swedish Church in Berlin sheltered many Jews in the church's compound, in the very capital of Nazi Germany. Pastor Albert Delord, in Carmax, southern France, enlisted his parish to help disperse Jews in the neighborhood. Pastor Vladimir Kuna, an evangelical minister in the Lutheran church, sheltered Jewish children in his orphanage in Mikolsz, Slovakia, and in a nearby village where he was forced by the authorities to relocate due to the fighting between Germans and Slovak rebels. Kuna claims to have been motivated "solely by that love which is described by Saint Paul in chapter 13:4–7, of his first Epistle to the Corinthians: 'Love is patient and kind; love is not jealous or boastful; it is not arrogant or rude. Love does not insist on its own way; it is not irritable or resentful; it does not rejoice at wrong, but rejoices in the right. Love bears all things, believes all things, hopes all things, endures all things.'"

In Eastern Europe, fundamentalist churches stood out in their help to Jews. The Baptists, or Sabbatarians, in Ukraine were especially helpful, as they felt it a religious obligation of the highest priority to avoid the destruction of God's "first promise" and of a people who were still considered "chosen." David Prital, who lost his family to the Germans in Lutsk and found himself fleeing for his life, was sheltered by a Baptist community in the region. They tried to dissuade him from leaving to join up with partisan rebels in the forest; as they explained, his arrival in their community was God's way of testing their religious faith and he, therefore, had to allow himself to be helped by them as a sign of divine condescendence of the community's religiosity.[17]

In the Catholic church, some clergy acted on their own without co-opting their elders and colleagues in their efforts to save one or several Jews. Father Jean

Adrien, of the Marist order in Lyon, hired several Jews, who were already equipped with false identities, to teach art and the German language in a nearby Catholic seminary. In deference to the religious loyalties of these hapless persons, forced to pose as Catholics, he instructed them how best to simulate the required religious gesticulations during the Mass: "Just move your hand a bit before your chest so that the pupils and others, accustomed as they are to making the sign of the cross, are led to believe that you did likewise in a good Catholic manner." Don Beniamino Schivo, a priest in Citta di Castello, Italy, took a stranded Jewish family under his personal care and had them moved to different locations for their safety. On one occasion, he had the Jewish mother and daughter dressed as nuns and locked in a convent room, with only the mother superior knowing of their presence, until the particular danger had passed. Raymond Vancourt, a priest and professor of theology at a religious college in Lille, France, hid a Jewish family in his home. Irene Kahn, one of his beneficiaries, recalls the dread of German searches. "Mr. l'Abbé would go to the door. . .and politely direct [the Germans] away from the house, towering over them, determined, sure of himself and probably praying with every fiber of his being. . ., but he never let me know." While in hiding, Irene, who was from Germany, helped the learned Abbé translate an important philosophical work from German to French. It was published in 1945, the year the war came to a close.

Not a few of these Catholic clerics who acted on their own were nevertheless inspired by the words and deeds of some of their elders and superiors. Authoritative students of the Vichy regime in France agree that the celebrated pastoral letter of Monsignor Jules-Géraud Saliège, of Toulouse, in July 1942, had a tremendous impact, even beyond the confines of his diocese in southwestern France (see more on page). It is believed to have played an important role in swaying public opinion in France toward a more active role in helping Jews elude the Nazis and their Vichy collaborators. In Belgium, Father Louis Celis, of the small hamlet of Halmaal, near Liège, admits to having being swayed by his superior, Monsignor Kerkhofs of Liège, to shelter fleeing Jews. One such family was sheltered in the village, and Father Celis took special care to facilitate the family's observance of their religious requirements even under the trying conditions of the war years.

Many Jewish children were also offered hospitality in monasteries and convents. One wonders how much pressure was exerted on these impressionable minds—lonely, disoriented, and under great stress—to forego their religion and convert to Christianity. We know from many sources that such exertions—some subtle, others more forceful—did take place, and many Jewish children were lost to their people through the unwillingness of their religious guardians to relinquish them to their fold after the war. But we are here concerned with those brave brothers and sisters who behaved otherwise; who rescued the hapless children at the time of their greatest need, then faithfully and without outside inducement returned them to their families and people.

The name of Abbé Joseph André, a priest in Namur, Belgium, comes immediately to mind. Although most of the more than two hundred Jewish children that he was instrumental in rescuing were hidden with laypersons, his dedication to these children and his attention to their Jewish religious needs have caused him to be admired by those who met him during and after the war. The same can be said for Father Bruno Reynders, who cooperated with a clandestine Jewish organization in dispersing close to four hundred children in the Belgian countryside. He was so successful in this undertaking that he was placed on the Gestapo "wanted" list and had to go into hiding himself.

In Poland, mention should be made of Sister Matylda Getter, of the Sisters of the Family of Mary in Warsaw, Pludy, and other places, where many Jewish children were sheltered and protected in spite of Nazi searches of the premises; and of Sister Alfonsa and her colleagues in the Saint Joseph's Heart orphanage in Przemysl, where 13 Jewish children were admitted. Upon the city's liberation, the children were faithfully turned over to the newly formed Jewish committee in order to reunite them with their people.

In Belgium, Sister Marie (Mathilde Leruth), of the Saint Vincent de Paul order in Verviers outside Antwerp, sheltered Jewish children whose parents had been deported. In the words of Sister Marie, the motivation for helping these young souls was a combination of spiritual, humanitarian, and maternal considerations. At a Yad Vashem ceremony in her honor, she stated: "In welcoming them and especially in loving them with all my heart, I only did my obligation as a woman and Daughter of Love. Their parents having been deported to Germany, it was only right that I impart to these dear little Jewish children the maternal care and especially the warm affection that they lacked."

In Budapest, Hungary, Pastor Gabor Sztehlo of the Good Shepherd Committee, a Protestant welfare organization, sheltered dozens of stranded Jewish children whose parents had been lost, either shot and dumped into the Danube River by the vicious Arrow Cross pro-Nazi militia or otherwise dispersed in the confusion of a city in the throcs of siege and revolution. He is credited with saving more than a hundred children.

Don Aldo Beccari, a priest in the mountainous Italian town of Nonantola, arranged for more than a hundred Jewish children (refugees from various countries) to be temporarily hidden in the city's religious institutions, before arranging their flight to the Swiss border, which they eventually crossed safely. When the Nazis discovered that their plan for the children's capture had been foiled, they gave vent to their rage by arresting and torturing the good padre. They released him only after failing to extract any information on the children's whereabouts.

We cannot end this section without mentioning the roles of other persons in religious garb whose rescue feats were perhaps more modest in scope, but whose courage and dedication are no less praiseworthy. Brother Bernardinus (Leonard Hendriks), a monk near Helden in southern Holland, was in charge of a juvenile delinquent rehabilitation center. Two Jewish children were hidden by him for a lengthy time. To camouflage their identity, he instructed them to act and behave as the others; that is, to be difficult, unruly, and lacking in manners and self-discipline. This made the two boys blend in with their new environment and assured their survival.

Sister Joseph of the Sisters of Charity of Saint Vincent de Paul in Calamari, Greece, took a one-year-old Jewish girl under her personal care during the years of the German occupation. When the Germans came to search the premises, she took the child on a boat at sea until it was safe to return. In 1947, when the child's parents had been relocated in Paris, the child was put on a plane to be reunited with them.

Sister Maria-Angelica Ferrari, the mother superior of a Dominican convent in Fossano, northern Italy, sheltered a Jewish girl who, together with her mother and brother, had fled southern France to Italy, where they were told they would not have to fear apprehension. But the Germans had overrun that country in late 1943. Regina's mother was hospitalized after she jumped from a train, while Regina was placed in Sister Maria-Angelica's care. To Regina, her protector "looked like the Madonna. Her soft eyes seemed sad, yet warm and deep. And she became my Mother—`mia Madre'—watching over me and treating me like her own special child. In her presence, I always felt safe and secure." The other nuns in the convent were not told the child's true identity. After the war, Regina was reunited with her mother and brother, who had been hidden elsewhere by a priest. To their great surprise, the family's father, who had been deported earlier, had lived through the rigors of several concentration camps, and thus the whole family miraculously survived the Holocaust.

Noteworthy too is the story of Sister Marie-Gonzague Bredoux, who was mother superior of a convent in the Corrèze region of France. She admitted the 19-year-old Betty Dornfest and her mother, and made great efforts to make it possible for the two women to practice their religion as if they were in their own home. Thus, Mother Marie brought candles and oil from the church for use to welcome the Sabbath on Friday evenings. When Passover approached, Mother Marie carefully noted down the prescriptions on the eating of unleavened bread (matzot), then brought the two women the necessary ingredients and special pots and dishes so they could prepare their food and eat it in comfort in the convent kitchen during the eight days of the holiday. The Germans visited the convent on several occasions, once almost discovering the two Jewish women's hideout. In September 1944, one month after the area's liberation, Mother Marie arranged for the two women to attend Rosh Hashanah services in a nearby synagogue. They then returned to the convent, where they stayed for another six months. "Words are insufficient to tell and describe what this admirable woman was capable of," the religiously devout (and now Israeli) Mrs. Dornfest writes in her testimony. There are few instances (certainly none before the Holocaust period) of Jews helped to practice their religion inside Catholic convents!

Finally, let us recall the exemplary behavior of two deeply religious persons. Father Jacques (Lucien Bunel), a priest of the Carmelite order, was head of a boys' religious boarding school in Avon, France, where he sheltered and personally cared for three Jewish boys. Betrayed to the Gestapo, Father Jacques was arrested and sent to several camps. He died from exhaustion three weeks after the end of the war. When his emaciated body was returned for burial in France, a Jewish rabbi attended the funeral service. The three Jewish children were deported to Auschwitz, where they perished. Father Jacques's parting words to the children before he was seized by the Gestapo, "Au revoir les enfants" (goodbye children), became the title of a well-known French film produced by one of the non-Jewish children who was witness to this sad but courageous episode of humanitarian valor.

A second person who suffered martyrdom in the cause of humanity was Elizaveta Skobtzova, better known as Mère Marie, of the Russian Orthodox Church branch in Paris. Together with her assistant, Father Dimitri Klepinin, she transformed the church's facility in Paris into a refuge for Jews. Disregarding threats to their personal safety, both were eventually arrested by the

Gestapo in March 1943 and deported to Dora and Ravensbrück camps, where they perished. Among her personal notes, the following words give testimony to the woman's altruistic fervor: "At the Last Judgment, I will not be asked whether I satisfactorily practiced asceticism, or how many bows I have made before the divine altar. I will be asked whether I fed the hungry, clothed the naked, visited the sick and prisoner in his jail. That is all that will be asked."

Other Hiding Places

Heads of public and private educational and welfare institutions could also choose to accommodate Jews on the run and register them under assumed names. The dangers for them were as real as for individual harborers of fleeing Jews. At the same time, institutions were better situated than private persons to make use of connections with trustworthy government agencies and public officials who supervised or regulated their activities and were inclined to extend a helping hand by passing over in silence the presence of Jews in these institutions. This complicity somewhat alleviated the feelings of loneliness and personal jeopardy with which individual rescuers had to contend. A good example of official collusion in clandestine rescue operations is that of the state child welfare agency in Belgium (known by its acronym ONE), which was headed by Yvonne Nevejean, a person of exceptional character and moral integrity. She lent her vast authority to facilitate the hiding of Jewish children (who were referred to her by the clandestine Jewish Defence Committee) in the homes she supervised. At a later stage, the children were dispersed with private families.

Private boarding schools also served as ideal hiding niches, especially for Jewish children on the run. In Cannes, France, Alban and Germaine Fort headed Le Rayon de Soleil, a private boarding school for disadvantaged children. During the period of Nazi manhunts for Jews, in 1943–44, the Forts admitted some 33 Jewish youths under assumed names in the Rayon's comfortable home. Other children sought shelter in preventoriums (children's convalescent homes). Arieh Reichelberg was admitted to a home for children suffering from tuberculosis in a village in the Savoy region of France, headed by John and Juliette Charrière. About twenty other Jewish children were there under assumed names—half of the home's total population.

Adults also sought refuge in hospitals and nursing homes. Paul Tzaut, an officer in the Salvation Army, sheltered 17 Jews in his nursing home in Escoutet, France. Marcel Billières, in Tarbes, France, did likewise in the hospital that he directed. One Jewish fugitive was appointed as his private secretary. Says the fortunate Jew: "Thus, I, a man hunted by the Gestapo. . .a tracked person, there I was, typing correspondence while the director attended to the Germans who regularly visited the hospital in search of wounded partisans or of hidden and sick Jews." Likewise, at the Feher Kereszt hospital in Budapest, Hungary, Dr. Geza Petenyi, head of the pediatrics department, falsified X rays so that fleeing Jewish refugees sheltered by him could be listed as suffering from tuberculosis and other ailments and hence be allowed to stay in his ward until they ostensibly recuperated.

Other hiding places were improvised, sometimes without much advance warning, but with no less care and precision. In Saint Gaultier, France, Pierre Dubuis hid two Jews for two weeks behind a screen in the cinema he owned. Georges Guichard hid the Wertheimer couple in a room above a classroom in the school where he taught. Mrs. Wertheimer's advanced pregnancy necessitated the finding of a place where the child could be safely delivered (other than a hospital, which was off-limits to Jews). With the help of an official in the Lodes municipality, an old unused building was located, which lacked light and electricity, and a midwife was brought in from a nearby village to help with the birth.[18]

In Vilnius, Lithuania, Juozas Stakauskas, the chief government archivist, blocked off a basement corridor with a shelf of heavy volumes. Behind it a dozen persons were hidden for a long period, while simultaneously Germans and Lithuanians were busy reorganizing the archives in the rooms upstairs. In Lvov, Poland (now in

Ukraine), a noted rabbi was hidden in a church library. The rabbi spent most of his time acquainting himself with church literature; during emergencies, he darted into a cubicle between two shelves and stayed there until the alarm was over.[19]

In Tarnopol, Poland, Irena Gut Opdyke hid Jews in a laundry shop (which served German army personnel) until a Nazi liquidation raid in the nearby ghetto was over. She later moved them to the basement of the home of the German commander of the officers' club, where she worked as housekeeper. The Sagal family in Paris was hidden in a room above a workshop that belonged to the family of Suzanne Boclet, the Sagals' former secretary. The workshop was situated in a block of buildings where other craftsmen had their ateliers. The four members of the Sagal family remained there for two years. A more imaginative method was that of Dr. Jan Zabinsky, head zoologist of the Warsaw zoo. He hid persons in emptied animal cages that had been heavily damaged at the start of the war in September 1939. One hidden person calls the place "a Noah's ark, where man and animals resided." In Nadworny, southeastern Poland, Wawrzyniec Bruniany hid two persons for 17 months in a nonfunctioning brick factory stove. One person died in hiding, the other survived. Similarly, in Tarbes, France, a baker named Lucien Legrand hid two Jewish persons in a room above the bakery's operating oven. The two persons were instructed to sprinkle water on the floor whenever it got too hot as a result of the oven's heat.

Condemned and otherwise bombed-out buildings could also offer excellent hiding opportunities. In Berlin, capital of Nazi Germany, many Jews hid in bombed-out and dilapidated buildings, between stops at homes of occasional benefactors. In one such case, Leo Witkowski and his wife found temporary shelter on a boat docked on the Spree River, before finding a more permanent hiding place in the home of a kindhearted woman.[20] Likewise, Charles Modijetsky shared quarters with students from a nautical school on a small boat near Amsterdam. Only the boat's owner and a nearby baker (who provided Modijetsky's food) knew of his Jewishness. When the boat no longer proved safe, he fled to the home of Clazina Struik, who operated a public phone from where Modijetsky had made secretive calls at a safe distance from the boat. In her home, he hid in an upstairs room until the city's liberation in 1945.

The 49 persons aided by the Pole Wladyslaw Kowalski, a former army colonel, did not enjoy such amenities. They hid in the ruins of a bombed building in Warsaw after the Germans had leveled the city in October 1944, and they remained underground for 105 days. The daily ration per person was three glasses of water, one piece of sugar, and some vitamin pills. By the time they were liberated in January 1945, they had been reduced to eating fuel.

Thick forest regions offered natural barriers against detection and afforded ample advance warning in case of danger and therefore constituted ideal hiding places—that is, for those prepared to brave the elements (especially the cold winters), constant foraging for food, and movement from place to place. The fugitives had to stay a step ahead of German gendarmes and policemen, as well as locally organized vigilante groups on kill-and-destroy raids against Jews in the forests. Here too, in order to survive, alone or in small groups, refugees needed help from friendly local inhabitants. Young Donia was hidden in a forest cave by the Ukrainian Olena Hryhoryszyn, whom she had only recently met. Olena was grilled by Ukrainian militiamen to disclose the whereabouts of the adolescent girl's forest lair, but to no avail. Jelena Valendovitch, from Minsk, Belarus, took a foundling Jewish child to a forest hideout, where she joined with friendly partisans and eventually met the child's mother, who had escaped earlier from the Minsk ghetto and had joined a different partisan unit. Even in the flatlands of the Netherlands, a particular wooded area could serve as refuge with the help of friendly hands in a nearby settled habitation. Thus Albertus Zefat, a farmer in the village of Valthe, cared for 13 persons who hid in a nearby wooded area and visited him at night for hot meals. This lasted until Zefat was betrayed to the authorities and shot in front of his house.

Other unsuspected hiding places included the ancient catacombs in Florence, where Father De Simione hid a group of fugitive Jews; the church garret of the Reverend Brillenburg-Wurth's chapel in Rotterdam, where a group of Jews were sheltered and told to be silent during services below them; or a hole in the ground, covered with potatoes, where Karolina Kmita from the Kovel region in Ukraine hid a lone Jewish adolescent girl over the winter of 1942–43. In the words of the fortunate girl: "In the winter, she came wrapped up in a white sheet so as not to stand out against the snow, and she blurred her footsteps with a twig."

To forestall the deadly fury of the Nazis, persons were willing to do the unthinkable and even seek refuge in the most unlikely places, such as inside unused tombs. Manko Szwierszczak, a cemetery janitor in Buczacz, eastern Poland, hid five persons in an emptied tomb over the winter months. A statue of Mary was placed over the tombstone to prevent persons from tampering with it. Pelagia Lozinska, of Lvov, Poland, hid her Jewish husband in a cemetery tomb. When she learned that several other Jews in distress wished to join her husband, she felt somewhat relieved, "since my husband would thus not remain alone in a grave." Before the cover was placed over the tomb, Pelagia took fright. "My husband was about to be buried alive! Everyone tried to calm me by saying they were prepared to remain in a grave until the end of the war since, in their words, life in a grave was preferable to death in a gas chamber."

In an epic of unprecedented heroism, Leopold Socha hid 21 Jews in the sewers of Lvov for 16 harsh months. To stay clear of the sudsy, stinking waters that flowed through the sewers, the persons gathered boards and stones. The saturated boards dried gradually with the warmth exuded by the people's bodies. Daily they struggled with hordes of sewer rats. To keep their meager food secure from these rodents, it was stored in a portable kerosene stove suspended from the roof with a string. During heavy storms above them, the water level in the sewers rose to dangerous heights, forcing people to stand on their toes to avoid drowning until the waters had subsided. Through all this tortuous period, Leopold

Socha faithfully supplied them with food, comfort, and encouragement. When Lvov was liberated in July 1944, as the rescued persons stepped out of the sewers they were blinded by the daylight, for they had lived in total darkness for 16 months. Only gradually were their eyes able to readjust to the light. Without the help of Socha, they unquestionably would not have survived in the dank and rat-infested sewers for such a long period. A sanitation worker, Socha before the war had dealt in stolen goods, which he stored in sewer niches known only to him. The brutalities of the Nazis effected a change of heart in the man. At first, he thought of hiding Jews in the sewers in return for payment. He then dropped this demand and devoted himself fully to the survival of the Jews in his care in the city's sewers until the city's liberation. He died in a road accident soon after the war. The many survivors he rescued continue to cherish his memory—in testimonies, books, and documentary films.

Chapter 3

The Art of Passing

Testimony of Cesar Mendes, nephew of Aristides de Sousa Mendes (Portugal)

In the year 1939, my father was ambassador of Portugal in Warsaw, Poland. To keep up with my plans of musical studies with [violinist] Jacques Thibaud, I left for Paris, then followed him to San Juan de Luz for the summer. In 1940 the German invasion was under way in France. My uncle, Aristides de Sousa Mendes, was then consul general for Portugal in Bordeaux. He was on his way to Bayonne, about 30 kilometers from San Juan de Luz, to settle matters about the refugees with the consul there. In these circumstances, I decided to interrupt my studies and join my uncle.

Later on when I arrived in Bordeaux and approached the consulate of Portugal, I noticed immediately that a large crowd of refugees was heading that way. The closer I got to the consulate, the larger the crowd. They wanted desperately to get visas to go to Portugal. Inside, the dining room, the drawing room, and the consul's offices were at the disposal of the refugees—dozens of them of both sexes, all ages, and mainly old and sick people. They were coming and going: pregnant women who did not feel well and people who had seen their relatives die on the highways killed by airplane machine-gun fire. They slept on chairs, on the floor, on the rugs. The situation was out of control. Even the consul's offices were crowded with dozens of refugees who were dead tired because they had waited for days and nights on the street, on the stairways, and finally in the offices. They did not eat or drink for fear of losing their places in the lines. They looked distraught; they had not washed or changed their clothes or shaved. Most of them had nothing but the clothes they were wearing. The sidewalks, the front door, the large stairways that led to the chancellery were crowded with hundreds of refugees who remained there night and day waiting their turn.

In the chancellery, they worked all day long and part of the night. My uncle got ill, exhausted, and had to lie down. He considered the pros and cons and decided to give all facilities without distinction of nationality, race, or religion and bear all the consequences. He was impelled by a "divine power" (these were his own words), and gave orders to grant free visas to everybody.

As his orders were not obeyed by the consul in Bayonne, he decided to go there himself. The refugees there received him with great joy and renewed their hopes to be saved. The consulate of Bayonne was under the jurisdiction of the consulate of Bordeaux. My uncle then drove to the frontier to help the refugees "in loco." From there, he went to San Sebastián to meet the ambassador of Portugal to Madrid, who insulted him, but my uncle did not give up. He continued his humanitarian action saving refugees until the end, when he was recalled to Lisbon. Before the German invasion, the Portuguese government granted visas. Then it stopped answering requests, and consequently the work in the chancellery concerning passports and visas froze. This way the number of refugees increased frighteningly, leading to a dramatic climax. This is when my uncle made up his mind to help all the refugees.

Not everyone was cut out for a life in hiding, of being uncomfortably cooped up in one place for an unspecified period of time at the mercy of others. Not everyone was prepared to revert to a childlike dependence where one's welfare and care, including the procurement of food, was entirely in the hands of others. Some felt they stood an equal, if not better, chance of surviving by masking their true identity and passing as non-Jewish residents of the local population.

It is not known how many chose the course of "passing," but, judging from various source material, it may fairly be estimated that there were as many Jews who lived an ostensibly free and legal existence by mixing with the local population as there were those who lived in hiding and were sheltered by non-Jews. Many did not even bother to change their Jewish identity but relied on the goodwill of local non-Jews who were not particularly keen to turn them in to the authorities. This passive type of help prevailed especially in France and Italy, but also in the Netherlands (for example, in the Friesland region). Most Jews on the run, however, understandably felt safer under the guise of a different name and religious affiliation.

In all this, help by non-Jews was indispensable in order to procure false credentials (identification cards, birth certificates, and labor cards), without which a routine inspection by the police could mean the difference between life and death. Many of those who went into hiding also tried at one time or another to pass as non-Jews. One dared not travel the streets of Nazi-dominated Europe without a set of ostensibly bona fide documents. Help was needed in procuring such documents or duplicates thereof, or fabricated papers carrying false names and other vital information.

Pierre Couvret-Damevin was asked by his former army buddy Jacques Pulver (a Jew who was working for a clandestine Jewish organization during the occupation of France) to lend him his identity card. In Pulver's words: "He did not respond, but asked me to wait a minute; he went up to his room and returned with his identity card, his ration card, his baptismal certificate, and other credentials that I no longer recall. He placed them on the table and said, 'Make good use of them.' I had them all copied by our experts, with my signature and photo on the identity card. He knew he was risking his life." A routine police examination would have uncovered the fact that Pulver's supposed credentials were really issued to another person, and that person would have been in serious trouble. They were both lucky that the Gestapo did not chance to check these credentials while Pulver circulated freely about the streets in France.

Mireille Philip, in France, reportedly carried a suitcase with seals that she used for issuing new identities for children while they were en route from the Le Chambon region to the Swiss border. In Poland, Father Jan Pod-debniak issued a set of false papers to the two Bass sisters, whose parents had been killed in Majdanek camp. With these vital credentials, they were able to register for labor in Germany as hospital attendants. In Athens, police commissioner Angelos Evert issued hundreds of false credentials for Jews trying to pass as Christians, signing many of these documents himself. Wladyslawa Choms helped Jews flee from Lvov with the help of false credentials that she acquired through the Polish underground. Waclaw Lada, a train employee in Warsaw, was arrested in 1943 for providing eight Jews with false papers. He was sent to Auschwitz, then Buchenwald camp; he survived. Barbara Makuch-Szymanska, a lecturer at an agricultural school, was arrested by the Gestapo on a train heading for Lublin carrying forged papers destined for Jews. She was sent to Ravensbrück camp, which she survived.

Trying to pass as a non-Jew was not a simple matter. One had to be well attuned to the customs of the local population, to the nuances of its language and slang, its quips and jokes, eating and drinking habits, religious customs and culture. Speaking an educated Polish when one's false credentials showed one to be a blue-collar worker could raise suspicions; so could a 30-year-old woman carrying in her purse a brand-new missal (Polish Catholics receive their missals during confirmation; by the age of 30, the prayer book would show the marks of age). Sad or too inquisitive eyes could give a Jew away, whatever his or her papers showed. A hurried gait, constant glances to the side and behind to double-check that no one was following, a piercing glance, a worried look—all these were gestures one had to avoid when venturing onto streets of a city that the authorities had declared off-limits to Jews on pain of death.

There was also the possibility of being recognized and pointed out to the police by a former non-Jewish acquaintance; or by a Jewish informer forced to work for the Gestapo, which was holding the informer's family hostage; or by professional informers, such as the *schmaltzovniks* in Warsaw and other cities of Poland, whose trademark was detecting and exposing Jews on the run, fleecing them of their belongings, then turning them over to the authorities. Spotting a Jew on the street had become a sort of sport in Warsaw. Dr. Alexander Bronowski, a Jew posing as a Catholic Pole in Warsaw, was tapped on his shoulders by two German military policemen; although his papers and appearance were in order, he had been pointed out by a former acquaintance from Lublin, Bronowski's prewar city of residence. He was about to be taken for a grueling encounter with the Gestapo, but was saved at the eleventh hour through the generosity of a good-hearted Polish prison warden.[1]

Not everyone was cut out for this type of nerve-wracking existence. Many, especially in Eastern Europe, preferred the temporary sheltering cushion of life in a ghetto to the tensions and fears of passing as a Jew on the "Aryan" or non-Jewish side of the city—the life of a hunted person, constantly on the run, free to be molested at will, with the constant fear of being exposed and doomed to death.

Zofia Kubar, a young Jewish woman who had fled the Warsaw ghetto and decided to pass as a non-Jew, relates that she stopped wearing glasses, for spectacles accentuated the "autumn look" of her face, a demeanor that characterized many Jews at the time. Once she forgot herself and, passing a store, pulled out her glasses to check the prices in the display window. It was a mistake. A man approached her and peremptorily told her: "You are Jewish. . .. Either you pay or we go to the Gestapo headquarters." She began haggling with the man, and soon a crowd gathered. Kubar's situation worsened, and only with much difficulty was she able to extricate herself from this dangerous encounter.[2] To make herself look inconspicuous, she wore a gray hat over her forehead, then later took to wearing vivid colors and heavy makeup. She thought of bleaching her hair, and finally settled for a self-disciplined, carefree appearance. "It's a beautiful day," she would tell herself.[3] She then chose the right mix of colloquialisms and acceptable language mistakes peculiar to her milieu. Imagine a Bostonian trying to pass as a Texan in Dallas with a New England accent! In her words: "I had never realized how many nuances there were in manners, gestures, facial expressions, and jokes. We had to invent credible identities and sustain them in every particular. One mistake could be fatal."[4] She was lucky and survived, but not without the aid of two friendly and supportive Gentile women.[5] Miriam Peleg, who was posing as a Catholic underground operative in the Cracow region, discovered that nonchalantly walking a dog on the street "looks quite Polish."[6] One method of avoiding dangerous train station inspections was to search for a woman leading several children, then offer to help her by leading one child by the hand when walking through the inspecting guards. The Germans generally let women with children pass on without much ado.[7]

Men faced the added risk of being called on to remove their pants to see whether they were circumcised. If so, there could be no mistake—the man was Jewish. In Poland circumcision was unknown among non-Jews. Some, such as Dr. Felix Kanabus and Prof. Andrzej Trojanowski, undertook the dangerous and painful operation of removing the signs of circumcision for a few trusted Jewish friends.

The acquisition of an array of false but ostensibly legal documents was an indispensable preliminary to any attempt to blend in with the surroundings. Every person, Jew or non-Jew, had to have on his or her person an identity card, known as a *Kennkarte*. Without this indispensable document, one was in serious trouble. Under German occupation, every inhabitant had to procure a new ID card, and this could be done only by producing a valid birth or baptismal certificate. For a Jew on the run this meant turning to non-Jews for help in obtaining this important document, and the role of the clergy was crucial in this endeavor. Father Riquet, in Paris, is reported to have issued hundreds of such false certificates. For those who feared to register at the municipality because of an obviously Jewish appearance, the *Kennkarte* had to be procured through a third party, with all the consequent dangers this implied for the other person in case of apprehension. And yet, many undertook this dangerous mission, and either handed valid credentials (their own or of others) to fugitive Jews or fabricated such documents listing fictitious names.

In Western Europe, where Jewish assimilation into the host societies was well under way before the war, more Jews sought to blend in with the population than in Eastern Europe, and hence there was greater need for false documents. Father Benoit, the famed Capuchin monk from Marseille, whose aid to Jews in distress has since become legendary, produced such documents in the basement of his home. Similarly, Father Albert Gau, a priest in Carcassonne, southern France, issued false baptismals to a clandestine Jewish organization that found hiding places for Jewish children. In his words: "I gave each Jew a baptismal certificate, under the sole condition that he does not undergo baptism." In Annecy, close to the Franco-Swiss border, Jeanette Maurier, who was employed at the local prefecture, issued false credentials and ration cards to numerous Jews who were temporarily staying in Annecy while en route to the Swiss border, which they hoped to cross clandestinely. We have already noted the role of Father Jacques in Avon, France, who dissimulated the presence of three Jewish children in his seminary and was betrayed to the Germans by an unknown informer.

In Poland, Dr. Olga Goldfein, a Jewish physician, traveled from Pruzana to other locations dressed in a nun's habit that had been given to her by her traveling companion, Sister Dolorosa (Genowefa Czubak). They stopped en route to rest and to tend the sick. Her patients did not suspect that the healing advice of "Sister Helena" was not due to any miraculous divine intervention but to her medical experience. Sister Dolorosa was expelled from the Saint Ignatius of Loyola order after the war for flouting monastic rules—for leaving the convent in order to accompany a Jewish woman dressed as a nun, and assure her survival.

In Czortkow, Poland, another Jewish woman discovered the saving grace of human compassion. Sylvia Berger was passing as a Ukrainian in a city emptied of its Jewish residents. Her blond hair, blue eyes, and youngish looks (she was then 20) added to her confidence and self-assurance. Her papers showed her to be Stefania Subtelna, employed with a German firm. She attended church regularly with her landlady, Anna Sekreta. One day, Berger learned of the violent death of her family in a nearby ghetto and could not control her weeping. Sekreta questioned her intently on this. Finally Sylvia, alias Stefania, broke down. "I'm Jewish," she told the startled Ukrainian woman. She describes in her testimony what then transpired. "I no longer cared whether I lived. I wanted to die like my mother, my sisters, and the rest of my family." The startled Anna Sekreta motioned the weeping woman to a corner of a room and whispered in her ears: "Listen! If you wish to live, then stop weeping. We will all help you. No one needs to know who you are. We won't tell anyone. Remain with us as family until the end of the war." As told by Berger: "These words are echoing in my ears to this day."

In Eastern Europe, the clergy who extended assistance to Jews were few and far between, but there were notable exceptions. In Kiev, Ukraine, Father Aleksey Glagolev, of the Russian Orthodox Church, gave a Jewish woman his wife's credentials, making it possible for her to pass as a Christian in a distant village. With Mrs. Glagolev's passport and certificate of baptism in her hands, Mrs. Minkin went to see a farmer whose expertise included falsifying the data on documents. Luckily for her, the documents had been damaged during a fire in Glagolev's home and had been drenched with so much water that the seal on them was smudged and faded. This made the erasure and changing of names easier. At a later period, when she felt threatened by disclosure, Mrs. Minkin and her daughters were readmitted to Glagolev's home. This Russian Orthodox priest is credited with helping other Jews in like manner.

Although no exact figures are available of persons living under such false pretenses, from the evidence on hand it is clear that this phenomenon was widespread in all countries occupied by the Germans. This was especially true in Western Europe, where the process of acculturation had removed many of the distinguishing marks of the Jewish population and made their blending in with the host societies relatively easy.

In Hungary, a unique situation prevailed during the period of the German occupation. The pro-German regime of Nicholas Horthy, under pressure from neutral countries, had agreed to a scheme devised by the embassies of Sweden, Switzerland, Spain, the Vatican, and the Red Cross, under which Jewish persons holding "protective passes" from these governments and international agencies were not to be harmed. These were meant to be temporary passports for persons supposedly on their way to the countries that had issued the documents. The ruse, devised by the Swiss diplomat Carl Lutz and amplified by the Swedish diplomat Raoul Wallenberg, was copied by other diplomatic representatives in the Hungarian capital, including Giorgio Perlasca, an Italian who posed as the representative of the Spanish government; Friedrich Born on behalf of the International Red Cross; and Valdemar and Nina Langlet on behalf of the Swedish Red Cross. Mention should also be made of Monsignor Angelo Rotta, the papal nuncio in Budapest, who issued numerous such documents (as well as false baptismal papers) on behalf of Jews in need. One of Rotta's couriers in this undertaking was Sandor Ujvary, to whom he gave hundreds of blank documents, forged protective passes, and faked baptismal certificates. He told the startled Ujvary: "My son, your action pleases God and Jesus, as you are rescuing innocent people. I grant you absolution in advance. Continue your work to the glory of God!" Thanks to this scheme, and to singular persons like Monsignor Rotta, thousands (at times, tens of thousands) of Jews were able to save themselves during the turbulent period accompanying the decline and fall of the pro-Nazi regime in Hungary in 1944–45.[8]

The role of the church hierarchies in Hungary has been criticized severely for their timidity in the face of the government's collusion in the destruction of that country's large Jewish population. No one can question, however, the singular humanitarianism shown by

Father Janos Antal, head of the Salesian Saint John Bosco order in Hungary during 1944–45. In the turbulent days of December 1944, with Budapest in the throes of rioting and excesses by the pro-Nazi Arrow Cross militia that had seized power two months earlier, a young Jewish man fleeing for his life had been directed to the Salesian main center. He was shown in to Father Antal, the provincial, or head of the order. The young Istvan Anhalt described his plight before the priest. Father Antal then pointed to a priest's cassock on a nearby chair and said, "Try this on." The next morning the priest handed Anhalt the identity paper of Istvan Zserdeny, a seminarian in the order who lived in a place already in enemy hands. For the next two weeks, Anhalt walked the streets of Budapest and rode its streetcars in a priest's habit ("At times older women offered their seat to me, a young `priest'"), contacting family and friends and helping them in many ways.

On the night of December 14, the Salesian house, where Anhalt invariably returned to spend the evening, was raided by Arrow Cross militiamen. Anhalt's papers were in good order and his demeanor raised no suspicion. But in the building's basement, some forty Jews were found hiding. Father Antal was arrested together with his wards and taken in for a brutal interrogation. Anhalt rushed to the Vatican nunciature in the city to appeal for its intercession on behalf of the priest, before heading to a friend's house for a new place of hiding. After the war, Anhalt learned that Father Antal had been brutally beaten and threatened with death for hiding Jews in the monastery's compound. Father Antal is reported to have replied to his interrogators (Catholics of a different kind): "I would do the same, even after this; I would provide help to my fellow human beings in need, and under persecution, and if the consequence of this would be death, I put my life in the care of the Lord." The Vatican nunciature's intervention came in time, and he was released. The apprehended Jews were of course doomed. In the meantime, from his new hideout, Anhalt continued to pose as a priest. Once he was given ten minutes to arrange Catholic last rites for twenty fallen soldiers. With the capture of Budapest by the Russians in February 1945, Istvan Anhalt's role of a Catholic priest was over, and he resumed his Jewish identity as well as his musical profession.

Janina Zemian, a fugitive Jewish woman in Warsaw, in a postwar statement lists some helpful survival advice for Jewish girls posing as non-Jews. Her suggestions include the following: (1) Always smile; sad eyes, especially when their color is not blue, may identify you as Jewish. (2) If you are followed by a stranger, turn to him and ask brusquely: "Excuse me, do you know where I can find this or that street?" You will thereby prove to him that you speak infallible Polish, without a foreign accent, and that you are on the street for a specific purpose. Make sure to stare him in the eyes. (3) When this does not help, and he questions you, "You're Jewish, aren't you?" try one of the following three tactics: (a) If he's young and handsome, ask: "Is this the new style for making out with girls?" If he takes an interest in you, arrange to meet him at a street that you are sure never to cross. (b) Start screaming: "Hey, folks, he's insulting me! He claims I'm Jewish! How dare he? He should be ashamed of himself!" People will flock; a commotion will ensue, and you will be able to sneak away. (c) Look around, and if you notice a German soldier, walk up to him and say in Polish: "He's saying I'm Jewish." The German will probably respond (in German) that he does not understand Polish, and will turn the other way. You will then go on your way. (4) Learn to drink vodka—a small glass in one sip—without losing your balance. For everyone knows that "Jews can't drink." (5) Learn by heart the most important prayers, such as "Our Father in Heaven," or "Hail, Mary." Also know how to cross yourself properly. (6) Learn carefully important church laws and proscriptions, even the uncommon ones, so as to be able to respond to all questions without much ado. For instance: How do you know when it is your turn for Confession while waiting at the other end of the priest's cubicle when he is still busy with another person at the other end? Clearly, it is after three knocks by the priest.[9] Questions like this one were often asked to entrap Jews in Poland, most of whom were far removed from the world of the Catholic faith. In order to pass undetected as a native in a very Catholic country, a Jewish fugitive needed the tender guidance of a believing Catholic.

In spite of all of Janina Zemian's expert advice, she could not continue her clandestine existence without the help of trusted Poles who knew her secret and kept it to themselves and aided her when the going got rough, in spite of the risks to themselves. Some were recognized by Yad Vashem as Righteous among the Nations.[10]

Chapter 4

Movement from Place to Place

Testimony of Christian Mamen (Norway)

It was in the fall of 1942 that the arrest of Jews started in full. Hundreds were imprisoned, but about an equal number had hidden themselves away. One day I got an SOS call from one of these families. The father and a son were hiding in a small apartment in Oslo where they could stay no longer. The Jewish family had arrived in Norway from Berlin as refugees a few days before the German invasion. The wife's aged father had been arrested but had taken his life with poison. My parents agreed that we should take in Dr. Winterfeld and his 16-year-old son, Gerhard. This could not be a permanent arrangement, however. I had contact with an "export route" to Sweden. It was not one of the simpler ones, but we had to act quickly. One had to go to Mysen [Norway] on one's own, but these German Jews were unacquainted with the country and the language. I had to accompany them myself. I chose a combined milk-transport and bus-wagon. Fortunately, I had a good friend in Mysen. If stopped by authorities, I would say I was on my way to visit him. And that turned out to be no lie.

One of the difficulties was that we could not take too many people on the milk wagon to Mysen. Winterfeld's son had to stay behind and wait for a later transport. The three other members of the family and I took the train to Oslo. We pretended not to know each other. We repeated that on our walk through the city to the

Station Square, and again when we got on the milk wagon. They had to buy tickets separately, and had been instructed that all they should say was the name Mysen. The journey went by without interruption. In Mysen, one by one we entered the bakery of Rev. Andresen's father and disappeared into the private apartment on the next floor. Here we had to wait until evening. During the day, I contacted the man in charge of the "export-route," the chauffeur Nyte. Everything was in order. We could come to the garage when it got dark. The chauffeur would allegedly take a trip to Orje to fetch a load of wood. The three Jews were to hide under a tarpaulin on the loading place of the truck. It worked.

Later, we went down to the Rodnes Lake, which we crossed in a small boat. In utter darkness we crossed fields, stepped over barbed wire, and waded across streams and fountains. Those few kilometers felt like an eternity. Close to Klund Chapel on the eastern shore of the Rodnes Lake was the farm that was our next station along the road. Here we were well received and were given food and reports on the latest German moves in the region. From here onward there is a dense forest right across the border and far into Sweden. Before starting on this last leg of the trip, we were allowed a little sleep, fully dressed. Before dawn, we started up again. It was a wonderful feeling to reach the border-clearance in the woods. On the other side of the border, the Winterfeld family could really start breathing again.

Once I carried the three-year-old son of a dentist across the border to Sweden. He began to sing as he sat on my shoulders through the woods, but we managed to silence him by telling him not to disturb the birds who were sleeping. I still remember his strong grip in my hair and how he bent down and looked at me with his dark eyes. A son of Abraham, and a good Norwegian boy he was. The meaning was that this little boy and all of his race were to be killed, but he was saved from the gas chamber. It was my privilege to see the boy's family safely across the border, where they were received by Swedish soldiers and could start talking loud again, just as it was time for the birds to awaken. But we heard no bird songs. It was November 1942, and darkness ruled Europe. In Amsterdam, Anne Frank was hiding in a loft.

Flight across Borders

For those not prepared to spend an indefinite period in hiding at the mercy of others, and at the same time not possessing the psychological stamina and strong nerves needed to circulate nonchalantly under an assumed name and fabricated identity, there were other options. The alternatives were no less dangerous, but held out the prospect of avoiding immediate arrest by the Nazis: to flee to a less dangerous region not under direct control of the Germans, or to remain in territory where danger lurked everywhere, but to stay constantly on the move—a few days in one place, then on to another. This flight could last until the fugitive had crossed a frontier into a neutral country, or until strength and energy were exhausted and further running was no longer physically and mentally feasible.

Several European countries maintained their neutrality throughout the war, and these became the goal and hoped-for destinations for many Jews on the run. For those in the occupied countries of Western Europe, Sweden, Switzerland, and Spain were within relatively easy reach and consequently offered the best chances of safe havens. Switzerland, one should remember, was not too happy (to put it mildly) to admit Jewish refugees; many were forcefully turned back across the border. Even countries that were allied with Nazi Germany could still be viewed as havens, as the anti-Semitic policies pursued by these regimes were at times milder by comparison with Nazi Germany. Slovakia, Hungary, Romania, and Vichy France may be included in that category.

In addition, even German-occupied countries differed in the level and scope of direct Nazi control of their internal affairs. In Western Europe, direct German control was not as thorough in Belgium and northern France as in the Netherlands. The same was true of northern Italy (even after September 1943, when the country came under direct Nazi control) and Albania by comparison with Serbia. Moreover, the Italian zone in France (up to September 1943) proved a haven for fleeing Jews unequaled by any other region in France. Fascist Italy, an ally of Nazi Germany, adopted a milder form of anti-Semitism, and many within its leadership were appalled at the inhumane methods of their German ally, especially the mass slaughter of Jews. Whenever they could, Italian diplomats and generals, whether in Greece, Yugoslavia, or France, tried to stem the Nazi killing avalanche. The news spread quickly that the Italian Fascists had not completely jettisoned common decency and human feelings, and many Jews tried desperately to reach regions under Italian administration. With Jews forbidden the use of public transportation or travel outside their restricted zone, any movement depended on the goodwill and support of friendly non-Jews.

In France, where two-thirds of the country, including Paris, was under direct control by the Germans, civil matters were still handled by the government of "free" France, installed in Vichy, which held sway over the southern third of the country. Although the Vichy government adopted an anti-Semitic policy of its own, it proved less brutal than the anti-Semitism practiced by the Germans. Many tried fleeing from the Netherlands (under tight Nazi control) to Belgium and thence to the "free" zone of France, where they could hope for milder treatment, though their movements and economic pursuits were severely restricted. Additional escape routes led either to the Swiss and Spanish frontiers, or to the Italian-held territory in southeastern France, or even to Fascist Italy. For Jews in northwestern Europe, the trail of freedom from Denmark and Norway led directly toward neutral Sweden, which after 1943 placed no obstacles on the entry of Jews.

In Eastern Europe, especially Poland, where the German occupation was the harshest, attempts at flight from direct Nazi control were directed either northward toward the Baltic countries (before these came under German rule in June 1941), eastward toward Russian-held territories, or southward toward Hungary via Slovakia (a nominally independent state since 1939, but sporting a Nazi-style fascist regime). Hungary, an ally of Nazi Germany, implemented restrictive measures against its Jewish population, but until March 1944 the bulk of its 750,000 Jews was not physically harmed. When the situation there deteriorated and Jews began to be deported to the death camps, many attempted to flee to Romania, where the anti-Jewish policies of the Ion Antonescu regime had somewhat moderated by 1944. To the south of Hungary, in Yugoslavia, Jews attempted to flee either to the hills to seek refuge with partisan forces led by Josip Tito, or to adjacent Italian-held territories in Dalmatia and Albania, where persecution of Jews was for a time unknown.

In Greece, most Jews lived in the German-held region in and around the city of Thessaloniki, and only a few managed to flee to the Italian-administered region centered in Athens. When the Germans eventually took over direct control of the whole country in late 1943, Jews attempted flight either to the hills, to join forces with the partisans, or across the Aegean Sea to Turkey, which maintained a neutral stance throughout the war and continued its age-long tradition of tolerance toward the Jewish population.

In all these escape attempts, the hope for success depended on help by non-Jews, prepared to jeopardize themselves in order to facilitate travel on trains and buses for Jews forbidden the use of public transportation; to arrange dangerous border crossings over formidable geographical barriers (the Alps, Pyrenees, and Carpathian mountain ranges, as well as rivers and seas); and to negotiate other potential danger spots, such as border controls, spot checks on the highways, and registration at overnight lodgings. Their help was also needed in acquiring credentials, most of which were clandestinely fabricated and then handed to persons whose tenor and language did not always match the information on the documents. Not everyone who helped did so for altruistic reasons; there were those who exacted large payments in exchange for the needed documents or for facilitating crossings of guarded frontiers. In this volume, however, we are concerned with those who helped mostly out of altruistic considerations. Thousands of Jews were able to survive the Holocaust and rebuild new lives thanks to the selfless help of good-hearted voyage companions and trustworthy border smugglers whose main satisfaction was in having lent a hand to save innocent lives.

Movement and flight over long distances did not necessarily have to end in border crossings. In the Nazi world of controlled terror, there were temporary relapses, respites from persecution, and loopholes—places that proved a safe haven for brief spells of time. A Jew from Lvov may have felt safer circulating the streets and passing as a non-Jew in the much larger city of Warsaw, where he or she was not known. Or one could try fleeing a ghetto that was in the process of liquidation to another ghetto where the persecution of Jewish inhabitants had not reached a critical stage. In regions where partisan units operated, some Jews thought of joining up in the hope of being admitted to their ranks, even among insurgent groups not known for their friendliness to Jews. Hence flight from a ghetto to a partisan-held area, usually in the deep forests or impenetrable mountains, seemed to many a viable option.

In France, fleeing from the occupied to the unoccupied zone brought a temporary respite from physical persecution, especially if the Jew was a native of France. Refugees who had entered the country previous to the war were more likely to be handed over to the Germans, even if they had served in the French army. Other Jews on the run entertained no notions of being treated better in other places under Nazi control (especially in Eastern Europe), but were prepared to move from place to place as conditions warranted, without any specific destination. They stayed on the move until they found safe refuge and permanent shelter in a friendly home, where they could remain until the war's end; or else they moved again to another sheltering home. In all these instances, success or failure depended largely on the help obtained from friendly non-Jews, persons prepared to risk their own safety and lives to guarantee the safe passage of a harried Jew.

In Western Europe, many sought to cross into Switzerland, in spite of the attendant dangers. Pastor Roland De Pury, a Protestant minister in Lyon, allowed his home to be used as a transit point for dozens of Jews on their way to the Swiss border. It was also necessary to find trustworthy companions for the long journey to the border. Mireille Philip, whose husband served as minister in Charles de Gaulle's government-in-exile, led many children from the hilly region of the Le Chambon area toward the Lake Leman area, where a crossing would be attempted into Switzerland. René Nodot, an employee in the refugees department of the Vichy administration, took advantage of his position to organize border crossings at various points on the Franco-Swiss border, himself accompanying the fugitives to these crossing points. Helga Holbek and Alice Synnestvedt, both Quaker operatives, helped smuggle children out of the Gurs detention camp in southern France, and then led them on a long trek toward the Swiss border. The destination was the town of Annemasse, where a crossing was attempted when the Swiss and French customs officials were having their lunch break inside their cabin. Alice Muller, whose attorney husband was on the Gestapo wanted list for having been involved in a suit filed against Nazi leader Julius Streicher on charges of molesting a French girl during World War I, fled with her husband and their children to the Swiss border near Annemasse, where Father Gilbert Pernoud was waiting for them. "He told us to keep the utmost silence and march one behind the other. We reached the barbed wire. My husband crossed first; Pernoud then helped the girls cross, and I passed the last. Just after passing, we were stopped by a Swiss border patrol, who took us to Geneva, where we were made to sleep on hay. We were then taken to Camp Au Bout-du-Monde."

John Weidner, an experienced skier, used this skill for quick crossings into Switzerland when pursued by the Germans, who correctly suspected him of heading a network that smuggled persons across the border. Known by the code named "Dutch-Paris," the network organized surreptitious crossings of Jews and political refugees from as far as the Netherlands. His textile store in Annecy, some 25 kilometers from the border, served as a front and staging point for these crossings. He was always on the move and covered great distances. As a student before the war at an Adventist college in Collonges near the Swiss border (across from Geneva), he had meticulously studied the roads and byways of this picturesque region. This knowledge stood him in good stead during the war years. He often recited the following prayer before the beginning of a mission: "My

Father, help me to be kind to those I try to help. Where they have known only hatred, help me to be loving. And give me the confidence that this work will accomplish what you have placed me in the world to do." Arrested several times, he managed to escape and elude his captors. The Nazis, however, captured his sister and deported her to a concentration camp, where she perished.

If guiding fleeing Jews to a border crossing was a risky venture, assisting in the crossing itself compounded the dangers. Rolande Birgy, affiliated with a Catholic welfare organization (JOC), had perfected the art of smuggling dozens of Jews over the Swiss border. In the words of Jacques Pulver: "She accompanied us, as though we were on an excursion, alongside a frontier road, and then suddenly raised the barbed wire and made everyone cross. We had hardly managed to cross when a German patrol car appeared and she barely managed to flee with the pushcart we had brought along for transporting our twin daughters. A second too late, she would have fallen into the hands of the Germans."

The Swiss Red Cross established several homes on French soil for orphaned and abandoned children, refugees of the Spanish civil war and the recent European conflict. Maurice Dubois and Anne-Marie Im Hof-Piguet, who headed one such home at Château La Hille, not far from the Swiss border, took matters into their own hands and, disregarding Red Cross regulations, organized and carried out the illegal flight of Jewish children across the Swiss border. The decision to spirit them across to Switzerland was taken when they received word of an impending German raid on the home.

On the Swiss-German frontier, Major Paul Grüninger, the commandant of the Sankt Gallen border post, flouted government instructions forbidding access to fleeing Jews, and allowed hundreds to enter the country illegally. He was in turn suspended, demoted, tried, fined, and expelled from the service, forfeiting the retirement benefits he had accrued during many years of faithful service in the Swiss police. As this book goes to print, the Swiss government (Sankt Gallen canton) has again refused to grant the late Grüninger a full rehabilitation but, bowing to growing public pressure, has declared the man innocent of merely "political" faults. In 1971, Yad Vashem awarded him the title of Righteous among the Nations and planted a tree bearing his name in a spot overlooking the Hills of Judea.

When Germany occupied Italy in September 1943 and expanded its reign of terror on that country's Jews, many sought refuge by fleeing north toward the Swiss border. The previously mentioned Don Beccari, in the mountainous town of Nonantola, central Italy, arranged for more than one hundred Jewish children, who had previously been sheltered in his seminary, to cross the Swiss border safely. Alfonso Canova at first helped Jewish refugees from Yugoslavia, whom he met in Bologna, in various ways. Sensing that the Gestapo was on their trail, he also arranged for their flight to the Swiss border. Lydia Cattaneo, who lived near the Swiss border, accompanied Jewish refugees on their flight to and across the border with the help of trusted passers. On two separate occasions, women refugees sprained their legs on the tortuous mountain roads and had to be taken back and hidden until they had recuperated well enough to attempt a second crossing.

Switzerland was the obvious choice for fleeing Jews in France, but others preferred Spain. This was especially true for those residing in southern France, where the Spanish border was within easy reach. But, while the terrain at the Swiss border in the Annemasse-Geneva region presented no insurmountable obstacle, the formidable Pyrenees mountains made the crossing into Spain physically strenuous. Some refugees, losing their way in the mountainous peaks or abandoned by their paid guides, froze to death on the snow-covered trails. Dangerous conditions also prevailed for Jews attempting to cross the Franco-Italian border in the Alps region.[1] In spite of these risks, many preferred the Pyrenees route because it was less rigorously guarded than the Swiss border.

A well-known story in this regard is that of Joop Westerweel, who organized groups of Jewish youth in the Netherlands, led them across occupied Belgium and France, and bade them farewell on the Pyrenean peaks before they crossed into Spain. No less dramatic is the story of Aristides de Sousa Mendes, the Portuguese consul general in Bordeaux, France, who issued Portuguese transit visas to thousands of Jews stranded in that city on the eve of its occupation by the Germans in June 1940, in spite of clear government instructions to the contrary. This made it possible for them to cross into Spain in advance of the approaching German army, then continue to Portugal. The case of Varian Fry is no less remarkable. Arriving in Marseille in August 1940 as a representative of the U.S.-based Emergency Rescue Committee, he used unorthodox methods to smuggle out of the country several hundred celebrated German and Austrian fugitives of Nazi terror (most of them Jewish), before being nabbed by the Gestapo, whose tentacles reached into the far corners of Vichy France.

Sweden was the hoped-for destination for Jews wishing to escape Nazi rule in northern Europe. From Norway, Sweden could be reached either by sea or via difficult mountain terrain and fjord crossings. This, of course, could not be done without outside help. Hans-Christian Mamen led many fleeing Jews across the Swedish border. His luck held out on several occasions when the bus that took him and his wards to the border region was boarded by Norwegian police. Although the papers held by the fugitive Jews were patently false, the policemen overlooked this serious offense. On another occasion, Mamen carried a three-year-old boy all the way across the border. "I still remember his strong grip in my hair and how he bent down and looked at me with his dark eyes. A son of Abraham, and a good Norwegian boy he was." In nearby Denmark, when the tiny Jewish community of eight thousand persons was threatened with deportation in October 1943, the Danish underground arranged, supervised, and carried out the flight of almost all Jews to Sweden aboard fishing boats. The whole operation lasted a fortnight, and by the time the Germans woke up to the fact, some seventy-two hundred Jews were safe and sound in Sweden. This is the only instance where a plan by the Nazis to destroy a country's Jews was foiled by that country's underground movement.

Some Jews were also helped to flee to Sweden from Germany. Pastor Erik Myrgren, of the Swedish Church in Berlin, organized the flight of dozens of Jews in sealed boxcars aboard trains heading to a seaport on the Baltic coast, with the help of bribed officials and local trustworthy Germans. The boxcars were supposed to contain furniture and other goods belonging to Swedish diplomatic personnel in Berlin. Upon arrival at Lübeck, the sealed boxcars were loaded onto ships heading to Sweden, together with the secret cargo of hidden Jews.

In Lithuania, Sempo Sugihara, the Japanese consul general in Kaunas, issued Japanese transit visas to thousands of Jews who had fled from Poland and found themselves stranded in Lithuania. He did so in spite of government instructions to the contrary. This visa on their passports enabled them to cross into Soviet Russia, then proceed to Japan. They left the country just in time, before the German invasion struck Lithuania in June 1941. Upon his return to Tokyo, Sugihara was peremptorily expelled from his country's diplomatic service.

In Poland, many sought to reach the Soviet lines, but as German forces penetrated ever deeper into Russian territory, this option became less and less feasible. The other possibility was to attempt a crossing into Hungary via Slovakia. Hungary, though an ally of Nazi Germany and itself applying anti-Semitic measures against its Jewish population, stopped short of physically harming them. This lasted until the Germans took direct control of that country in March 1944. Andrzej Kostrz was one of the few Poles who led many Jews across the Carpathian Mountains into Slovakia, and thence to Hungary. He was lame in one leg, but this did not prevent him from spiriting Jews out of the Cracow ghetto, arranging temporary shelter for them in his home, then guiding them through difficult terrain across Nazi-allied Slovakia into Hungary by way of Kosice.

Zevi Zimmerman relates how he and fellow fugitive

Jews from Cracow were helped by the Pole Michal Lomnicki to flee toward the Slovakian border, where they rendezvoused with the Slovakian forester Stefan Kocun. They too arrived safely in Hungary by way of Kosice. Back on the Polish side of the border, the Kobylec family home in a mining town near Katowice served as relay station for Jews fleeing toward the Slovakian border. One of the family's sons was drafted into the German army (the region had been annexed to Germany). The Germans were finally able to track down the source of this escape leak, and the Kobylec family was arrested. The elder Piotr and son Mieczyslaw were carted off to Auschwitz camp, where they suffered immensely but survived.

When matters took a turn for the worse in Hungary, many attempted to cross into Romania, which in 1944 was already wavering in its loyalty to the Axis cause and had toned down the persecution of its Jews. In German-occupied Yugoslavia, many Jews sought shelter with Tito's partisans, or in the Italian zone of occupation, or in Italian-administered Albania. Mustafa Hardaga, a Moslem from Sarajevo, arranged the flight into Italian-held Mostar of his friend Josef Cavilio, who joined his family who had fled there earlier (also with the help of Hardaga). In the Macedonian city of Skopje, which was annexed by Bulgaria, Anna Popstefanova, an actress married to a Bulgarian police officer, arranged the flight of the Jewish family Kariv to the Albanian frontier (under Italian control), which they successfully crossed. Farther south, in occupied Greece, Dr. Kostas Anagnostopoulos provided shelter to a Jewish family, then led them to a rendezvous with the captain of a fishing vessel for their flight across the Aegean Sea to Turkey. Also in Greece, Pouris Demosthenes helped the two Cohen brothers to flee to Turkey. The rest of the family was in hiding in the palace of Princess Alice, whose son Philip is now Duke of Edinburgh, married to Queen Elizabeth II of Great Britain. Princess Alice is one more dignitary embellishing the Righteous Roll of Honor at Yad Vashem.

Movement within Nazi-Controlled Lands

Compared to fleeing across well-guarded international frontiers, moving from one place to another within enemy-held territory seemed to many an easier, more manageable, and less dangerous option. In France, for instance, geographical and political conditions favored movement within the country. Many areas were less accessible than others, such as the Protestant redoubt in Le Chambon and the Cévennes, and the Lozére region. An additional attractive haven for fleeing Jews was the Italian zone of occupation in the Nice and Savoy areas, which offered excellent refuge prospects by comparison with the rest of the country, since the Italians, though allied to the Germans, did not persecute Jews in the Nazi style. In fact, they considered the whole preoccupation with the "Jewish Question" a boring nuisance and an interference with the greater goal of winning the war. Jews arriving in the Italian zone of France sighed in relief; they were no longer a hunted species. Moreover, the Germans did not have the requisite SS and Gestapo manpower to undertake massive manhunts of Jews throughout the country (as they were able to do in Poland); they had to rely on the local police and gendarmes, who in many cases proved unreliable.

An example of help in moving Jews from one place to another inside France is the case of Father Jean Fleury in Poitiers, who helped disperse Jews of his region to various distant locations. Hélène Durand, one of his aides, was especially adept at this. In the words of one of the rescued Jewish women: "She accompanied us to the nearby Catholic women's seminary and there we were hidden for one evening. The following morning, we left on foot to a farming family in a village, 15 kilometers away, who hid us for two weeks." From there they proceeded to Lyon and Grenoble.

Renée Gaudefroy helped the OSE, a Jewish children's welfare organization, move 150 children to various safe locations, using arguments and threats to get people's consent to help her in this endeavor. Likewise, Marinette

Guy and Juliette Vidal arranged sheltering places for many children in the Chamonix area of France. Camille Mathieu, a guard at the Drancy detention camp in the Paris region, helped three men and their wives cross into the Vichy zone of France in 1941, after he had arranged the men's flight from the camp. There his family cared for them in the succeeding years.

In the Netherlands, the small size of the country, its stringent control by the Nazis, and the undiversified nature of its territory made movement from one place to another more difficult. But the country's active underground, with its excellent contacts, compensated for the many difficulties standing in the way of fleeing Jews. The underground helped move fugitives from place to place in quick succession. Thirteen-year-old Ruth, for example, was first taken to the home of Arie Verduijn, an engineer in Helmond, where her family had occasionally visited. She was then moved to the Postuma home in Helenaveen, where Ruth shared the bed of one of the eight children in that household. Thence she was taken to the Driessen home in Sevenum, where she stayed with the Reverend Mr. Gommans for four days, then went to the Verhaags, followed by a stay with the Ulens family. She then moved back to the Verduijns, and to the Ulens as well—all this in order to better her chances of survival.

The case of the De Zoete family is another example of a family desperately trying to stay one step ahead of its persecutors. The three De Zoete children were moved separately to eight different locations. At one of these places, one of the girls had to leave because of marital problems in her hosts' home. The parents, in turn, moved to five different locations, ending up in the church garret of Rev. Gerrit Brillenburg-Wurth of the Dutch Reformed Church in Rotterdam, where they were hidden with other Jews and told to keep especially quiet while services were in session. The De Zoete family survived the Holocaust intact.

In Eastern Europe, conditions were more precarious for the local populations and even more so for the defenseless Jews. Sara Diller had served as a private tutor to the sons of Anna Bogdanowicz, who was married to an anti-Semitic mayor of a large city. When Sara was threatened with deportation, Anna arranged for her to flee from Jaslo to Kielce and helped find several hiding places for her in the region. Anna Bogdanowicz was eventually arrested by the Gestapo and sent to Auschwitz, where she perished.

Tadeusz Soroka, who worked for the railways in Grodno, northern Poland, took along nine Jews on several nighttime journeys on top of German military trains en route to the Russian front. The plan was to flee the Grodno ghetto, which in early 1944 was slated for destruction, to Vilnius, several hundred kilometers away, where conditions had stabilized after several killing spates in the nearby Ponary forest. From Vilnius one could also attempt to join the partisans who were operating in the vicinity. The journey in the cold night of March 1944 took place on top of a military wagon, and as the train approached Vilnius, the Jews jumped off and hid in the fields until they could mingle with a group of Jewish laborers on their way back to the ghetto. Soroka made five such trips aboard German military convoys.

There are many similar stories of Poles helping Jews escape from ghettos and labor camps, then taking them to other regions within the occupied country where hiding places were prepared for them. Leon Sliwinski helped the 12-year-old David Friedman flee a German labor camp near Kielce, with the consent of Sliwinski's parents and Friedman's parents. Leon sneaked up to the fence and pulled two strands of barbed wire apart so that David could squeeze through. Both then hopped on a train carrying lumber, going in the direction of Sliwinski's home. There David remained hidden until the area's liberation. Edward Marciniak spirited children and grown-ups from the Warsaw ghetto to temporary shelter in his home, then secretly moved them to other locations. In command of a partisan unit, he was able to move persons from place to place with relative ease. Similarly, Feliks Rajszczak helped move Jewish underground fighters of the Warsaw ghetto, as they emerged from the sewers in flight from the burning ghetto, to a hideout on the Aryan side of the city (which was off-limits to Jews on pain of death). He later sheltered some of the Jews in his Warsaw apartment for an extended period until they were able to relocate. Zofia Glowiak agreed to smuggle out of the Tarnopol ghetto the sister and daughter of a Jewish person (who was passing as a non-Jew) she had recently met at her workplace. The fugitive Jewish women were at first hidden in Glowiak's home in Tarnopol, then moved to other locations. When their luck ran out in a village near Lvov, they returned to Zofia, the "savior angel, the faithful guardian," in their words, with whom they stayed intermittently.

A fantastic rescue story of moving from a dangerous place to one paradoxically more dangerous is that of the teenager Julian Goldman. He was first hidden on the Aryan side of Warsaw by Celina Ceglewska, his family's former governess. When the Germans evicted the population of Warsaw following the Polish uprising of 1944, Celina decided to take Julian with her (declaring him as her son)—to Auschwitz camp, of all places! She felt he stood a better chance of surviving close to her in the area of the camp reserved for political prisoners, rather than by himself on the ravaged streets of Warsaw. In Auschwitz, she managed to keep him with her in the women's section where she could watch over his every move. When the camp was evacuated in January 1945, Celina took Julian to a labor camp near Berlin, where both remained until the end of the war.

In Vilnius, Lithuania, Ona Simaite, a librarian at the main city library, at first smuggled out precious Jewish literature from the ghetto, then helped move persons to the Aryan side. Sofija Binkiene, a writer in Kovno, turned her home into a relay station for Jews escaping the nearby ghetto, some of whom she personally picked up on the streets. She forwarded them to various sheltering places. The Rakevicius family, who lived outside of Kaunas, helped smuggle out some thirty Jews from the doomed ghetto and dispersed them in the countryside among friendly farmers. Among those saved were seven-year-old Aaron Barak and his mother (he was smuggled out of the ghetto inside a sack, which one of the Rakevicius sons carried a long distance until he reached his home); Barak is currently serving as President of Israel's Supreme Court.

Bronius Gotautas, a wandering Lithuanian monk who peddled religious books and pamphlets, arranged hiding places for many Jews who had fled the Kovno ghetto. Sarah Finkelbrand, one of his wards, describes him as small in stature, his faced covered with a reddish beard, and dressed in a heavily patched cassock and with a sack pulled over his back. He lived in extreme poverty, walked barefoot (except in winter), and ate sparingly. He had no permanent place to sleep, lodging for the evening wherever his wanderings took him. He was venerated by many as a saint. His popularity made it possible for him to find sheltering places among his admirers for fleeing Jews.

The story of Leah Korlendchik is a further illustration of survival by life on the run. Until 1943, her family was inside the Kaunas ghetto. With the help of a paid Lithuanian, they were able to flee the ghetto and reach their former birthplace, near the town of Vishay (Veisiejai). They looked up an old acquaintance and asked for his help; he turned them down. Destitute and at a loss what to do next, Leah's family considered drowning themselves in a nearby lake. "Suddenly we recalled another Lithuanian we knew, Margialis, also a former customer of our store. He admitted us to his home, the three of us." He kept them only two days, for fear that his son, a policeman, would turn them in. He then led them to a friend in a nearby village. There a hiding place was built underneath the kitchen. When the neighbors began to glance suspiciously at that home, it was time to move again. They reached another village and another friendly sheltering home. That family supplied them with false credentials, with which they were able to hire themselves out as handymen on local farms, and thus pass undetected until the area's liberation.[2]

Temporary hiding places for people on the run included hospitals and pension homes. Dr. Stanislaw Swital sheltered members of the Jewish resistance of the Warsaw ghetto in his hospital outside the city. To avoid detection by the Gestapo, he placed a sign over the wards where the Jews were kept, reading: "Warning! Typhus Infection!" No German dared go through that door. Janina Szandorowska claims to have opened the doors of her Warsaw pension to as many as one hundred refugees from the Warsaw ghetto who stopped there to rest. A clandestine Jewish organization referred the fleeing Jews to her. Those with clearly Semitic features remained indoors. From the pension, they proceeded to other prearranged sheltering places inside and outside the city.

As strange as it may sound, for Jews living in occupied Poland, where Nazi terror was at its most brutal, Germany seemed a less threatening place, especially if one arrived there under a pretentious non-Jewish name as part of a contingent of forced laborers to perform various assignments in industrial installations, on farms, or as domestics in German homes. Conditions for Jews passing as non-Jews in Nazi Germany were more tolerable than in occupied Poland, where Nazi terror was relentless and local anti-Semitism even stronger than in Germany. Thus when Leonard Glinski overheard a work colleague and his wife, in Warsaw, contrive to throw out on the street a 16-year-old Jewish girl in their care, he arranged through his underground contacts for her to be provided with a new set of credentials and registered for domestic work in Vienna. Thanks to this ruse she survived.

The Bass sisters, after losing their parents to the Germans in Majdanek camp and hiding in various unsafe places in nearby Lublin, were able through the intercession of Father Jan Poddebniak to be registered for labor in Germany. They found themselves assigned to a hospital that treated wounded soldiers as well as sick and injured foreign laborers. Father Poddebniak continued writing the sisters letters on various subjects, including the supposed state of health of their fictitious family, so as to give credence to their false identities. Young women doing labor in Germany who received no mail from home could raise suspicions among their colleagues, and Father Poddebniak understood this well.

Dora Sagalowicz moved, under an assumed name,

from Lvov to a farm in Germany. She was accompanied by the two Ukrainian sisters, Vera and Nadezhda Izmalkova, in whose home she had previously stayed. The three women lived out the war years on a farm near Weimar, Germany.

Many similar cases are recorded of Jews in Poland who, with the aid of local Poles or friendly German officials, were able to leave for Germany under assumed names. Most survived the war years with their true identity a secret. Others were discovered and deported to the death camps, as was the case of Malke Livne and her sister, who wound up in Auschwitz after the Gestapo had uncovered their Jewish identity.[3]

These cases of survivors constitute drops in the bucket; the paths of the large majority of Jews did not cross those of friendly non-Jews, or of persons prepared to risk their own safety for the sake of the distraught Jews. They are not here to testify, for they make up part of the doomed six million; their ashes lie spread across the fields of Europe, in ditches and unmarked graves, near Auschwitz, Treblinka, Sobibor, Belzec, Chelmno, Treblinka, Babi Yar, Bergen-Belsen, Dachau, and Buchenwald.

In some instances, German military or civilian officials attached with the Polish occupation administration arranged employment in Germany for their Jewish workers to protect them from the killing raids of the SS and Gestapo, who operated with greater freedom and brutality in Poland than in Germany itself. The previously mentioned Major Helmrich arranged for a dozen Jewish women to be sent to Germany under assumed names, where his wife Donata arranged domestic assignments for them, thus assuring their survival. After the war he explained his motivation in the following words: "We preferred for our children to have dead parents than cowards as parents. After this decision, everything was relatively easy. We figured that after we had saved two Jews, we were both equally guilty before Hitler if we were apprehended. Therefore, each additional person we saved, we considered a bonus to us."

Not far from Drohobycz, in Lvov, Konrad David, a German civilian working under contract for a construction firm, learned that his housekeeper, Nusia Koerner, was Jewish and was being blackmailed by a Ukrainian policeman. Instead of dismissing her, he hid her temporarily in the house of a friend who was away on leave. Later, in April 1944, when the construction firm was relocated to a safer location (the Russians were within reach of Lvov), David took Koerner and her five-year-old daughter with him to the firm's new location, where she was assigned to prepare food for the workers. He later arranged for her further transfer inside Germany.

Once in Germany, Jews passing as foreign laborers found it best to stay put in a single place. But this was not necessarily true for local German Jews. Like their compatriots in other Nazi-ruled countries, they learned to survive by not staying too long in one place. For instance, the former film producer Max Krakauer and his wife moved to more than forty different locations (mostly with the help of ministers of the Confessing Church) during the war years; they survived unharmed. After the war, Krakauer detailed these peregrinations in a book entitled *Lichter im Dunkel* (Lights in the Darkness).[4] The Wolffenstein sisters, who had been baptized into the church but by Nazi racist definition were considered "full" Jews, were also helped by ministers of the Confessing Church to move to distant places within Germany.[5]

Founded in 1934, the Confessing Church consisted of ministers of various Protestant denominations who were opposed to the Nazi-controlled main church organization as well as to the Nazi ideas of the primacy of race, leader, and soil. Though in most cases blindly accepting the centuries-old anti-Jewish theological prejudice of their predecessors, they saw in Hitler and Nazism the greater danger. They helped many baptized Jews (and other Jews) elude their captors.

An unusual story is that of Siegmund and Marga Spiegel and their small daughter Karin, alluded to earlier. A recipient of the Iron Cross for his services in the German army during World War I, Spiegel earned a living as a cattle merchant in Ahlen after the war. Learning of his impending deportation to the camps, he contacted some of his former clients, and from February 1943 to

May 1945, they helped the Spiegels move from place to place and arranged shelter on different farmsteads in the Münsterland area. In some places, the family stayed for only a few days, in others for several weeks or longer. Their rescuers knew their true identity; others were told that they were refugees from nearby cities enduring Allied air raids. When danger threatened, they fled at a moment's notice, but were fortunate to find shelter on another farmstead. Recalling one of these farming families, the Aschoffs, Margot writes: "These acts of kindness can never be repaid. I came to these courageous people, who didn't even know me, ate with them, and was received as though I belonged with them." The Spiegels were among the few lucky Jews of Germany—the majority of their brethren who remained in Germany perished in the camps.

Similar examples of flight attempts occurred in other occupied European countries. In Yugoslavia, in December 1943, Olga Bartulovic led the Jewish Nachmias family over a 4-kilometer trek to a hilly region controlled by Tito's partisan forces, where they were safe. In Hungary, in October 1944, when Jewish internees in a camp in Satoraljaujhely were about to be handed over to the Germans, the Czismadia family (whose house bordered the camp) arranged the flight of some thirty men to nearby villages. One survivor relates that when they had to cross a certain guarded railway bridge, Malvina Czismadia approached one of the Hungarian gendarmes and asked for a match to light a cigarette. She struck up a conversation with the guard, allowing enough time for the men to cross the railway tracks undetected. "Half an hour later, when I fell down exhausted," relates one survivor, "Malvina forced me to continue walking. It was a superhuman thing to do with all those sights on the way: corpses of workers from the labor units left hanging, and dead cattle in the ditches." Malvina's sister Olga did likewise for another group of men.

In Greece, Dimitris Spiliakos, an attorney in Thessaloniki, cleverly arranged for some of his former Jewish clients to flee the local ghetto in early 1943. Since the Germans allowed a limited number of Jews who claimed Italian nationality to leave Thessaloniki for Athens (where, under Italian administration, Jews were not molested), Spiliakos was able to produce false credentials for his Jewish protégés, and after arranging their flight from the Jewish ghetto, had them board an Italian military train leaving for Athens, where they were safe.

In Italy, the Catholic priest Beniamino Schivo, already mentioned earlier, led the Jewish Korn family from Città di Castello, where they were originally interned, to various hiding places in the hilly countryside. In the words of Ursula Korn: "He took off his habit and, together with another young priest, marched us by night through German patrols eight hours up into the hills to a summer village of the Salesian nuns. There he broke down a side door, and there we hid for a month in the dark with all windows closed, sleeping on the bare floor." When they no longer felt secure in that place, he took the family's father farther up into the hills, while mother and daughter were hidden in a convent dressed as nuns, locked in a room, with only the mother superior privy to their presence. They all survived.

At times, simply moving at random from place to place was no guarantee of survival. One needed to stay constantly one step ahead of the enemy to better the chances of nondetection. An unusual story in this regard, previously alluded to, is that of Dr. Olga Goldfein. She was a practicing physician in Pruzana, northeastern Poland (today in Belarus). On a medical errand, she met Sister Dolorosa of the Order of Saint Ignacy of Loyola and treated her illness. Later, when the Germans decided to liquidate the Jews of Pruzana, Olga fled to Sister Dolorosa's convent. Told that she could not admit the forlorn woman within the walls of the convent, Sister Dolorosa decided to leave and take up the life of a wandering nun. She took with her the Jewish woman, who was given a nun's habit and a name to go with it—Sister Helena. The two women supported themselves with alms in return for prayers and healing advice. Dr. Goldfein was introduced as a former student nurse who had taken a nun's vows; she was revered as a healer. They finally arrived at Sister Dolorosa's hometown of Rozyce, where they stayed until the country's liberation. Sister Dolorosa was thereupon expelled from the order for breaking monastic rules; she reverted to her original name of Genowefa Czubak. Dr. Goldfein moved to Israel and resumed her medical practice in a Haifa hospital.

In the Kosov region of southeastern Poland, the Ukrainian Olena Hryhoryszyn cared for a 12-year-old orphan named Donia whom she had met by accident. She wandered with the forlorn girl to different places while supporting herself with odd jobs. At times, she hid the girl in a forest hole, coming out at night to feed her and massage her frozen legs. Hryhoryszyn told Donia: "For as long as I live, so shall you. Only now do I realize that my life has a meaning.... My single wish is that God allow me to keep you strong and healthy so that you live to experience happiness. I ask nothing in return. Only, when I die, you bury me." In the spring of 1944, while Donia was in the forest, she was accosted by a Ukrainian pro-German militiaman. She fled across the Pruth River and into the Russian-held zone. She survived and dedicated a book to her rescuer, whom she never saw again.

In another story involving a Ukrainian helper, Miriam Baratz was helped by Jakob Suchenko to move and flee from one place to another in the Kiev region, until he was apprehended and shot by the Germans.

In Croatia, Julija Dajc, who had lost her husband to the Nazis, found herself constrained to be constantly on the move, and worried where she would deliver the child she was carrying. Staying one night at the home of the Bondzic family, she slept together with Grozdana, the house matron, who did not turn on the light lest the children wake up and see the strange woman. She gave birth to a child in another home, then continued her wanderings. "From the day of my son's birth [in March 1943], until the end of June 1943, I took refuge in 24 different houses in the vicinity of Aleksandrovac. Slobodan Knezevic [one of her benefactors] used to visit me from time to time at night on his donkey, and, in spite of the curfew, take me through byways from one sheltering place to another, carrying my baby in his arms."

Fleeing from Death Marches

Survival through quick movement, in its most acute form, is exemplified in the stories of "death march" escapees. In early 1945, with German armies reeling before the Soviet juggernaut, whose armies had penetrated German-held Poland, the Nazis decided to evacuate Jewish prisoners and lead them at gunpoint on forced marches, in subzero weather, to the interior of Germany. Thousands of marchers, their strength gone, fell from exhaustion and were shot by Nazi guards. Those who reached their destination—another concentration camp—underwent new deprivations and ongoing struggles to survive. Elie Wiesel, for one, describes the harrowing death march from Auschwitz in January 1945 in which he and his father participated (his mother and siblings were lost in Auschwitz). After much more harrowing suffering, Wiesel survived to witness liberation at Buchenwald camp. His father's strength gave out several weeks before liberation.[6]

A few others tried their luck by fleeing from the dwindling ranks of the marchers. Those caught were shot on the spot; others who were hidden by friendly people survived to tell their ordeal. One was Michael Gilad. Born in 1925, he lost his parents and sisters in the Belzec death camp. Being able-bodied, he was conscripted into a labor gang, and in November 1943 was dispatched to Auschwitz. On the night of January 17, 1945, he was led with 14,000 prisoners on a long march in the cold night, through sleet and cold, surrounded by armed SS guards. "We marched some 100 kilometers that night. The shots [of those falling on the way] did not stop for a moment. With our last strength, we arrived at dawn to an abandoned camp near Gliwice." After a short rest, the marchers were loaded on an open cattle wagon, then forced to descend and continue on foot. Through all this tormenting march, they were not fed. "When I felt fully exhausted, I decided that rather than falling during the march, I had better try escaping, clearly risking being shot during my flight, but I was not going to give in."

Gilad and several friends reached the village of Wielopole, sneaked into the attic of a barn, and dug themselves into the deep hay. A while later, they heard German voices, which they inferred were of SS guards seeking escaped prisoners. Throughout that night, they heard shots and the howling of dogs. The next morning a young girl climbed to the attic and left a pitcher of milk and a loaf of bread. At first they feared a trap, but hunger overcame them, and they emptied the pitcher and gobbled down the bread. That afternoon the same girl appeared with additional food. Stefania Zimon and her parents decided to shelter the three fugitive Jews for several weeks, in spite of the risks to themselves, until the front had passed that area. The three survived. After the war, Gilad moved to Israel and joined a special police team that prepared the case against Adolf Eichmann, one of the chief Nazi architects of the "Final Solution," who was apprehended in Argentina, brought to Israel in 1960, and tried and executed.

A similar story is that of Anna Salzberg and her sister Malka Livne. After a three-day forced march in deep snow from Auschwitz camp, they arrived at the village of Jastrzebie-Zdroj. "My feet were badly frozen and swollen, and it became almost unbearable to continue," Anna recalls. That evening, they were able to slip out unnoticed and reach the nearby farmhouse of Erwin and Gertruda Moldrzyk, where they were sheltered until the arrival of the Russians several weeks later.

Bruno and Bronislawa Jurytko, of the village of Ksiazenice, sheltered a group of 14 Jews who had escaped from a column of "death marchers" from Auschwitz after the German guards, annoyed at having to watch over their straggling prisoners, opened fire on them. SS troops searched for the Jewish escapees in nearby villages; those caught were killed on the spot. Samuel Lieberman and his group of fugitives were among the lucky ones who survived, thanks to their fortitude and the kindheartedness of a local farming couple. Before leaving the house of their benefactor, they added their signatures to the following statement: "We, the undersigned from Auschwitz camp, confirm that Bruno Jurytko, from the village of Ksiazenice, at the risk of his life and of his family, sheltered us for eight days and fed us, and helped us in other ways; all this, while the Germans and SS were pursuing all escapees in the region, thus saving our lives in return for no material compensation—only because he is an honest and straightforward person."

Escapees from other concentration camps include Eva Erben, who formed part of a column of prisoners led out from Gross Rosen camp. After her mother collapsed and died during the march, she decided to escape and wandered into the Czech village of Postrekov. She was found unconscious in an open field by Kristof Jahn, who took her home and together with his wife Ludmila nursed the teenaged girl back to health.

Erna Haertel, a German farming woman in Moldinau, East Prussia (today, Poland), took in Frieda Kleiman after she escaped from a mass massacre of Jewish women prisoners on the shores of the Baltic Sea. These thousands of women had been forced to march in deep snow from Stutthof camp, which was evacuated in January 1945 at the approach of the Russians, toward the Baltic Sea coast, where they were told they would be taken aboard boats to the interior of Germany. Instead, upon reaching the coast, German machine gunners opened fire on the scantily dressed women. Kleiman found herself in the ice-cold water of the Baltic. After wading ashore, she began to walk aimlessly until she reached the home of Erna Haertel. Kleiman recalls the expression of horror on the face of her benefactress: "This the Germans did?" Haertel asked in consternation. Kleiman adds: "I looked like a monster." Then, Haertel, "with tears in her eyes, quickly swept me into her home, embraced and comforted me. From that moment she cared for me like a mother." After bathing her and washing her lice-infected hair, Haertel put the forlorn woman in a comfortable bed (for the first time in years) and said: "Now you are a person like the others. You shall stay with me until the war's end."

Similarly, Celina Manilewitz and her two women companions, who had also escaped the Baltic Sea massacre, reached the home of Loni and Albert Harder in the village of Sorginau. "It was almost too much. It was like a dream—having a proper bed again, for the first time after long years of concentration camps.... Here in the midst of our enemies, the Germans, we three Polish girls—Jewish, too—had suddenly found a mother." They survived, a handful out of the original ten thousand, thanks to the compassion of a German farming couple.

Hannah Rigler, who had been on the same death march, slipped out of the column after her mother fell from exhaustion, and wandered into a barn that was manned by British prisoners of war who had been brought there from a nearby camp for their day's chores. She was discovered by Stan Wells, who alerted several of his friends; they consulted on what to do with this fugitive girl. One of the men, in an entry in his diary dated January 26, 1945, describes the condition of the women prisoners: "They came straggling through the bitter cold, about 300 of them, limping, dragging footsteps, slipping and falling—to rise and stagger under the blows of the guards—SS swine. Crying loudly for bread, screaming for food, 300 matted haired, filthy objects that had once been Jewesses!" He writes of his reaction to this sight: "I was struck dumb with a miserable rage, a blind coldness which nearly resulted in my being shot. Never in my life have I been so devoid of fear of opening my mouth." The men conspired to save the lone woman who had straggled into the barn. They smuggled her into their camp where, inside the men's compound, she was washed and nursed back to health. After several weeks, the British POWs were moved out, but not before they had arranged for Sarah to be cared for by a paid Polish woman. Sarah survived the war and years later reestablished contact with her POW friends, and together they took part in a moving ceremony at Yad Vashem.

Support by the Clergy

Members of the clergy were also involved in moving Jews from place to place. Priests, pastors, monks, and nuns had certain advantages and privileges usually not enjoyed by laymen, such as greater freedom of movement, access to baptismal papers that served as birth certificates, and inviolability of their persons and property (though sometimes honored only in letter rather than in practice). They were often shown somewhat greater consideration by the Nazis and their collaborators, who claimed that the cause they were fighting for would assure the survival of Christian civilization from the encroachment of Judaism and communism.

Clergy who lent a hand did so out of a sincere conviction that this was a religious obligation, coupled with an abiding theological belief that the Jews remained God's chosen people, though having "backslid" for not acknowledging the "true" faith. In spite of the continuous refusal of Jews to accept the Christian Messiah as their own, many Christians felt a personal obligation to protect the seed of Abraham from destruction from the hands of those perceived as representing a direct threat to the very core of Christian faith and civilization. It must be pointed out, however, that relatively few clergymen in Eastern Europe were involved in helping Jews, since the clergy there mirrored the intense anti-Semitism of the local populations. In Western European countries such as France, Italy, Belgium, and the Netherlands, larger segments of the clergy spearheaded the rescue of Jews.

Father Benoit, a French-born Franciscan monk stationed in Marseille, fabricated false credentials for Jews trying to flee the country. At first he directed them either toward the Spanish border or to Nice, which was under Italian administration. With the Gestapo hot on his trail, he fled to Nice in 1943 and persuaded the Italian Commissioner of Jewish Affairs, Guido Lospinoso, not to place obstacles in Benoit's rescue activities. This included an extraordinary plan to move thousands of Jews, via boat, across the Mediterranean Sea toward North Africa, recently liberated by Allied armies. The new Italian government of Pietro Badoglio, after the demise of Benito Mussolini, in July 1943 gave its blessing to the plan, and this was seconded by Pope Pius XII, with whom Benoit had a special audience. When the plan was foiled by the German invasion of Italy in September 1943, Benoit remained in Rome, and as "Padre Benedetto" helped hundreds of Jews elude the Nazi dragnet in that city. Dubbed "Father of the Jews" by his benefactors, he stated after the war: "What I did for the Jewish people…is but an infinitesimal contribution of what should have been done to prevent this most heinous and satanic slaughter of some six million Jews, which will undoubtedly remain mankind's foulest disgrace.… The Jewish people is not to be exterminated. It is by divine providence that the Jewish people wishes to fulfill its divine goals—at first, for its own good, then for the good of all mankind."

Many of his French colleagues may have entertained similar feelings in their heart. Father Louis Favre, for example, of the Juvenat seminary in Ville la Grand, personally facilitated the crossing of the Swiss border by fleeing Jews. One of Favre's colleagues, Father Raymond Boccard, had a room under the roof on the seminary's outer perimeter, which constituted the border between France and Switzerland. "From there, one sees very far. Thus I was able to observe easily the arrival of patrols. At a favorable moment, when the German border guards, who scrupulously followed all the curves of the wall bordering on the frontier, could no longer see what was happening in our region, I gave the signal from my window by raising my hat. The fugitives had two minutes and 30 seconds time to make the crossing. One, therefore, had to hurry." Father Jean Rosay, a priest in Douvaine, also on the Franco-Swiss border, also helped Jews cross the border from his parish, until his arrest by the Germans in February 1944.

In Italy, the majority of the Catholic clergy lent themselves (almost instinctively) to helping Jews, and much of the credit for the rescue of most of that country's 45,000 Jews is due them. We have already mentioned in this regard the role of Don Aldo Beccari, who with the help of others arranged for more than a hundred Jewish children and their guides to be taken on a long trek toward the Swiss border, which they crossed on Yom Kippur eve of 1943. Many monks and nuns were also involved in helping Jews move from one place to another.

The contribution of Protestant pastors as well is not to be overlooked. Roland de Pury, a Swiss pastor serving in Lyon, France, was arrested in May 1943 in his home together with 86 Jews whom he was temporarily sheltering while arranging their flight to Switzerland. He was incarcerated in the city's notorious Montluc prison, and his life was spared only due to his Swiss nationality. Earlier, in July 1940, when the majority of Frenchmen hailed the pro-German collaborationist regime headed by the aged Marshal Henri Philippe Pétain, Pastor de Pury preached a ringing sermon in his Lyon church: "Better a dead France than one sold; defeated than robbed. One may weep over a dead France, but a France which betrayed [the trust] that the persecuted place in her, a France which has sold its soul and renounced its mission…, this would no longer be France." Few Frenchmen took kindly to such words spoken in the early days of the Vichy regime.

In the Netherlands, Pastor Bastiaan Ader, a Protestant minister from Nieuw Beertha, appeared one day at the Jewish Invalid Hospital in Amsterdam and volunteered to help spirit patients and staff to safer locations throughout the country. He organized a network of persons who aided him in helping move numerous refugees. He also participated in raids on offices where food ration cards were kept. Placed on the Nazi "wanted list," he was finally arrested in Haarlem and executed in November 1944. It is reported that after the war, his Jewish beneficiaries contributed money for the repair of his church in Nieuw Beertha.

In Germany, too, ministers helped Jews move from place to place. We have already noted the role of the Confessing Church, which mostly looked after the needs of Jewish converts to Christianity. By Nazi definition such persons were full Jews because of their Jewish blood, which no religious conversion could change. Thus, the Wolffenstein sisters were assisted by clergy of the Confessing Church and helped to move from one end of the country to the other.[7] At a later stage, churchmen of the Confessing Church began aiding any Jews who needed help. As already noted, the Krakauers were constantly moved from place to place with the help of more than forty persons, the majority of whom were pastors in the Confessing Church. Some of these pastors were honored by Yad Vashem with the Righteous title. There is no other recorded rescue story in which so many clergy participated in the rescue of two Jews, fugitives of Nazi terror.[8]

In Poland, an exceptional priest in this regard was Father Stanislaw Mazak, whose parish was located in a wooded area of the Tarnopol region. He helped move Jews from one place to another and fetched provisions for those in hiding. He placed one child, whose mother was taken to Germany for forced labor, in a children's institute in Warsaw; after the war he made sure the child was returned to the mother. His help gained him the enmity of the Ukrainian Bandera partisan movement, which operated in his region, and it condemned him to death. He was forced to flee.

This section ends with the story of Father Bronius Paukshtys. He was a priest and monk of the Salesian order in Kaunaus, Lithuania. During the war he committed himself to helping as many Jews as possible to escape the city's ghetto in the Slobodka sector. He is described by those he saved as shy, good-hearted, friendly, and kind. Penina Tory, one of his beneficiaries, writes of him: "Of all my terrible and hair-raising memories of the Holocaust, one ray of light shines forth—the image of a wonderful person, Father Bronius Paukshtys. The very appearance of this man instilled in our hearts the hope that not all was lost, that not all men had turned to predator beasts or cowards; that there are still people with morals, good conscience, good-heartedness, and compassion." Paukshtys arranged for fleeing Jews to meet him at his office; they would either be temporarily lodged in his own quarters, or taken to more secure places with relatives in nearby farms. Penina Tory remembers being welcomed by him "with a smile on his lips," and staying in his room with his daughter for 10 days.

Rachel Levin, desperately looking for a hiding place after escaping from the Kaunas ghetto in early 1944 and after being turned away by a person to whom she had been referred, was welcomed by Paukshtys and given a room adjoining the church for a two-week stay until more permanent arrangements could be worked out. "Father Paukshtys visited me every day; he would bring me books and talk with me. He spoke to me about himself, his studies, his life as a monk in Italy, his family and his work. He spoke of the importance of moral issues, of love for fellow man, religious tolerance, nonviolent resistance. He was concerned with the question of 'vengeance.' He was a very religious person, but not once did he raise the religious question, and he respected me for my outspokenness. I gave him to understand that I was not religious, but that Jewish values were sacrosanct to me."

Father Paukshtys is credited with saving several dozen Jewish lives. To Avraham Tory, Paukshtys revealed that he was reprimanded by his superiors for jeopardizing the church in Lithuania by raising doubts in the eyes of the Germans about the value they could place on the Catholic church's declared allegiance to the German cause. His wards kept in touch with him after the war. To Penina Tory, who visited him immediately upon liberation, he returned her valuables, including a ring. She asked him to keep them as a contribution to his church, but he refused. His beneficiaries tried to persuade him to join them in fleeing Lithuania. His response: "I cannot abandon my flock; here I belong, and I must fight the Bolsheviks as I fought the Nazis." To Masha Rabinowitz, who came to him with the news of her engagement to a Holocaust survivor and asked for his blessing, he responded: "If you wish to respect my feelings, please marry according to the law of Moses and Israel, with my friend Rabbi Oshri [who later settled in the United States]."

In 1946, Paukshtys was arrested and exiled to Siberia. His Jewish beneficiaries pleaded with the Soviet authorities for leniency, citing his personal role in their rescue, but to no avail. When he returned home in 1956, Masha Rabinowitz visited him. "He seemed at peace with himself, his goodness shone from his whole being." He died in 1966 at the age of 69. Many of his former wards attended his funeral. Earlier, he had written to a colleague in the United States: "I did what I could at the expense of my family [i.e., the monastic order to which he belonged]. At times, I had nothing in my pockets, not even a few cents to buy the most basic foodstuff for my family. In order to help others, I was forced to flee my home thrice from the Gestapo.... How many worries, how many sleepless nights, how many tiring wanderings and fears were my lot?... I did not pride myself..., but was guided by the following single thought: `work in the cause of others, and with love.'" Reminiscing about Paukshtys, Rachel Levin, one of his wartime charges, states: "At a time of the eclipse of the world's light, the image of the Lithuanian priest Paukshtys beckons as a shining star, and this noble Christian person is worthy that his memory not be forgotten."

Help by Clandestine Networks

All European countries under Nazi rule had underground movements of various sizes and importance, and of differing political definitions. They could facilitate the flight of Jews from more to less dangerous locations. In general, the underground movements in Eastern Europe were intensely anti-Semitic; in Poland some factions themselves participated in the killing of Jews. In the Netherlands, by contrast, underground networks were helpful and active in the movement of Jews from place to place.

One of the most celebrated cases is that of Arend Smit from Apeldoorn. He is credited with saving several dozen Jews—some claim as many as one hundred. A member of the Dutch underground, he met Jewish persons upon their arrival in Apeldoorn, usually arranged by his network colleagues, and he secured for them hiding places and false credentials. In some cases, the fleeing persons were sheltered in his home for short periods of time. In the words of Geertruida Finkelstein, one of his beneficiaries, "Arend Smit was in charge of organizing everything, from stealing ration cards, to getting doctors to the sick, to getting barbers for haircuts for all those (how many we never knew) under his care, to issuing us false identification cards." He was eventually apprehended by the Germans and dispatched to the Neuengamme concentration camp, where he perished.

Piet Meerburg, another Dutch network rescuer, is credited with saving about three hundred Jewish children. In 1940 he preferred to resign as a student rather than take a loyalty oath to the new occupation regime. Together with other former students, he created a network for the rescue of Jewish children. Most of these were stealthily spirited out of the Crèche, a former day nursing center in Amsterdam that the Germans had turned into a giant assembly point for children. From there they were taken by members of Meerburg's group to distant parts of the country—mostly to the southern Limburg province, where they were in turn dispersed among friendly farmers.

Others in the Netherlands who created clandestine networks include the legendary Joop Westerweel, a Montessori educator in Utrecht, who led groups of Jewish youth across occupied Belgium and France to the Spanish frontier, where he bid them farewell. He too suffered martyrdom in the cause of freedom. Joop Musch and Jaap Woortman created a cell known as the NV Group (in Dutch, the Anonymous Association) for the purpose of saving Jewish children. These were spirited out from the Crèche in Amsterdam and dispersed in the Limburg province. Musch and Woortman were eventually betrayed to the authorities and died after undergoing torture. A statue in Brunssum evokes the heroism of the NV group. Arnold Douwes (of whom more will be told in chapter 6) found hiding places for many fleeing Jews by scouring the countryside in the Nieuwlande area in northern Holland. He was aided by Max Leons (nicknamed Nico), a Jew from Amsterdam who posed as a seminarian from a distant province. Both managed to save the lives of more than several hundred Jews.

In Belgium, a Jewish clandestine organization initiated the rescue of thousands of children by scattering them in the countryside, aided by Belgian persons from all walks of life: priests, laymen, professionals, persons in high positions, and plain working people. The Jewish

Defence Committee (CDJ) laid the blueprint and infrastructure; others, mostly non-Jews, did the tedious work of fetching the children and accompanying them to their new homes, then checking up on them to see if they were well cared for. Yvonne Nevejean, who headed the country's main child care center (ONE), and Jeanne Daman, a noted child care worker, lent themselves in this giant rescue operation that aided more than three thousand children. Two prominent child dispatchers who were constantly on the move to check out the condition of the hidden children were Ida Sterno (Jewish) and Andree Geulen (Catholic). During a ceremony in her honor at Yad Vashem, Andrée Geulen stated: "I never had the feeling of having done something heroic. Even today, in this sacred place, listening to the words of praise—I feel a bit ill at ease. All this has always seemed to me so natural. For, actually, what could be more spontaneous for a normal human being but to extend help to children whom the barbarians decided to exterminate?...I never felt one needed a particular courage. And as for fear, when one is imbued with the certainty of being right, fear does not touch you."

In France, some Catholic and Protestant organizations helped in passing Jews from one place to another. We have already mentioned the role of Rolande Birgy of the Catholic labor movement (JOC), who spirited many Jews across the Swiss border. Madeleine Barot, of the Protestant CIMADE movement, helped move threatened Jews from one place to another. These welfare organizations were also involved in many clandestine operations during the war years to help those threatened by the Nazis, with Jews topping the list. Some individuals created their own operations, like the previously mentioned John Weidner's Dutch-Paris network, which helped Jews move over long stretches and across borders.

In Poland the main umbrella underground organization, the Home Army, better known by its acronym AK, was generally unsympathetic, to put it mildly, to organized efforts to help Jews. Various elements within that large and powerful underground actually took part in hunting expeditions against Jews hiding in forests or private homes; those men, women, and children caught were immediately shot. There were only a few isolated exceptions to this rule. One was the Zegota organization, created by representatives of the Polish underground to help Jewish children flee the doomed ghettos and arrange their reception by adoptive families. One of the principal heroines in that endeavor was Irena Sendler, who helped smuggle out some two hundred children from the Warsaw ghetto. She was betrayed, arrested, and condemned to death. Hours before her scheduled execution, she was freed after members of the Jewish underground successfully bribed the Gestapo agents responsible for her imprisonment. Members of Zegota in other regions of Poland also helped Jews flee the ghettos or cross the Slovakian border.[9]

A unique case of military assistance in Poland is that of Henryk Iwanski. Immediately after the country's occupation in September 1939, he created his own independent cell (known as the KB), which he opened to Jews with military experience. His was the only underground network that openly accepted Jews; others accepted only Jews who were able to mask their identity. He later participated in the Warsaw ghetto uprising of April 1943, helping Jewish combatants with arms, fighting alongside them, leading them out of the doomed ghetto through the sewers (which exited near his home), and helping them flee to other parts of Warsaw. He is reported to have lost a son in that endeavor; another son was lost during the Polish uprising the following year. Iwanski himself was severely wounded in an engagement with German troops during the Warsaw ghetto uprising, leaving him disabled in one leg. His wife Wiktoria became infected with tuberculosis, which she contracted from a Jewish woman whom she aided, and suffered from this disease for many years thereafter. Some of Iwanski's colleagues in the underground turned a cold shoulder to Jewish combatants; his exceptional behavior, hence, stands out all the more.

Other Poles served as emissaries and messengers for Jewish underground networks. Jan Karski was a Polish underground agent who left for England and the United States, where he tried to alert civic, religious, and political leaders to the full extent of the Holocaust as he himself had witnessed it. Many listened—but few believed, and the Jews were left to their fate.

Inside Poland, Irena Adamowicz relayed messages between Jewish networks in Warsaw, Lublin, Bialystok, Kaunas, and Vilnius, thus helping them coordinate clandestine activities. Henryk Grabowski, a former member of the Polish scout movement and a colleague of Adamowicz, was the first emissary to relay to the people of Warsaw the terrible news of the slaughters in the Ponary forest outside Vilnius in September 1941. His house on the Aryan side of Warsaw served as relay station for Jewish underground operatives on the move, and a place for the storage of weapons. Marian Brust kept the lines open between clandestine members in the Warsaw region and those in the Czestochowa region. He was shot during one of his missions but managed to swallow a paper that contained the names of network members. He died under torture without revealing these names.

In Yugoslavia and Greece, many Jews were able to survive after joining up with guerrilla forces operating in the hills and moving with them from place to place. We have already mentioned how Olga Bartulovic moved a Jewish family from Split into a hilly region controlled by partisan forces headed by Josip Tito. A similar typical case from Greece is that of Abraham Barouch, who was helped to move from Trikala, in the Thessaly region, to a hilly region occupied by Greek partisans. There he met other Jews seeking shelter with the underground. Wherever they went, villagers, including priests, helped them. Barouch worked as a bookkeeper for the resistance in exchange for food and other necessities. He stayed with them until the country's liberation in October 1944.[10]

In Russia, various partisan groups halfheartedly admitted Jews to their ranks, especially the young and militarily able. Some widened this to include the combatants' wives and children, who fled into the forest depths and were constantly on the move with the men's fighting units to assure their own survival. Gennady Safonov, a supply officer in a partisan unit, extended much help to Jewish families who fled into the forests of

Belarus from nearby ghettos; this, in spite of the reluctance of his partisan unit to admit noncombatant persons, or even assist them in other ways. Simcha Fogelman relates how he and a companion fled from a ghetto in the Vilnius region into the forests of Belarus. Those left behind were lined up before ditches and machine-gunned to death. "We roamed around without food.... The farmers used to give us a piece of bread and a bottle of milk that would suffice us a few days.... That was how we roamed around for five months." When the Russian winter arrived and the temperature dropped to 40 degrees below zero, Fogelman and his friend realized they needed help. They ran into Safonov, who appeared "like an angel from heaven who brought us warm clothes and sometimes bread." To other Jews roaming the forest, he brought potatoes, bread, and occasionally meat. After the war, he erected a memorial over the common grave of eight hundred Jews slaughtered by the Nazis in 1941.

Serafin Alekseyev escaped from the Nazis as a Russian prisoner of war, then created his own Russian partisan unit in the Zelechow region. Alekseyev's unit established contact with a clandestine Jewish military organization operating in the region, and the two units carried out successful raids against German facilities in the region. The help received by this Russian partisan unit also assured the survival of these fighting Jews through the difficult days of the German occupation.

A fitting finale to this section is the story of Kustyk Kozlovsky, a Belarus farmer. His farmhouse stood astride the Lida-Novgrodek road and served as way station to many Jews fleeing the ghettos and labor camps toward the forests to join a Jewish partisan unit headed by Tuvia Bielski and his brothers. Thanks to Kozlovsky, dozens (some say hundreds) of Jews were able to reach the partisans. Fleeing Jews, arriving at his farmhouse, would be greeted by the mustachioed Kozlovsky with the words: "Welcome, you're probably hungry; you fled from the ghetto. You have arrived at a safe place. Come, have some bread and milk; eat and drink. You'll stay the night here, and early tomorrow I will take you to a hiding place" (usually a hole in the field where potatoes were stored). He then arranged for the Bielski partisans (a Jewish unit) to come and fetch the new recruits. They in turn assigned him various errands, such as delivering important messages, food, and medicine to the remaining Jews inside the Novgrodek ghetto. Those helped by him refer to Kozlovsky as "a saint."

Civil and Military Officials

Persons in high positions could facilitate the movement of Jews out of a dangerous zone or, alternatively, place them under the protective custody of the governments they represented. Examples of the first type (already described in the previous chapter) include the Spanish consul general Aristides de Sousa Mendes in Bordeaux, France; the Japanese consul general Sempo Sugihara in Kaunas, Lithuania; and the Swiss border police officer Paul Grüninger in Sankt Gallen, Switzerland. Examples of the second type (previously mentioned) include the diplomats Raoul Wallenberg, Carl Lutz, Giorgio Perlasca, and Monsignor Angelo Rotta, respectively representing Sweden, Switzerland, Spain, and the Vatican, and all posted in Budapest, Hungary.

Even officials of lower rank could be of immense help. Marcellin Cazals, the head of the local gendarmes in Malzieu in the Lozère region of France, "blew the whistle" by giving ample early warning to Jews of anticipated roundups that he was ordered to carry out, thus enabling them to flee in time. He provided some of the Jews with false identities for use in their other places of residence. His superiors correctly suspected that he had a hand in the failure to arrest any of the more than one hundred Jews in that town—they were never to be found in their homes when the gendarmes came looking for them. By the time officials planned to take corrective action against Cazals, the area had been liberated. More than one hundred lives were saved due to Lieutenant Cazals's sabotaging of instructions from above, orders that conflicted with his belief in a higher moral ethic.

Police officers Édouard Vigneron and Pierre Marie in Lille, France, alerted the Jews in that city of an upcoming raid in July 1942, urging them to be away from their homes during that time. They provided a few of the fugitive Jews with new false identities (without the incriminating "J" sign that was obligatory for all Jews), with which they were able to cross the demarcation line into the unoccupied zone. Gilbert Lesage, a senior Vichy official who was responsible for supervising the movement of foreigners in the country, on several occasions sounded the alarm to heads of the Jewish scout movement of an impending raid on the children. Lesage's timely warning made it possible for the scout leaders to disperse the hundreds of children in their care to new secure places.

German military personnel also could be of immense help in this endeavor. They enjoyed freedom of movement and were generally exempt from harassments and humiliating inspections to which the local population was subjected. Hugo Armann, a sergeant in the Wehrmacht stationed in Baranowice, Poland (today Belarus), helped Jews escape from the ghetto to nearby forests. His military assignment consisted of arranging space on trains for German soldiers home on leave, and this gave him much latitude and freedom of movement. Aided by the Pole Eduard Chacze, he took the fleeing Jews aboard his military van, and even supplied them with light weapons to defend themselves in the forest. There is no need to dwell on the consequences to Sergeant Armann in the event his superiors learned of his involvement.

Sergeant Anton Schmid, stationed in Vilnius, was responsible for directing soldiers returning from leave to their units, which in the meantime had relocated. Making contacts with Jewish underground operatives in the Vilnius ghetto, he furnished them transportation to other cities in his military van and helped them coordinate resistance acts against the Nazis. He was apprehended, court-martialed, and executed in April 1942.

In Novi Sad, Yugoslavia, Lt. Roman Erich Petsche helped a Jewish family escape a deportation order in 1944. He took some of the family with him on a night train journey to Budapest, where he arranged for their stay inside a convent.

Mention should also be made of the labor battalions of Hungary, which were composed of Jewish conscripts and commanded by non-Jewish officers. These units were sent to the Russian front (Hungary was allied with Germany) and assigned noncombatant duties. In some cases these included not merely the grueling work of digging trenches, but also the more dangerous task of clearing minefields. During the retreat of the Hungarian armies after the stunning defeat at Stalingrad in February 1943, some commanders facilitated the escape of their Jewish conscripts. Noteworthy in this respect is the case of Capt. Jeno Piller, commander of Battalion 107/11. When ordered to turn his Jewish laborers over to the Germans, he instead contrived to have them surrender to the advancing Russians, who by late 1944 had reached Lake Balaton inside Hungary, thus saving the more than four hundred Jewish conscripts of his unit. Earlier, he had insured the men's survival when he obtained from Monsignor Angelo Rotta, the papal nuncio in Budapest, certificates claiming that the men were under the protection of the Vatican. After the war, former battalion conscripts added their signature to a citation to their former officer, which reads: "Now that we are free, we think of you. You are worthy of our appreciation, for thanks to you we were saved from the edicts and decrees, which had you abided by them, we would have been lost. You took upon yourself risks when, in opposition to an order, you went over to the Russian side. Be assured that the whole company thinks of you with love and thanks."

Other labor battalion commanders who treated their men kindly and made it possible for them to escape include Col. Imre Reviczky and Capt. Bela Kiraly. The former was overall commander of several labor battalion units. His humanitarian behavior toward the Jewish men in these units almost cost him his life. Kiraly, during the retreat from Russia into Hungary, had his men dressed in the uniform of regular Hungarian soldiers, thus assuring their protection from harrassment and harm by hostile elements in the country.[11]

Help to Children

The next chapter deals exclusively with the saving of Jewish children, but mention must also be made here (if only in passing) of those who exerted their energies to moving children to safer places. In France, we have already noted Renée Gaudefroy, known better by her code name "Pauline," a social worker from Limoges, who helped the OSE to hide some 150 children in various places. We also spoke of Marinette Guy and Juliette Vidal, who arranged the transfer of children to convents and other hiding places. They purchased a hotel in Chamonix where Jewish children were temporarily sheltered. Sensitive to the children's religious needs, they brought them ritual objects so that they could maintain their religious practice even under the perilous conditions of the war years. Already noted too are the roles of Father Beccari in Italy in arranging the flight of more than one hundred Jewish children to the Swiss border, and of Irena Sendler in Poland in facilitating the flight of more than two hundred Jewish children from the Warsaw ghetto to temporary shelter.

In the Paris region, Suzanne Spaak, a mother of two, insisted that the Jewish children who were temporarily kept in special Jewish children's homes (whose leaders were responsible to the Gestapo for the children's presence) be turned over to her, so that they could be saved. To find secure shelters for these children, in the words of a colleague in the underground: "She pounded on doors of priests and demanded that they take a stand in the face of persecutions. She went to see judges and writers, reminding them of their sacred obligation to do something; she traversed the length and breadth of Paris.... There were no obstacles and dangers which could stop her." Arrested in October 1943, she was jailed, then shot in August 1944, on the eve of France's liberation.

Monsignor Jules-Geraud Saliege, from Toulouse, France, who issued the famous pastoral letter in August 1942, in which he denounced the persecution of Jews.

Blaga Todorov from Skopje, Macedonia, and adopted child Betty Bechar, in wartime picture.

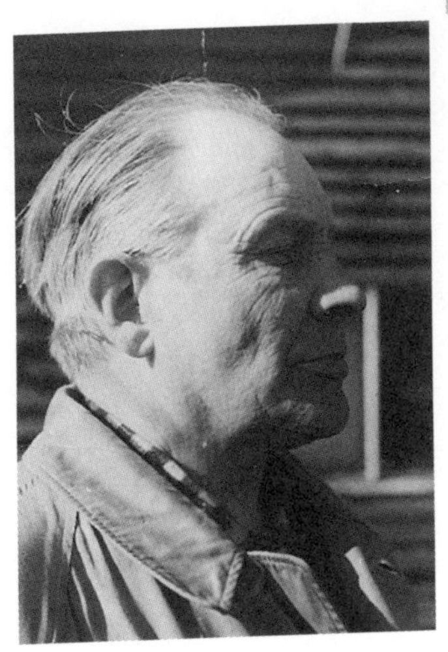

Jan Lipke, the dockworker from Riga, Latvia, who rescued some 40 Jews.

The famed Father Benoit-Marie, rescuer of Jews in Marseille, France, and Rome, Italy.

Joop Woortman, creator of NV network to rescue Jewish children in the Netherlands, was captured and executed.

Jan Karski, Polish underground envoy to the Allies, gave a searing eyewitness account of the murder of Jews in Poland by the Nazis.

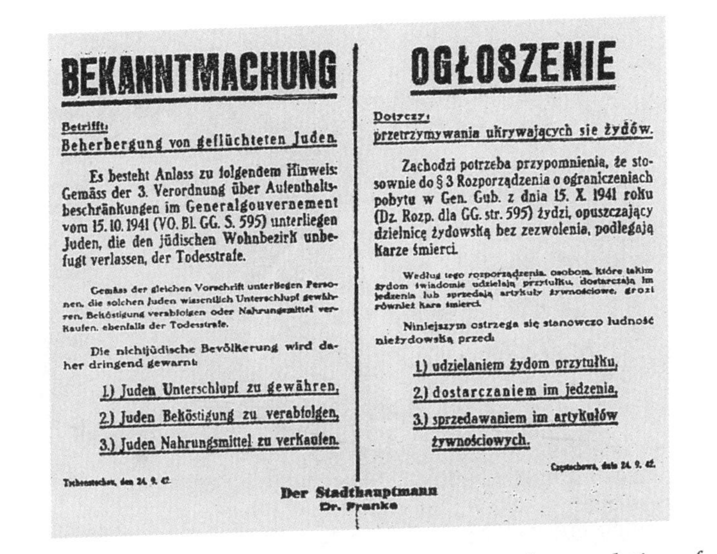

BEKANNTMACHUNG

Betrifft:
Beherbergung von geflüchteten Juden.

Es besteht Anlass zu folgendem Hinweis: Gemäss der 3. Verordnung über Aufenthaltsbeschränkungen im Generalgouvernement vom 15. 10. 1941 (VO. Bl. GG. S. 595) unterliegen Juden, die den jüdischen Wohnbezirk unbefugt verlassen, der Todesstrafe.

Gemäss der gleichen Vorschrift unterliegen Personen, die solchen Juden wissentlich Unterschlupf gewähren, Beköstigung verabfolgen oder Nahrungsmittel verkaufen, ebenfalls der Todesstrafe.

Die nichtjüdische Bevölkerung wird daher dringend gewarnt:

1.) Juden Unterschlupf zu gewähren,
2.) Juden Beköstigung zu verabfolgen,
3.) Juden Nahrungsmittel zu verkaufen.

Tschenstochau, den 24. 9. 42.

OGŁOSZENIE

Dotyczy:
przetrzymywania ukrywających sie żydów.

Zachodzi potrzeba przypomnienia, że stosownie do § 3 Rozporządzenia o ograniczeniach pobytu w Gen. Gub. z dnia 15. X. 1941 roku (Dz. Rozp. dla GG. str. 595) żydzi, opuszczający dzielnicę żydowską bez zezwolenia, podlegają karze śmierci.

Według tego rozporządzenia, osobom, które takim żydom świadomie udzielają przytułku, dostarczają im jedzenia lub sprzedają artykuły żywnościowe, grozi również kara śmierci.

Niniejszym ostrzega się stanowczo ludność nieżydowską przed:

1.) udzielaniem żydom przytułku,
2.) dostarczaniem im jedzenia,
3.) sprzedawaniem im artykułów żywnościowych.

Częstochowa, dnia 24. 9. 42.

Der Stadthauptmann
Dr. Franke

Warning by German occupation authorities to the population of Czestochowa, Poland, of the death penalty for sheltering Jews or providing them with food. Signed by Dr. Franke, city commander.

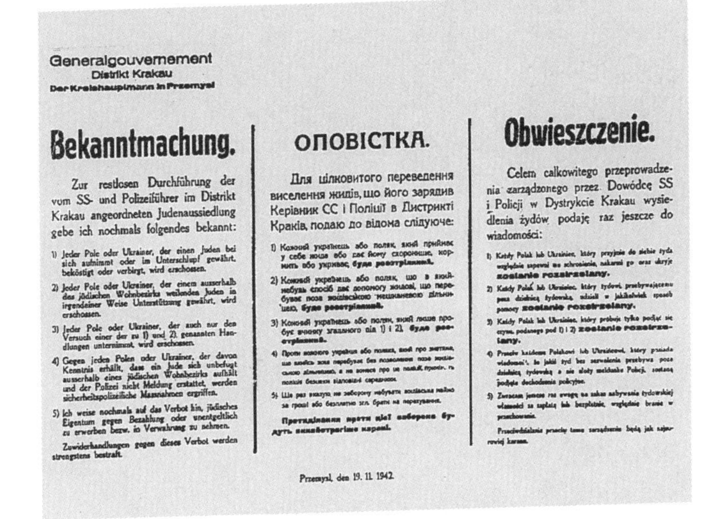

Generalgouvernement
Distrikt Krakau
Der Kreishauptmann in Przemysl

Bekanntmachung.

Zur restlosen Durchführung der vom SS- und Polizeiführer im Distrikt Krakau angeordneten Judenaussiedlung gebe ich nochmals folgendes bekannt:

1) Jeder Pole oder Ukrainer, der einen Juden bei sich aufnimmt oder im Unterschlupf gewährt, beköstigt oder verbirgt, wird erschossen.
2) Jeder Pole oder Ukrainer, der einem ausserhalb des jüdischen Wohnbezirks weilenden Juden in irgendeiner Weise Unterstützung gewährt, wird erschossen.
3) Jeder Pole oder Ukrainer, der auch nur den Versuch einer der zu 1) und 2) genannten Handlungen unternimmt, wird erschossen.
4) Gegen jeden Polen oder Ukrainer, der davon Kenntnis erhält, dass ein Jude sich unbefugt ausserhalb eines jüdischen Wohnbezirks aufhält und der Polizei nicht Meldung erstattet, werden sicherheitspolizeiliche Massnahmen ergriffen.
5) Ich weise nochmals auf das Verbot hin, jüdisches Eigentum gegen Bezahlung oder unentgeltlich zu erwerben bezw. in Verwahrung zu nehmen.

Zuwiderhandlungen gegen dieses Verbot werden strengstens bestraft.

ОПОВІСТКА.

Для цілковитого переведення виселення жидів, що його зарядив Керівник СС і Поліції в Дистрикті Краків, подаю до відома слідуюче:

1) Кожний українець або поляк, який приймає у себе жида або дає йому схоронище, кормить або укриває, буде розстріляний.
2) Кожний українець або поляк, що в якийнебудь спосіб дає допомогу жидові, що перебуває поза жидівською мешканевою дільницею, буде розстріляний.
3) Кожний українець або поляк, який лише пробує вчинку згаданого під 1) і 2), буде розстріляний.
4) [illegible]
5) [illegible]

[illegible]

Obwieszczenie.

Celem całkowitego przeprowadzenia zarządzonego przez Dowódcę SS i Policji w Dystrykcie Krakau wysiedlenia żydów podaję raz jeszcze do wiadomości:

1) Każdy Polak lub Ukrainiec, który przyjmie do siebie żyda względnie zapewni mu schronienie, nakarmi go oraz ukryje **zostanie rozstrzelany.**
2) Każdy Polak lub Ukrainiec, który żydowi przebywającemu poza dzielnicą żydowską udzieli w jakikolwiek sposób pomocy **zostanie rozstrzelany.**
3) Każdy Polak lub Ukrainiec, który próbuje tylko podjąć się czynu podanego pod 1) i 2) **zostanie rozstrzelany.**
4) [illegible]
5) [illegible]

[illegible]

Przemysl, den 19. 11. 1942.

Warning by German occupation authorities (in German, Polish, and Russian) to the population of Przemysl, Poland, of the death penalty for helping Jews escape a planned Nazi liquidation raid in November 1942. For text, see page 162.

Japanese diplomat Sempo Sugihara with wife, children, and work colleagues.

Hetty Voute with a student friend in a wartime picture, Netherlands.

Hetty Voute (left) and Gisela Sohnlein (middle) upon arrival after their release from Ravensbrueck Camp (March 1945).

Father Joseph André, of Namur, Belgium, surrounded by the Jewish children he saved. At his right is U.S. chaplain Lt. Rabbi Marc Saperstein, to whom the children were turned over at the end of the war.

SCHUTZ-PASS Nr 81/23

Name: Frau Ludwig Frisch
Név: geb. Ilona Blumenfeld

Wohnort: Budapest
Lakás:

Geburtsdatum: 17. März 1888.
Születési ideje:

Geburtsort: Lugos
Születési helye:

Körperlänge: 165 cm.
Magasság:

Haarfarbe: grau Augenfarbe: braun
Hajszín: Szemszín:

Unterschrift:
Aláírás: Özv. Frisch Lajosné

SCHWEDEN SVÉDORSZÁG

Die Kgl. Schwedische Gesandtschaft in Budapest bestätigt, dass der Obengenannte im Rahmen der — von dem Kgl. Schwedischen Aussenministerium autorisierten — Repatriierung nach Schweden reisen wird. Der Betreffende ist auch in einen Kollektivpass eingetragen.

Bis Abreise steht der Obengenannte und seine Wohnung unter dem Schutz der Kgl. Schwedischen Gesandtschaft in Budapest.

Gültigkeit: erlischt 14 Tage nach Einreise nach Schweden.

A budapesti Svéd Kir. Követség igazolja, hogy fentnevezett — a Svéd Kir. Külügyminisztérium által jóváhagyott — repatriálás keretében Svédországba utazik.

Nevezett a kollektív útlevélben is szerepel.

Elutazásáig fentnevezett és lakása a budapesti Svéd Kir. Követség oltalma alatt áll.

Érvényét veszti a Svédországba való megérkezéstől számított tizennegyedik napon.

Reiseberechtigung nur gemeinsam mit dem Kollektivpass. Einreisevisum wird nur in dem Kollektivpass eingetragen.

Budapest, den 26. September 1944

KÖNIGLICH SCHWEDISCHE GESANDTSCHAFT
SVÉD KIRÁLYI KÖVETSÉG

Kgl. Schwedischer Gesandte

One of Raoul Wallenberg's "Protective Passes" issued to a Jewish woman in Budapest, 1944, and signed by the Swedish Ambassador Carl Danielsson.

Zayneba Hardaga upon arrival in Israel from Sarajevo, Bosnia, in 1994. During World War II, she and her husband saved a Jewish family. The Israeli government reciprocated by removing her from her war-torn country and bringing her to Israel with her family.

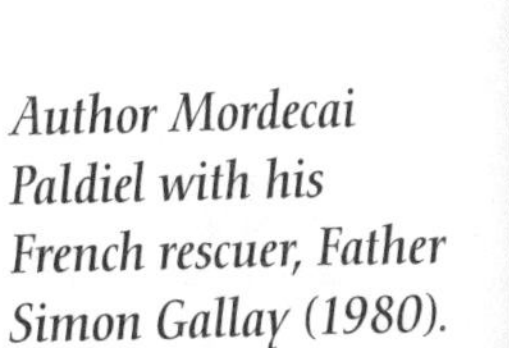

Author Mordecai Paldiel with his French rescuer, Father Simon Gallay (1980).

Varian Fry, the only American listed as a Righteous among the Gentiles at Yad Vashem.

Mordecai Paldiel, of Yad Vashem, holds a special Scroll of Honor to be presented to the community of Chambon-sur-Lignon, France, which is read by Jacques Pulver, member of the Yad Vashem Commission for the Righteous. To Paldiel's right is Israel's Ambassador to France, Ovadiah Sofer (October 1990).

Yad Vashem medal for the Righteous (in Hebrew and French).

All photos (except Varian Fry) courtesy Yad Vashem.

Chapter 5

Children on the Run

Testimony of Julien Engel (France)

My parents, both born in Poland and educated in Germany, married and settled in Dortmund, where Father established a successful furniture business. In mid-1933, very soon after Hitler came to power, they decided to seek refuge in Belgium. At the border town of Aachen, they were imprisoned for two weeks by German frontier police. Mother was then in very advanced pregnancy. I was born two weeks after their arrival in Antwerp, on September 6, 1933. My brother Georges was born there in 1938. After the armistice and the German occupation of Belgium, the family made its way to Nice, sometime in June or July 1940.

Life under the Vichy regime was tolerable at first, but quickly became less so. The family somehow managed to survive from day to day, despite the many constraints imposed on refugees, by means I have never quite figured out. The situation took a sharp turn for the worse in mid-1942, and the family once again set off in search of a refuge, this time in Switzerland. A French guide was to smuggle us over the frontier at Annemasse. Within sight of the frontier station a few hundred yards away, we were apprehended by French border police. After keeping us in detention for several days at the police commissariat of Annemasse, they took us, handcuffed and guarded, by regular passenger train to the Rivesaltes concentration camp. Some two weeks later, Georges and I, along with perhaps twenty or thirty other Jewish children, were freed from the camp, probably through the intermediary of internation-

al humanitarian agencies still operating in Vichy France. Our parents took the route to Auschwitz.

After our release we were taken to a children's home somewhere in the Toulouse region. My mother's cousins in Nice soon undertook to have us released into their care, probably in early 1943. We returned to Nice very uncertain of what the future would hold. In late April or early May, Mother's cousins were arrested in a street roundup while they were out shopping in the center of Nice. They were never heard from again. Fortunately, they were in the company of a Gentile friend, who was left free. She hastened back to the house to warn us. Georges and I instantly made for the house of a neighbor, whose garden adjoined our own. After putting us up for a day or two, he arranged to have us taken in hand by the Catholic authorities in Nice. The archdiocese operated an underground rescue scheme to spirit Jews out of Nice and place them into safe haven in the rural back country. It is through them that Georges and I were presented to and warmly welcomed by Alban and Germaine Fort at the Rayon de Soleil of Cannes. We were to remain there for three full years.

The Rayon de Soleil was a family-type, privately supported home for homeless children. It was one of a chain of some eight such homes founded in France during the interwar years by high-minded and dedicated individuals, deeply concerned about the condition of parentless children, those orphaned, abandoned, or judicially removed from incompetent parents. At the Rayon the children were made to feel as members of a community bound by mutual affection and common purpose. During our stay there, the Rayon family numbered from forty to sixty children. About a quarter were infants abandoned by their mothers and available for adoption. A number of Jewish children had preceded us at the Rayon and had been taken to other places. A few were there when we arrived and left in subsequent months, as did others who arrived after us. At the time, the Rayon was housed in the American-owned Villa Clemente, located in the hills directly above Cannes, which it obtained cost-free for the duration. It had ample, parklike grounds, elaborate facilities, and rich decor.

For Jews in France, this was a time of very great fear. Arrests and disappearances were a feature of daily life. The Forts sheltered Jewish children through the darkest days of the war, when the consequences of discovery for them would have been deportation, and for the Rayon, to which they had dedicated their lives, a future in very great jeopardy.

Our identity cards carried our family name slightly altered. The addition of an e *to the Germanic Engel (Engele) gave it a French or Italian intonation. Our very French first names happily required no tampering. Though we were no more than two or three miles from the center of Cannes, the physical isolation of the Villa Clemente, its relative self-sufficiency, and particularly the inward-centered ambiance set by Alban and Germaine Fort, enabled us all to lead almost a life apart, buffered from the brutal realities of the world outside. The Rayon received many visitors, including on one occasion, disconcertingly, a group of German officers.*

I have always felt immense gratitude for the Forts. Their extraordinary courage, generosity, and strength of character have left an indelible mark on me. Paradoxically, these were happy years for us, at a time when so many others in Europe lived in sorrow and suffering.

The wholesale Nazi murder of Jewish children was unprecedented. It is estimated that some 1.5 million Jewish children were murdered during the Holocaust years. Never before in history had children been singled out for destruction for no other reason than having been born. Children, of course, were no match for the Nazis' mighty and sophisticated killing machine; their only chance for survival was outside help. Those who helped Jewish children survive this massive, government-orchestrated infanticide did so at the risk of their own lives. This chapter is devoted to the rescue of some of these children.

Hiding children created many problems, not the least of which was trying to impart to them a sense of the special dangers they faced. It was difficult to explain to them that it was necessary for them to deny their identity (which was still in the process of being shaped and molded), their recent past, their natural parents—everything, indeed, to which children feel especially attached—and to accept strangers as their guardians. Children of a more understanding age, eight and above, were told to look, think, and act as non-Jews and to practice the religion of their new social milieu. They were also warned to be alert to attempts by others—that is, potentially hostile children and adults—to betray them to the authorities; the forces of law and order represented a mortal danger to them. They found themselves forced to mature at a relatively early age, while at the same time remaining fully dependent on the goodwill of their host families.

For the rescuers, it seemed a daunting challenge to try to instill confidence in a child who felt torn away from his or her natural parents. Then came the time when the child had to be returned—to parents or distant relatives or, worse, to children's homes and orphanages. The child was told to renounce his or her recently acquired new name, and perhaps religion, to revert to the original family name and readapt to a new cultural-religious milieu. Many surviving children still bear the scars of these youthful traumas. They have created new lives, but the excruciating psychological pains of their tender years have not fully healed for many.

The following story illustrates some of the traumas experienced by children. Eva was five years old when her father ("an eternal optimist") took her for a fateful walk outside the Staszow ghetto in Poland in 1941. On the way, he explained that she was going to live with the Szumielewicz family, with whom they were acquainted. She would stay only a short time, he explained, for the war, this "madness," was sure to end quickly. "After several hours of walking hand in hand and mostly in silence," she recalls, "I knew that this was a very significant journey. We were both overwhelmed with emotion and could barely speak." She was never to see her father again. Writing in 1980, Eva recalls:

> In looking back over the 44 years of my life, that day, when I let go of my father's hand, was the most difficult and traumatic day of my life. I was only five years old but I knew that I was letting go of my whole life; my family, my world. A metamorphosis took place within me. I ceased being a child and became an introspective and shrewd observer of life with an innate skill for survival. When I felt Wiktoria's warm but unfamiliar hand on mine, I was engulfed in the deepest grief; perhaps I knew that I would never see my beloved father's face again; perhaps I knew that this was a farewell like no other before it; this was the final farewell of death.

In 1945, when Eva was told of an aunt in Canada who wanted to adopt her, "I did not want to hear about it.... I did not want to be a Jew again now that my parents were dead." Subterfuge was used to persuade her to leave her new home; she was falsely informed that her parents had miraculously survived and were waiting for her in Cracow. When she arrived there, she was placed in an orphanage, then taken out of the country, and eventually sent to Canada, where after several years she resumed contact with Wiktoria Szumielewicz, whom she continued to remember tenderly. "In the vortex of a world gone mad, my father carefully placed my hand in the hand of Wiktoria Szumielewicz.... My father chose wisely," Eva wrote in her deposition.

Many children were rescued single-handedly, or nearly so. In France, Dr. Rita Breton, a physician in Paris in the service of the OSE (a Jewish child welfare organization), helped disperse some two hundred children in villages and hamlets in the Normandy region. Clergy of the Catholic church were better positioned than most to handle such large groups. Father Joseph André and Father Bruno Reynders, in Belgium, worked closely with the clandestine Jewish Defense League in finding accommodations for hundreds of Jewish children who had been separated from their parents. After the war, Father André, who lived in and operated from a house in Namur across from the German local command, met U.S. Army chaplain Rabbi Lt. Marc Saperstein and arranged for the children to be returned to their relatives and religion. In the words of one Jewish witness: "He never thought of trying to convert these children. On the contrary, he always emphasized the duty of maintaining every person's own faith to the extent that the children under his care all knew the *Hatikvah* [the Jewish national anthem]."

Father Bruno Reynders, a Benedictine monk near Louvain, is credited with saving several hundred children. "How many are the homes that I knocked on their doors!" he stated during a ceremony in his honor in Jerusalem after the war. "Even Almighty God will have to deal with me kindly in the World to Come," he added facetiously. The following testimony by Esther Krygier gives an idea of Father Reynders's dedication to his youthful wards:

> He was very kind, very fatherly. He imparted in us a certain security. At 12, one can distinguish the difference. He kissed us in a very fatherly way. He took us by the hand, and explained to us that where we were going one must not say one is Jewish; to do exactly what we're told to, not to trust even another child, but keep everything to ourselves. He emphasized the need to be discreet. Father Bruno represented safety and hope.... He was the only one who had the gift to remove the fear within us. This, I don't know how to explain why.[1]

Father Reynders was eventually forced to remove his cassock and go underground after the Gestapo raided his home at Mount Cesar. The Germans continued searching for him until the country's liberation in September 1944.

Further to the south, in Jamoigne-sur-Semois, in the Ardennes forest region of Belgium, Marie Taquet-Mertens operated a children's home. Under the patronage of the Queen Mother of the country (Elizabeth), the home had originally been created as a center for feeble children. In this comfortable nest, tucked away in the deep forest, some eighty Jewish children were sheltered and their cares attended to during the war years. In the words of one of the former children: "This period that I spent at Jamoigne was my childhood best; . . . this especially so, since I found there, for the first time that I can ever remember, a loving and caring home..., which was to a large degree due to Mrs. Taquet, who imparted, as much as conditions permitted, warmth and love."

In the Netherlands, a clandestine organization named the NV group was created by Joop Woortman and Jaap Musch, respectively a former cab driver and a laboratory technician, to facilitate the escape of Jewish children from Amsterdam to distant localities in the south of the country (mainly the Brunssum region). To fetch the children, they relied on trusted couriers, such as Anne Marie Van Verschuer, who recalls some of the difficulties in finding suitable hiding places for the children: "If you found a place willing to shelter a Jewish child, you took down the information. They ordered a child, approximately four years of age with dark eyes. You passed the message and brought them the dark-eyed boy. The bright-eyed eight-year-old girl remained in the Crèche [the main assembly point of Jewish children in Amsterdam under German control]. This is how it was." Children were spirited out through the backyard of the Crèche in milk cans, knapsacks, laundry bags, and potato sacks, then taken by train to distant farmhouses in the Friesland or Limburg regions. Some children passed through many hands, for a variety of reasons; one boy, named Hanoch, passed through 20 different places by the time the war was over. The young Ed Van Thijn, the future mayor of Amsterdam, passed through 14 hands. Musch and Woortman, the heroic chiefs of this vast operation, were betrayed and died at the hands of the Germans. Their sole crime was helping children to survive. The NV network successfully brought almost all the children in its care safely through the war.

Hetty Voute and Gisela Sohnlein belonged to a student group based in Utrecht that also dealt in saving children. Their principal task was to fetch children from private homes and urge hesitant parents to release the children to them. Voute recalls: "As a young girl, we entered an unknown home of unknown people. We did not mention our name, but the parents gave us their children in confidence, and we thanked them for their trust." Voute and Sohnlein were arrested at a train station at the end of one of their errands. They went through a grueling interrogation and several concentration camps, including the notorious Ravensbrück camp north of Berlin. They somehow survived the cruelties of that camp.

Hester Van Lennep, another courier of Dutch children, recalls when a bundle was left at her doorstep. "When I opened it, I saw a baby inside. Its diapers had not been changed. Its skin was festered with wounds. It was an awful sight. I took it to my family doctor De Groot. Each time I returned to him with another infant, he never said a word." Others in Holland who helped children on a grand scale were the Bockma farming family in Limburg; Hanna Van der Voort of the village Tienraij, where more than one hundred Jewish children passed through; and Nico Dohmen, who dealt with some 120 children and arranged placement with local farmers, acting as their guardian or surrogate father, giving them pep talks and counseling on a host of problems, including bed-wetting.

Still another Dutch rescuer, Marion Van Binsbergen (today Pritchard), recalls arriving at a small town with a Jewish baby in her arms; she was to turn the infant over to a certain person for safekeeping. At the train station she was informed that the man had been betrayed and arrested. It was late in the day, and the informant invited Marion to his house to spend the night. She was at a total loss what to do with the child but, fully exhausted, she fell immediately into a deep sleep. When she woke up, she noticed that the host's wife had changed and fed the baby, and was explaining to her children that "I was a sinner, that I had this baby out of wedlock, and that my punishment was that they were going to keep the baby, and I would never see it again." Thus, a solution was found to satisfy all parties concerned, including the villagers who would be fed a seemingly credible story. An additional child had been saved.[2]

Margaretha Van Dijk, in a lengthy and moving testimony, relates how she became involved in rescue activities. In 1938, at the age of 18, she was hired as a typing and shorthand teacher in a business school in The Hague, Holland, operated by a Jewish couple, Jacob Moses and his wife. When the deportation of Dutch Jews began in 1942, Mrs. Moses told Gre (short for Margaretha) that in the event of a summons for deportation, Gre would take the Moses' little son, Dikki. Gre spontaneously responded ("without understanding the implications of my words"), "I will take care of Dikki." When the feared summons arrived, Gre took Dikki to her home, then moved with relatives to the distant Brabant province. "Each week I visited the parents (hidden elsewhere) to keep them posted on news of their son. In the meantime, I continued to operate the business school."

When she began to arrange hiding places for Jewish students of the school, Van Dijk was surprised to meet others who were also in the business of helping Jews on the run. "It was like a revelation! There were other people who were aiding persecuted ones." She eventually moved with Dikki from place to place, after her own parents were arrested by the Germans together with the six persons hiding in their home. Dikki had pronounced Semitic features; this added to the danger of sheltering him, and Van Dijk experienced several close calls with the police. This did not dim her determination, and she also accompanied adult Jews to their new hiding places.

When the war ended, she recalls, "I was completely exhausted—perhaps not as much physically as mentally. We had devoted all our energies to them [the persons rescued], but did not have time to 'recharge' our own batteries. I thought to myself: The war is over, the children are back in their places, the adults have blended anew in their social environment and need me no longer. Why maintain contact and arouse unpleasant memories of those unhappy years?" What was her wartime motivation? "We did what we were required to do.... My behavior was simply a matter of course; nothing extraordinary, just a natural thing, and a way of resisting the cruelty of the Nazis. One writer called that period `the holy years.' Why so? For it was a period where the hallowed values were clearly defined, more than ever afterwards. I helped according to my capacity whenever there was a need."

In yet another Dutch rescue story, Carolien Elzas sought a sheltering place for her daughter, Karin. A friend in Amsterdam told her that her sister in Dordrecht would be willing to take the child. Carolien insisted that the sister be told the truth about the child's origin. The woman's response, as reported by her brother, was: "I wept bitterly when all the Jews in Dordrecht were evacuated from their homes and were forced to squeeze in with their families in a closed section of Amsterdam. I simply wept. I don't know why, but I forced myself to the train station. When I saw the train there, and all the innocent Jews, who had harmed no one and wearing the yellow star, mounting the train; when I saw all those children with their pale faces staring through the train windows—I thought to myself: `God! How much I should want to take a child from that train and save it. And now, the opportunity has presented itself to save a

Jewish child, and I shall do so.'" Little Karin stayed with Alida Van den Berg until the war's end.

In Belgium, Lea Diamant was told to bring her four-year-old son Nathan to a Brussels train station, where she was to turn him over to an underground operative. Nathan was taken to the home of Lucien Brunin, a justice of the peace in Ghent, where he stayed until the country's liberation. Brunin arranged new credentials for the boy and enrolled him at school. At home, a picture of his parents was placed at his bedside so Nathan would not forget them. Two years after the separation from her son, and fearing she was on the point of being arrested, Lea Diamant asked to be allowed to see him. When the two met at a prearranged location, the mother saw a smiling, happy-looking and well-dressed boy. Both sides maintained strong links in the postwar years.

Years later, Lucien Brunin showed Nathan the diary he had kept during the boy's stay with him. One entry reads: "You looked so sad and unhappy when you arrived at our place. We tried to distract your thoughts by giving you a little car toy and listening to music on the radio. But you kept saying, `I am staying for a little while; then I am returning to my mother.' You arrived with a toothbrush in your shirt pocket and with false papers handed over by the mayor of Canne, under the name of Albert Dumont, as well as with ration stamps for a month's duration." The last entry states: "Before your departure to Israel, you came to bid us farewell with your mother.... You were very anxious to know whether you could take your bicycle to Israel. So, that is the end of our good remembrances and our happiness of sharing a fraction of life with small Albert."

Arieh Reichelberg reports being sheltered in a preventorium, a rest home for children afflicted with tuberculosis, in a village in the Savoy region of France. He was registered as a convalescent child.[3] Not far from there, Felicia Cohen was sheltered in the home of a woman whom Felicia's mother, Zisla Przedborski, had met while seeking a hiding place for herself and her daughter. Fleeing from Lyon in 1942, Zisla had wandered into the village of Domène, near Grenoble. She proceeded to the municipality to get ration cards. She was directed to a young secretary, who appeared gentle and friendly. Felicia's mother decided to gamble everything. She told the woman: "I am Jewish; I am in great danger. I have an only girl, and I beg you to take her with you, for my husband and myself are in great danger." The young woman promptly responded: "Here's my address. Bring your daughter there this day." Anne-Marie Mingat was then 24 and married. When the 12-year-old Felicia arrived at the Mingats' home, Anne-Marie told her that henceforth she was to say she was a refugee cousin from Paris. Felicia recalls:

> She chose for me the name of Jeanne Chevalier, arranged all the papers, certificates of birth and baptism. She made me sleep in her room in spite of her husband's objection. She had me registered in the local school, placed a cross around my neck and purchased a missal, and we went to church every Sunday and on holidays. She was not a great believer, but she did it for me. She never influenced me in the Catholic religion. On the contrary, she would say to me, "One day you will be able to be a Jew again, but now you must forget that in order to save yourself."

Mrs. Mingat walked great distances to fetch fresh eggs and milk. Felicia ends her testimony with the following words:

> Anne-Marie was to me more than a mother who did everything to nourish me, to spoil me, to educate me, and to protect me. She also saved my parents, finding for them a place of hiding, and providing them with false credentials, and secretly providing for their needs. My father was hidden for two years. I did not even know they were in the same village. She did this because she was an exceptional woman, of great courage and goodness.... I owe her everything. She saved my life. My gratitude and love for her will remain eternal.

It all began as a random encounter at a village municipality, at a time when goodness was in short supply.

In Poland, the Nazis' brutal methods against the occupied population, coupled with a native anti-Semitism that was more manifest than elsewhere on the occupied continent, made the rescue of Jewish children more difficult. The rescuers there stand out all the more for their bravery and humanity. We have already noted the case of Irena Sendler, a social worker in Warsaw, who smuggled out some two hundred children from the doomed Warsaw ghetto and arranged for their accommodation with adoptive families.

The Sendler case represents the exception to the rule for, as we have already noted, most rescue operations involving many children were the result of group efforts. Individual rescuers, working on their own, without recourse to outside help, could at best save one or several children. The most common cover-up in such cases was to claim that the child was one's own, the result of an illicit affair, or a distant relative, or either orphaned or born out of wedlock.

Gertruda Babilinska, a governess with a Jewish couple in Warsaw, took their four-year-old son, upon the mother's untimely death, to her hometown of Gdansk (then known as Danzig), claiming the boy as her own. She had him admitted to a church choir; one of his tasks was to sprinkle holy water on heads of worshippers, including German officers of the Catholic faith. After the war, she kept her vow to the child's dying mother by taking the boy to Israel so he could be brought up as a Jew.

Janina Sycz, a teacher by profession and a divorced mother with three children of her own, agreed to take an 11-year-old Jewish girl from the Lvov ghetto, then move with her family to her father's residence in another city. To support herself, she did odd jobs. There was hardly enough food for all the children, but in the words of the Jewish girl, Irena: "Everything was divided equally among the four of us and if she ever showed any preference it was for me—as if trying to make it up to me for my double burden. She was a wonderful, brave human being and I loved her very much." When Irena left to join a distant aunt in the United States, the Sycz children wept bitterly.

Halina Assanowicz met Nina Danzig at her workplace in a sewing factory in Koretz, Ukraine, in 1942. The two women befriended each other, to the point that Nina felt comfortable enough to confide to Halina that she was Jewish and needed someone to save her newborn daughter. Halina contacted her mother, Maria, who agreed to take the child and raise her as her own. Later, Danzig found a more secure occupation as a cook in a nursing home for wounded German soldiers, and she wanted her child back. Maria was reluctant to return the child, toward whom she had developed strong affectionate bonds, but Nina was adamant. Maria returned the child with the following letter addressed to her mother:

> Please excuse me for acting so stubbornly towards you when you visited us, but you must understand that it was not on purpose. For in those days, I wanted to scream and hit my head against the wall, for during a year and a half I loved Lala as a mother loves her child, and I did not imagine you would take her now from me. I was sure it would be after the war.... But there's no choice, and I am happy that she will be with her parents, for it's good for her. But to root her out of my heart. . . this is too difficult for me. . . The only thing I ask of you: to inform me from time to time how she's doing, and at the first opportunity, please send me a picture of her. Should she be in danger, you must somehow send her back to me, for it would be a pity that all I've done for her was in vain.

Zofia Sendler, from Cracow, agreed to shelter a Jewish child in her home. The baby was smuggled out of the ghetto and brought to her, stuffed in a knapsack. To guarantee the success of the operation, the baby had been given an injection of a sleeping potion before her clandestine journey, but the dose was excessive and it took Sendler three days to revive her. During that critical period, Sendler refrained from breast-feeding her own two-month-old child, so as to allow the stricken baby to benefit from mother's milk. The girl recovered and survived.

An even more poignant story is that of Sarah Moshinska, who witnessed the decimation of her family near Koczery, in the Bialystok region of Poland. Escaping a Nazi execution raid, five-year-old Sarah, her 18-month-old sister, and their mother fled to the woods.

"We passed from forest to forest, from home to home, to seek some food and perhaps even sleep. We did not know what the morrow would bring; we slept in attics, on the floor of barns, and any other opportune place. In the forests, they hunted down Jews with searchlights. Death stalked every day." At one resting place, Sarah's mother handed over her other daughter to a willing Polish woman, only to learn later that the child had been murdered. At her wit's end, the mother turned over Sarah to another Polish woman, at one of their nocturnal resting places, in return for the few possessions she still had.

When that woman learned that Sarah's mother had been killed, and no further payments would be forthcoming, she chased Sarah out of the house. "The woman took pity on me, so instead of killing me, she took a broom and with it chased me out of the house, keeping with her the money my mother had given her for my upkeep." From that moment, Sarah was alone. Kindhearted farmers allowed her to stay overnight in their homes, then would tell her to move on the following morning. "My strength was waning. It was bitter cold, and I was not sufficiently dressed." She sat down on the wayside, rolling over to keep herself warm. Some people threw her some lettuce, but she was no longer capable of reaching out for it. Suddenly two women approached and lifted her up, taking her to their home. She was given milk to drink and a warm blanket.

Bronislawa Milkowski, from the village of Koczery, a mother of eight, was Sarah's delivering angel. The following morning, Bronislawa placed a cross around Sarah's neck and told her to henceforth address her as "Mother." Sarah stayed with the Milkowski family for two years. After the war, representatives of a Jewish welfare organization came to fetch her. Bronislawa refused to part with the child, even in return for a substantial monetary reward. Sarah was forcefully snatched away and eventually taken to Israel. In 1988, married and with children of her own, Sarah went back to Poland to be reunited with the children of her benefactress, who in the meantime had passed away. On that occasion, she lit a candle over the grave of her murdered baby sister. "On that day, June 16, 1988, I shed many tears, and that day I will remember forever."

Farther north, in Lithuania, Lea Gittelman gave birth to a girl in the Vilnius ghetto, and aptly named the child Getele ("of the ghetto"). In November, Lea's husband David was transferred to a labor camp outside the ghetto, together with his wife and little girl. This momentarily saved them. In the course of his work, David met Viktoria Burlingis. After surviving another killing raid in the labor camp, David contacted Burlingis, who agreed to take the child with her. Lea stayed with the child for a few days, until she had become sufficiently accustomed to Burlingis. One day, while visitors were in the house, Getele, at the other end of the house, suddenly began to sing a song in Yiddish ("I Am Queen Esther"). In the words of Getele's mother: "We had celebrated Purim in the camp shortly before the `children's action.'... I was not aware that Getele had memorized the song. Only here, in Viktoria's house, did she erupt with that song. Viktoria and her husband came immediately to me; I started to weep, but they reassured me that no one had heard a word. Since the child spoke Yiddish, however, they said they could no longer keep her. The next day, they told me they had found another hiding place for her." It turned out to be with a Polish nun by the name of Aleksandra Drzewecka.

In 1944, when Vilnius was still contested between Germans and Russians, with shells exploding everywhere, Lea and David managed to flee from the labor camp and reach Sister Drzewecka's home to find Getele safe and sound. "I could continue and write on this, on the miracles which occurred to us during those days," Lea Gittelman writes in her 1989 testimony, "but I no longer have the physical and mental strength for this. My daughter, Getele, is now known as Rina. She is married and the mother of three children." Lea excuses herself for writing so late about her rescuers. "First—every time we tried to write to you [to Yad Vashem], we would weep and stop writing. Second—several of my friends who were with us in the labor camp and in the ghetto, their children were killed by the Germans; they were not able to save them like we did ours. Now that my husband David has passed away, I decided to document the rescue of my daughter Getele, for I am the only one left still reliving these memories." In the postwar years, Lea lost track of the Burlingis family. But she maintained contact with Sister Drzewecka for many years, and the Gittelmans supported the kindhearted nun (who also sheltered another Jewish child) with packages, medicine, and money.

In Skopje, Yugoslavia, four-year-old Betty Bechar was turned over by her parents for temporary safekeeping to her father's business partner, Aleksander Todorov. It was March 1943, and the city's Jews were being rounded up to be deported to an unknown destination. The girl's parents could not know that their destination was the large killing facility in Auschwitz camp. Betty was reared by the rescuers as their own child. When she accidentally discovered in 1948 the truth about her origin, she decided to leave for Israel, yet without cutting her close links with her rescuer family. Bechar's support for her adoptive family has not waned, even with the current upheavals in Yugoslavia and the difficulty of maintaining contact with her adoptive rescuer family in Macedonia.

In the following story, the discovery of a child's Jewish origin did not diminish the adoptive mother's love for him. Maria Potesil, a World War I widow in Vienna, adopted a boy in 1927. She later discovered he had been fathered by a Jewish man. After Austria was annexed to Nazi Germany in 1938, Potesil was told she would have to let the child go. She refused. The boy was thereupon expelled from public school and made to register at a Jewish school. To add to the pressure, Potesil was told to move into the secluded Jewish quarter. When she remained determined to keep the child, the Nazis stepped up their harassment and seized the boy. After a stormy session with a Nazi chief who heaped verbal abuse on her, Potesil managed to have the boy returned to her. She was told that, in spite of her being a clean-cut Aryan, she would have to wear the yellow star sign, obligatory for Jews, as a mark of contempt, and she would henceforth be permitted to shop only in specially designated Jewish stores, which sold low-quality foodstuffs and only during short, specific hours. She endured all these humiliations and emerged from the dark Nazi period with young Kurt safe at her side.

Farther north, in Berlin, Ruth Abraham in 1942 went to her daily forced labor shift at a plant in the Tempelhof district that manufactured pharmaceutical products for the German army. She was eight months pregnant. On her long walk home from work (Jews were not allowed to use public transportation), she noticed a woman tailing her. Ruth told her to stop following her, for fear of alerting Gestapo agents who may have been tracking her. One day in late December 1942, the unknown woman brought a basket filled with food to Ruth's workplace. Maria Nickel, a Berlin working-class woman, told Ruth, "I couldn't eat my Christmas dinner knowing that you are hungry." A few days later, Nickel returned and volunteered to help the pregnant Ruth when the time came for the baby's birth. "Don't be afraid," she told the suspicious and distraught woman, "I only wish to help you. Please give me your address." The baby was born on January 5, 1943. A few days later, Ruth went underground, with papers provided by Maria. The baby was deposited in a blanket at the door of Maria, who adopted the child in addition to her own two children. Occasionally Maria sheltered Ruth and her husband Walter as well. All three members of the Abraham family survived in the heart of Nazi Germany.

An acute problem was what to do with Jewish infants left on the roadside and in off-the-beaten-track areas by fleeing parents who were desperately trying to save at least one member of the family. The following stories are but two of such instances in Yad Vashem files.

An eight-month-old infant girl was found abandoned in the woods outside the village of Dziczkowice, near Krasnik-Lubelski, Poland. Her parents and the other Jews in the forest had been hunted down by local Polish farmers, who had spared the infant girl. Nobody wanted her except Oldak Apolonia. She and her husband Alexander (who was being sought by the Germans for political reasons) decided to take the child into their home, treat her wounds, and feed the undernourished creature. Local villagers added to their difficulties. In Mrs. Oldak's words: "I tried getting some milk which was being distributed for the village children. Everywhere I was met with refusal. All claimed that a Jewish child had no right to milk.... All the time, the farmers did not approve the fact that we were keeping a Jewish child." Soon she was questioned by the German police about the child. Her reply was that the infant was not Jewish but a foundling Gypsy. After the war, adoptive mother and child moved to Israel, to allow little Basya to be close to her uncle's family, who had miraculously survived the war.

In the Minsk ghetto, today capital of the independent Belarus republic, a Jewish mother wishing to save her infant son placed him near an abandoned house outside the ghetto perimeter. The baby was picked up by a man who took him to Jelena Valendovitch. Later Jelena fled with the child to the woods to seek the protection of Russian partisans. The child's mother was also with a partisan unit, and the two were reunited deep in the Russian forest.

The preceding stories are but two of many such accounts, of thousands of Jewish children saved at the eleventh hour by compassionate persons moments before the parents were rounded up by the Nazis. Many of the parents did not live to reclaim their children.

Nursemaids could be extremely helpful in such dire circumstances. Helena Bereska, a nursemaid to a Jewish family, wandered with the family's daughter, born in 1938, from Cracow (where Helena's family threatened to denounce her to the authorities) to other relatives in Gorlice. Similar threats by those relatives forced her to wander once again, and she continued on to several locations in the Krosno district. She kept the child for years after the end of the war, releasing her in 1950 to an uncle who had come to fetch the girl.

Conditions were little more promising for Jewish children in occupied countries of Western Europe. Pieta Creuzberg, a nurse in Arnhem, Netherlands, saw the anguished look of a mother in the hospital maternity ward after she had delivered a child. The woman disclosed to the nurse the reason for her anxiety: she was Jewish. She and her husband had found a secure hiding place for themselves, but what were they to do with an infant? Its cries would surely give them away. Pieta's solution was to take the baby home to her parents. Reverend Jelis and Françoise Creutzberg cared for the child for 16 months, then returned it to its parents. The Creutzbergs, who lost one of their sons in the war, comforted themselves with the thought of being able to save the life of a child. They saw in this the hand of God.

A similar predicament faced the Bouwman family, who were living in hiding with a Dutch family while their two children were safely tucked away with another hospitable family. The problem arose when Sophia Bouwman discovered she was pregnant. This information reached Elizabeth Linschoten, who worked as a clerk in a firm that had once belonged to the Bouwman family, and she told her father. The Linschotens hatched a plan to save Mrs. Bouwman's infant. The baby was to be delivered in a juvenile delinquent rehabilitation center that Pieter Linschoten supervised; then it was to be taken the same evening to the Rowe couple, who would have the child properly registered as their own. Months before the birth, Catherine Rowe changed her attire to make herself look pregnant, and advertised her "news" to others. Moments after the child's birth, Pieter bicycled with it to the Rowe home, and the following morning, Mrs. Rowe proudly let it be known she had given birth to a boy. The child's parents returned to their original hiding place. After the war, the child was returned to his birth parents, and they now experienced the bureaucratic hassle of having the boy reregistered as their own. The Bouwman family were fortunate in having found a family who showed much compassion and hospitality—and no small amount of initiative, inventiveness, courage, and audacity. Thanks to this fortunate combination, all the members of the Bouwman family survived.

Those prepared to save a Jewish child had sometimes to undergo not only discomforts, but even social stigma. In obscuring a child's true origin and identity, some rescuers claimed that the child was the result of an illicit liaison. The rescuer then stood the risk of being ostracized for apparently promiscuous behavior. Cornelia Blaauw, a child welfare worker in Haarlem, Netherlands, had agreed to look after a child left in her care by parents who were deported to the Sobibor death camp. When police asked her why she kept the child's presence a secret, she claimed that the boy was the product of a liaison with a married German officer who was now stationed on the Russian front. That is why, she explained, she had failed to have the child properly registered at birth, fearing a social backlash that could have jeopardized her career. She was strongly reprimanded for this most uncivil behavior, but the child was left in her care, and saved. He is now a practicing psychiatrist.

In another village in the Netherlands, Gertruud Kruger claimed that the little girl the Dutch underground had brought to her family for safekeeping was actually the product of a past romantic liaison with an unmarried man. The inhabitants of this staunchly Calvinist village in the Friesland region did not take kindly to this avowal, and Gertruud courageously bore through the war years the stigma of supposedly being an unwed mother. On top of this, she found out that the man she was engaged to marry belonged to a pro-Nazi political group. She managed to keep him at arm's length and come out of the war unscathed—with the child alive.

Similar stories took place in other parts of Europe. In Poland, Irena Ogniewska, of Stalowa Wola, passed off a one-year-old adopted Jewish child as the product of her husband's affair with another woman. Likewise, Wiktoria Rodziewicz, a nurse in Vilnius (which before the war was part of Poland), helped spirit 21-month-old Sarah out of the Vilnius ghetto, then acquired a baptismal certificate listing the child as her illegitimate daughter. At first she stoically bore the stigma in her home village, to which she had fled, but when suspicions mounted as to the child's true origin, she left for another region. Midnight flights continued until she felt safe with the child. Wiktoria was able to keep her fears and anguish to herself, and impart to the child the motherly love she needed at such a tender age. After the war, Sarah was returned to her natural mother. Reminiscing years later on this dramatic episode in her early life, Sarah writes:

> Not only did Wiktoria save my life, which certainly would have been enough to ask of anyone, but she gave me so much love and, yes, security as well, that I never felt the fear and danger that she faced daily. She hid these from me so well that I looked forward to our midnight flights as adventures and not as ordeals. Not only did she save my life but she gave me a life worth living. She never transferred her fears to me, and I never suspected that my childhood was anything else but normal.

This chapter concludes with the story of a special person who compounded the risks to himself in a giant effort to see several hundred Jewish children safely out of Nazi hands. Bill Barazetti was born in Switzerland and studied in Prague, where he met and befriended Tomas Masaryk, who was later to become the first president of independent Czechoslovakia. Barazetti then left for Hamburg, Germany, to complete his studies. Shocked by the sight of Nazi brutality, he decided to enlist as a secret Czech agent. On the verge of capture by the Gestapo, he managed to escape and return to Prague. There, he joined a team of workers headed by Nicholas Winton. From his base in Great Britain, Winton tried to get as many Jewish children as possible out of a country that, during 1938–39, was on the point of dismemberment.

When the Germans marched into Prague on March 15, 1938, Barazetti was able to flee to Poland, with the help of the British ambassador. Conscience-stricken at having left the children still stranded on the Czech side, he returned to Prague under an assumed name. Contacting Czech underground operatives, he stayed in Prague for several months, until he had seen several hundred Jewish children safely out of the area and bound for England, where Winton had already arranged entry visas for them. The parents, unfortunately, had to be left behind, and most later perished. During this second stay in Prague, Barazetti—a man most wanted by the Gestapo—used whatever it took, including fabricated Nazi seals, to see the children safely out. He then fled again into Poland weeks before the start of World War II, and then continued to England, where he has lived since.

At a ceremony in his honor at Yad Vashem, one of the surviving children, Hugo Marom, thanked Barazetti in the name of the hundreds of children. "To thank you for saving us from going through hell; to thank you for giving our parents a gift that grew more valuable from day to day as they became entrapped by the agent of hell; to thank you on their behalf, as your gift of life to us grew from year to year as we matured.... You, Mr. Barazetti, were our savior. Just when our lives started—and to our parents, in the nick of time, before their lives were extinguished." To which the modest Barazetti responded: "Everything is to me quite simple.... It was not that I was extraordinary in doing this. It was the natural reaction of a man of 25, who was astonished and shocked that the rest of the world was doing nothing." His, we today know, was the "natural" reaction of only a select few.[4]

Chapter 6

Special Rescue Stories

Testimony of Moshe Bejski (at a reception in Israel, 1962, for the German Oskar Schindler)

Until the arrival of Schindler I was familiar, like all of us, with what had been told by those who worked with him in Cracow, while we were still in Plaszow camp. Which one of us did not dream of going there, compared with the regime of Amon Goeth, the commander of Plaszow? As for myself, I got to know Schindler only in Brinnlitz, and even there the contact was mainly through [Itzhak] Stern and my deceased brother. But Schindler was the first German since the beginning of the war of whom I was not afraid. On the contrary! And the same goes for every one of us! This was true to such an extent that we were not fair to him. Whenever a German passed through the plant, anyone who wasn't working pretended he was. But when Schindler entered the plant, nobody cared to even pretend, and the women went right on with their knitting of sweaters and underwear, from wool they had pinched from the neighboring Hoffman factory. And when Hoffman discovered the thefts and complained to the Gestapo, it was Schindler who saw to it that the case be dismissed, and also paid 8,000 marks for the stolen wool. Meanwhile, we were all dressed with sweaters and underwear.

Schindler's plant was the only one in which the building of the big presses was done for the addition of half a loaf of bread. It was in our own interest that these presses should be erected; it gave a better appearance to the plant, as we never really produced. Pardon me, there was some production. Each one of us produced for himself a shaving machine, spoons, eating utensils, and even cigarette lighters. Not only were we not afraid of Schindler, but whenever he entered the plant, everyone expected him to stop by. It so happened that whenever he stopped, he always "forgot" a package of cigarettes there, and in those days, even a cigarette butt was of great value. Sometimes, at night, he was seen walking and whispering for hours on end together with Stern. Only this morning did Schindler tell me: "What do you know of the lessons in Talmud I received from Stern?" And he added: "But do you know how every talmudic elaboration ended? With another request for an additional half loaf of bread for everybody! He certainly could have told me point-blank that he was talking about bread, and we could have saved time."

The case of the Goleszow people always brings back to my mind the picture of Mrs. Schindler, walking in the factory, and behind her two follow carrying pails full of porridge, which she had cooked herself. One must really have a golden heart in order to treat those who were even more miserable than we, comparatively. When SS Commander Liepold decided that the Goleszow men should also be put to work, they were still half-dead, in spite of Mrs. Schindler's porridge. Proper jobs were sought for them, mainly in the storeroom. Except for those who were found frozen dead after the cars were opened by welding torches, and a few more who passed away during the first days, all of them recovered and were released together with us, on May 8, 1945. And another unique episode in connection with the Goleszow people—the 16 frozen dead corpses had to be buried. This was no problem for Liepold—these could be cremated. But when Rabbi Levertov and Stern turned to Schindler, he ran around and arranged for a separate plot of land in a Christian cemetery, and Rabbi Levertov saw to it that they were given a proper Jewish burial, which he attended. Also, a proper signboard with Hebrew script was erected on the grave.

My dear friends, each one of us can conjure memories and innumerable stories, and still we shall not encompass all that should be said about this man Schindler, about his deeds and his attitude toward us. But from all things, always the humanitarian in him stands out. He made an indelible mark not only because of a single rescue operation, but for his constant fatherly attitude and self-sacrifice, which are indescribable; he passed a test that has no equal. And he stayed with us to the very end. He did not leave us until 10 minutes past midnight, on May 8, 1945, after the SS guard had left first, and the armistice was already in force.

It is difficult and unfair to grade rescuers according to criteria of courage, initiative, and personal involvement, from a hindsight of fifty years. All rescuers played for the highest stakes, and whether they saved one or several persons, whether the rescue operation lasted one week or many months, all of them placed their lives and freedom on the line. It is unfair to hold in higher esteem persons who hid a whole family in their barn for a full year and were lucky enough not to be apprehended, compared to others who hid one Jewish person in their attic for only a month. The circumstances of each rescue episode must be taken into account. In the final analysis, what really matters is that all rescuers risked their own lives and well-being to save others threatened with death.

At the same time, some rescue stories are of such magnitude, some rescuers so unique and their moral lessons so edifying, that they transcend the other no less meritorious incidents of aid to the helpless. The exceptional stories in this chapter, some of which have been briefly mentioned earlier, deserve special attention.

Giants of the Spirit

First we consider the special cases of those who acted out of religious compulsion. The aged and semiparalyzed Catholic bishop of Toulouse, France, Monsignor Jules-Géraud Saliège, was sitting quietly in his study one July day in 1942, when he was told of the forceful roundups by the French police of Jews in his diocese; of men, women, and children who were turned over to the Germans to be deported to an unknown destination. He immediately asked for a pen and paper to be brought to him, and he composed a pastoral letter, which he required to be read from the pulpit of all churches in his diocese the following Sunday. It reads in part:

> There is a Christian morality, there is a human morality that imposes duties and recognizes rights. These duties and rights refer to the nature of man. They come from God. One may violate them; no mortal being is capable of suppressing them.... Jews are real men and women. Not everything is permitted against these men and women, against these fathers and mothers. They are part of the human species. They are our brothers, like so many others.

His colleague in nearby Montauban, Monsignor Pierre-Marie Théas, equally minced no words in a similar strongly worded letter:

> I give voice to the outraged protest of Christian conscience and I proclaim that all men, Aryans and non-Aryans, are brothers, because created by the same God; that all men, whatever their race or religion, have the right to be respected by individuals and by states. Hence, the recent anti-Semitic measures are an affront to human dignity and a violation of the most sacred rights of the individual and the family.

Such blunt and unequivocal criticism of the regime's anti-Semitic policy by high-ranking Catholic clerics had been unthinkable only a few months before. The Catholic church in general looked kindly at Marshal Pétain's regime when it assumed power after the defeat of France in June 1940. Even the regime's anti-Jewish laws during 1940–41 were received with few serious misgivings. Reducing Jews to a second-class citizenship category, and even interning foreign-born Jews, were condoned by many French people. But the massive forcible roundup of Jewish men, women, and children by Vichy, in order to deliver them to the Germans for deportation to an unknown fate—that was something else. At this crucial juncture, French public opinion came to the fore, and the new sentiment was heralded by the public pronouncements of these two distinguished Catholic prelates. They had been warned by Vichy officials not to issue such strongly worded pastoral letters, but they paid no heed to this. Théas even enlisted Marie-Rose Gineste to disseminate his declaration to all his diocese's parishes; she did so by riding her bike, stopping at each of the diocese churches and parishes.[1]

These two princes of the church then gave instructions that Catholic institutions open their doors to admit Jewish fugitives being sought by pro-German Vichy officials. In June 1944, both men were visited by the Gestapo (by then the Germans were in full control of all France). Finding Saliège confined to a wheelchair, they proceeded to arrest Théas and incarcerated him. The liberation of France in August of that year spared Théas from being deported to a camp in Germany. The two pastoral letters of Saliège and Théas broke the silence of the Catholic church in France on the persecution of Jews; historians agree that these pronouncements, duplicated and disseminated throughout the country, had a serious impact in molding French public opinion for a more favorable disposition toward fleeing Jews. These letters encouraged many to extend aid to Jews in spite of the regime's intensification of Jewish persecutions. This change in public opinion in mid-1942 is one of the factors explaining the relatively low casualty rate of French Jewry during the Holocaust.

Some two thousand kilometers removed from France, in Greece, two officials of the Greek Orthodox Church took a similar stand. In Athens, Monsignor Damaskinos protested to the Greek prime minister in February 1943 against the latter's acquiescence at the treatment of Jews by the German overlords in the occupied parts of Greece. "Our holy religion does not recognize differences—superior or inferior—based on race and religion," the head of the Greek church reminded the head of the government. "One should not forget that one day the nation will judge the deeds done during this difficult period, even when done against our will and beyond our authority, and every one involved will have to bear responsibility. This moral responsibility will weigh especially on the nation's leaders on that Judgment Day if they do not dare make public the people's negative position concerning deeds such as the deportation of Jews, recently begun." The venerable churchman then ordered all religious institutions to throw their doors open to fleeing Jews. When told of the danger to himself in taking such a step, he responded: "I have made my cross. . .and decided to save as many Jewish souls as I can, even if that will endanger me." He then instructed the head of the Athens municipality to assist Jews with new identifications under assumed Christian names, based on false baptismals provided by his church. Angelos Evert, head of the Athens police, is reported to have issued several hundred new false identification documents. Many Athenian Jews availed themselves of this opportunity and were saved.

On the Greek island of Zakinthou, Bishop Chrysostomos confronted the local German commander, who asked to be given a list of the 275 Jewish inhabitants of the island. The bishop countered by writing his own name on a slip of paper and saying: "Here, take the list of the Jews of Zakinthou. I am at your mercy. You can arrest me, not them. If this does not satisfy you, then know that I will march together with the Jews into the concentration camps." Stunned by the bishop's stand, the German major relented, and the island's Jews were momentarily spared. By the time the Germans decided to move against them, the local Jews had been spirited out of their homes and hidden in the surrounding hills.

The small French Protestant community in France did not fail to produce giants of the spirit, such as the previously mentioned Pastor André Trocmé, the spiritual guide of the Le Chambon-sur-Lignon community in the hilly region of southeast France. He inspired his community to extend shelter to many Jews in need, and together with his wife Magda organized various sheltering places in the vicinity and arranged flight routes toward the Swiss border. To a visiting Vichy minister who asked about the many Jews who were reported being sheltered in the town, Trocme responded: "We do not know what a Jew is; we only recognize human beings." Fifteen days later, Trocme was summoned to the police and asked to draw up a list of the Jews under his care. He answered: "I don't know the names of these persons, and even if I knew them, I would not deliver them to you. They came to seek help and protection from the Protestants of this region. I am their pastor, that is, their shepherd. A shepherd's role is not to betray the sheep under his care."

A year earlier Trocmé had preached a sermon in which he denounced the persecution of Jews, and added: "The Christian church should go down on its knees and ask forgiveness from God for its current incapacity and cowardice.... I am saying this because I can no longer remain silent. I do not say it in a spirit of hate, but of sadness and humility, for the sake of the people of this country." He preceded many churchmen, Catholic and Protestant alike, in condemning the government's anti-Semitic policy. After repeated warnings to keep silent and cease further rescue action, Pastor Trocmé was finally imprisoned by the French authorities, but released thanks to pressures from Protestant church circles. Some five thousand Jews are reputed to have found temporary shelter in the Le Chambon-sur-Lignon region during the war years.

Not far to the north of Le Chambon, in Lyon, the second-largest city of France, General Robert de St. Vincent, the military commander of the city, was ordered in July 1942 by his government to place troops at the disposal of the police to facilitate a roundup operation of the city's Jews. The general refused to comply with this order; he was promptly dismissed from the army. This was the only known instance of a French general refusing to besmirch his name, and that of the army unit he commanded, by becoming a tool in the execution of a clearly inhumane act. It was later learned that the general had been a founding member of the Amitié Chrétienne, a clandestine religious group that was also involved in the rescue of Jews. General St. Vincent's name was added to the Righteous Honor Roll by Yad Vashem.

Farther north in German-controlled Paris, Mother Maria Skobtzova ("Mère Marie") of the Russian Orthodox Church was arrested in March 1943 for extending her church's hospitality to fleeing Jews. Earlier, when Jews were forced to wear the yellow star sign on their outer clothing, she penned a paean in praise of the star:

> Israel
> Two triangles, a star
> The shield of King David, our forefather
> This is election not offense
> The great path and not an evil.

Once more is a term fulfilled
Once more roars the trumpet of the end
And the fate of a great people
Once more is proclaimed by the prophet.
Thou art persecuted again, O Israel
But what can human ill will mean to thee
Thee, who has heard the thunder from Sinai?

After she declined, under interrogation, to commit herself to cease aiding Jews, she was dispatched to Ravensbrück camp in Germany, where she perished in March 1945. Her body was consumed by the flames of the camp's crematorium. The following entry in her personal notes gives testimony to the woman's altruistic fervor: "At the Last Judgment, I will not be asked whether I satisfactorily practiced asceticism, or how many bows I have made before the divine altar. I will be asked whether I fed the hungry, clothed the naked, visited the sick and prisoner in his jail. That is all that will be asked."

In the vast farmlands of Ukraine, a Baptist community was quietly cultivating its unique brand of Christian fellowship. During the terrible Holocaust years, these pious men and women stood out in their help to Jews who were being mistreated and killed by their Ukrainian compatriots. The young David Prital, fleeing a Nazi killing raid in the Lutsk ghetto, sought shelter with the Baptists in the region. When he knocked at one farmstead door, he was greeted with the words: "God brought us an important guest. Come, let us thank the Lord for it." Such welcoming greetings to Jews were rarely heard throughout Ukraine in those years. David was then rotated among different Baptist homes, traveling by night, for added security. On the eve of one such nocturnal journey, he asked why he was being moved so frequently. The response by Ivan Yatsyuk remains embedded in David's memory: "We usually place our trust in our fellow believers. But man is in the final account tested in adversity and in difficult situations. Tonight we shall take you to a certain farmer who does not know you. His attitude and response will test the sincerity of his faith. There is no danger in this for you. At the most, he will refuse you his hospitality and we shall take you elsewhere. But to us, his response will be a serious indication of the strength and depth of his faith." Many other hapless Jews were saved by the Baptists in Ukraine and adjacent lands, by benefactors who saw in the rescue of Jews the ultimate test of their Christian creed.

There were also those who acted not merely because of religious faith but because of a profound conviction that the Nazi challenge called for an immediate human response. Joop Westerweel, from Utrecht, Netherlands, was a staunch pacifist, iconoclast, and nonconformist; a person who previously refused to pay taxes because part of the funds was diverted for military expenditure; an innovative educator; a man who saw in all forms of nationalism the root cause of the twentieth century's evils—this man, at the sight of the massive onslaught by the Nazis on the Jews in the Netherlands, worked with a Zionist pioneering group to help save as many of their members as humanly possible. His personality was an amalgam of strong authority and limitless fervor, tempered by compassion toward the innocent and helpless.

A whole generation of Jewish youth was inspired by Westerweel's example. Those who met him during the summer of 1942 were immediately struck by the man's zeal and dedication. "The meeting with him was awesome and overwhelming," recounts one person. During that encounter, Westerweel told them: "Friends, this is the mission I have been waiting for all these days." He arranged for dozens of Jewish youth to be hidden with local Dutch people. Then, he devised a plan to send contingents of Jewish youth on long treks across occupied Belgium and France, right up to the Spanish frontier, on the Pyrenees mountain heights, where he bade them farewell. Some still recall his parting words during one of these sojourns in 1944: "You are on the threshold of freedom. Soon you will arrive in the land of freedom and you will fulfill your goal of building Eretz Israel [the Land of Israel] as a homeland for all of the world's Jews [this from a staunch antinationalist!].... Build up your land and erect a memorial for them, immortalizing their memory.... Remember the suffering in the world and build up your land in such a way that it becomes for all its inhabitants a source of freedom, hence justifying its existence."

Westerweel was eventually betrayed and arrested by the Germans, who sentenced him to death. An attempt by his Jewish comrades to release him failed, with tragic consequences for them. On the eve of his execution, he penned the following poem, which he managed to have smuggled out from his cell. It reads in part: "There they are... all my friends, standing in line next to me; together we marched this straight road, to face the enemy. Whether I die or live, it is now the same for me. A great light has dawned within me, enriching me much. It is time for silent thought. The night is dark and long. But I am fully enveloped by the splendor within me." Beneficiaries of his aid still gather to evoke his name and seek inspiration from his deeds. They speak of the tremendous influence of this strong-willed humanitarian on their lives.

Equally idiosyncratic was Arnold Douwes from the Netherlands. A gardener by profession, he joined a clandestine organization headed by Johannes Post (who was eventually apprehended and shot by the Germans), and together they turned the village of Nieuwlande and vicinity, in northeast Holland, into a haven for several hundred fleeing Jews, including many children. Douwes's method was to persuade every household in the village to take in a Jew, at least for a short time. In this endeavor, he was also helped by Max ("Nico") Leons, a young Jewish man posing as a Protestant seminarian. Years later, Douwes recalled the problems he faced with moving large numbers of people from place to place:

> Our work was not easy. The victims themselves presented the major problem. One had to invest great efforts in order to convince them. Many did not wish to acknowledge the dangers facing them.... One had to resort to lies in order to separate children from parents.... We told them stories about green pastures and similar inventions.... When we told people "one week," it really meant

> for a period up to the liberation. When we said "two days," we meant two years.... The technique used was to contact people in Amsterdam and implore them to let their children go, assuring them that there were safe places waiting for them. There were really no such places. Our thinking was that the moment that people arrived, we should find for them suitable places. These had to be found and they were indeed found: in homes, cellars, and attics or other forms of concealment.

Douwes personally met the children in Amsterdam or at the train station, kept secret tabs of every person's whereabouts, and moved people from one place to another whenever necessary. Says Lou Gans, one of his wards: "He was one of a few. You met him, looked in his eyes, looked at his tight-lipped face; then you understood that no brute force in the whole world could force such a man to talk against his will.... He not only saved my life, but also enriched it!" The Germans, desperately on the lookout for him, finally nabbed him. But on the eve of his execution, he was liberated by the underground in a daring raid on the jail. When the war ended, he returned to his old profession, gardening. Several hundred persons owe their lives to this humble man.

In France, Adelaide Hautval, a physician by profession, stands out for her dauntless character, unbroken in spite of the difficult challenges thrown at her. In 1942 she was arrested for attempting to cross, without a permit, the demarcation line separating the two parts of France—not too severe an offense but still punishable. While in jail, she protested the treatment of the Jewish inmates. The response from her German interrogator was simply: "Since you like them, you will join them." She was eventually placed aboard a convoy heading to Auschwitz, where she arrived in early 1943. She immediately caught the attention of the SS medical staff in that giant killing facility and was invited to join in the human experimentation done (without the use of anesthesia) on live victims. She refused.

Asked by Dr. Wirths, the SS head surgeon in the camp, why she was blind to the deep gulf that separated her from the Jews, she curtly responded that the only gulf separating her from others was the one between her and the interlocutor. This response in itself should have doomed her, but her luck held out. Still, she was sure she would not be allowed to survive. She told a fellow inmate: "The Germans will not allow for what is happening here to be known in the outside world, so the only thing that is left for us to do is behave, for the rest of the short duration that is allotted us, as human beings."

Somehow she survived the horrors of Auschwitz and Ravensbrück. In 1964, she testified in the slander trial of Dr. Dering versus the American author Leon Uris, who in his book *QB7* had accused the doctor of not using anesthesia on women patients in Auschwitz when their ovaries were removed on orders of the Nazis. Dr. Dering claimed that in a place like Auschwitz, the laws of civilized life did not apply and, to save his own neck, he had to comply with the inhuman demands of his captors. Dr. Hautval's testimony (which, according to Justice Lawton, made a deep impact on the court) showed that it was possible, for those who had the courage, to decline inhuman commands even in Auschwitz. Her own example and that of several others who testified at the trial were proof that the human spirit was not completely squashed, even in such a hellish place.

Diplomats in Service to Humanity

As mentioned earlier in this volume, certain diplomats played a crucial role in facilitating the rescue of many people. There were a few, moved by altruistic zeal, who went to unimaginable lengths, even jeopardizing their own careers in the process.

Aristides de Sousa Mendes, the Portuguese consul general in Bordeaux, France (briefly mentioned earlier), threw caution to the wind when, in June 1940, he acted against the express orders of his own government and issued transit visas to thousands of Jews. He had been repeatedly cautioned against this course of action, and when diplomatic dispatches from Lisbon failed to bring about his compliance, two emissaries were dispatched to bring the recalcitrant diplomat home. Earlier he had explained his motivations to his startled staff:

> My government has denied all applications for visas to any refugees. But I cannot allow these people to die. Many are Jews and our constitution says that the religion, or the politics, of a foreigner shall not be used to deny him refuge in Portugal. I have decided to follow this principle. I am going to issue a visa to anyone who asks for it–regardless of whether or not he can pay.... Even if I am dismissed, I can only act as a Christian, as my conscience tells me.

Upon his recall, he was summarily fired from his post and lost all retirement benefits. After his dismissal in 1941, he explained to Rabbi Haim Kruger, the man with whom he negotiated in Bordeaux the passage of thousands of Jews through Portugal, the reasons for his behavior: "If thousands of Jews can suffer because of one Catholic [meaning Hitler], then surely it is permitted for one Catholic to suffer for so many Jews." Mendes died forgotten and destitute.

In 1989, the Portuguese government recanted, and in a public declaration rehabilitated the late Mendes and restored to his family the pension benefits that had been denied him.

Barely two months after Mendes's forcible departure from France, another rescuer appeared on the scene, the American Varian Fry. He arrived in Marseille in August 1940 as a special emissary of the Emergency Rescue Committee, a private American relief group founded under the auspices of Eleanor Roosevelt for the purpose of saving exceptionally talented persons who were trapped in France, now a conquered nation. Fry carried with him a list of two hundred such people. These included artists, writers, musicians, intellectuals, and politicians, many of them Jews, who had fled Nazi Germany to France and were now in jeopardy of being turned over to the Gestapo by the pro-German Vichy government.[2] President Roosevelt had begrudgingly consented to his wife's demands for special visas to be granted to these endangered persons, but someone was needed to be on the spot to collect these people and bring them to safe harbor. This man was to be Varian Fry.[3]

"Friends warned me of the danger," Fry wrote in 1945. "They said I was a fool to go. I, too, could be walking into the trap. I might never come back alive." But buttressed with an overdose of self-confidence, Fry was sure that the job could be done within a month's time—"or so I believed."

Upon his arrival in Marseille, his first thoughts were of how best to search out and contact those on his list, most of whom were living in seclusion. No sooner had the word gone out that an American had arrived on a rescue mission, however, than a stampede ensued to Fry's temporary office at the Hotel Splendide. "The refugees began coming to my room the next day. Many of them had been through hell; their nerves were shattered and their courage gone. Many had been herded into concentration camps at the outbreak of the war, then released, then interned again." They had managed to escape, and now sought frantically to escape France, believing that the Germans were about to invade the southern unoccupied part of the country, or that the French would try to stall the Germans by surrendering to them all "undesirables" sought by the Gestapo.[4] Deciding who should be helped and who were possible undercover provocateurs was the most difficult part of his job. The solution adopted by Fry was "to give each refugee the full benefit of the doubt. Otherwise we might refuse help to someone who was really in danger and learn later that he had been dragged away to Dachau or Buchenwald because we had turned him down." But, as a precautionary measure, each person to be helped was asked to provide trustworthy references.[5]

To get people out of France, it was thought best to have them cross to Spain, then head for Portugal where, with the U.S. visa in their pocket, they would board a boat heading for the United States. As most persons in this category had no travel permits, false credentials were fabricated—French exit visas, fake Spanish transit visas, or passports from countries such as Lithuania, Panama, Czechoslovakia, Venezuela, and even China. Several crossing points on the Franco-Spanish border were utilized; most were located in the Cerbère/Bayuls region on the Mediterranean coast. The noted writer Franz Werfel, the Hebraic scholar Oscar Goldberg, the sculptor Jacques Lipchitz, and the noted artist Marc Chagall were among the more than one thousand persons smuggled out of the country. Fry also arranged, with the help of Mary Jane Gold, to spirit several persons out of the French internment camp at Vernet and then smuggle them out of the country.

Fry's troubles with the French authorities began early. He was targeted by the French police for constant harassment. His office and private dwelling were raided on several occasions. In each instance, he managed to destroy incriminating documents (frontier maps, false passports, visas, and identity cards) moments before his premises were thoroughly searched. Fry was secretly told that this was part of a campaign "to frighten me into leaving France of my own free will. . . . It's a classic maneuver."[6] In December 1940, on the pretext of Marshal Pétain's visit to Marseille, Fry was hauled away aboard a boat, the SS Sinai, and kept there incommunicado for three days. His was part of a massive arrest of 20,000 suspects to ensure Pétain's safety.

Undeterred by this constant harassment, Fry extended his original 30-day stay into months, up to his expulsion in August 1941. In the meantime, he set up a team of trusted aides who facilitated his work. His superiors in New York, mindful of Fry's successes, pleaded with him to stay on the job for as long as possible.

As Fry enlarged the scope of his rescue operation, he encountered friction from another direction—his own government. The U.S. State Department, concerned about U.S. relations with the Vichy regime, began to hamper Fry's freedom of movement. He was constantly urged by the U.S. consul in Vichy to cease operations and return home. "You must understand," a U.S. diplomat told him, "that we maintain friendly relations with the French government. . . . We can't support an American citizen who is helping people evade French law."[7] The consul general kept reminding Fry that "I'd be expelled any day if I were lucky enough not to be arrested and held on charges." In his book, written in 1945, Fry accuses the U.S. embassy of cooperating with the French police in bringing pressure on him to go.[8] Fry defiantly stayed on. As he explained: "Without an American there to protect them, [his staff people] would soon be arrested and sent to a concentration camp, and everything would come to an end. Our work was by no means finished. We had not succeeded in sending out everyone we had located.... Somehow, we had to find a way to get them out of France."[9]

When diplomatic proddings failed to move Fry, his passport was confiscated in January 1941. A secretary at the U.S. embassy told him, "My instructions are to renew it only for immediate return to the United States, and then only for a period of two weeks. So I'm afraid I'll have to keep it here until you're ready to go." From that moment, until his forced departure seven months later, Fry was without a passport. In August 1941, a French police officer warned him that he was on the point of arrest unless he left France. Fry asked, "Tell me, frankly, why are you so much opposed to me?" "Because you have protected Jews and anti-Nazis," came the reply.[10] When Fry paid no heed to this additional warning, he was arrested on August 27, 1941, given one hour to pack, conducted to the border, and turned over to Spanish authorities, with an expulsion order in his pocket.[11]

The newly constructed U.S. Holocaust Memorial in Washington, D.C., dedicated a special exhibit to Fry's rescue operation. A few of his original rescue team were present to recall the man and his motivations. To Mary Jane Gold, Varian Fry was a Scarlet Pimpernel, who wanted to pluck "half of the intellectual elite of Europe."[12] Fry once confided to her that during a visit in Berlin in the 1930s, he saw a group of Nazis brutalizing a Jew in a restaurant, thrusting a knife through the man's hand and pinning it to the table. "I think the image of that hand nailed to the table beside the beer mug had something to do with his decision to take on the rescue job." To Albert O. Hirschman (nicknamed "Beamish" because of his grin), Fry's outward "innocence" was his source of strength. "Had he known from the outset the odds he was up against he could never have achieved what he did. Indeed, his accomplishments exceeded all that was predictable or probable under the circumstances." Willi Spira ("Bill Freier"), the cartoonist, who helped by forging false credentials, sums it up: "Varian Fry is certainly one of the great men of this century. America can be proud of him." Yad Vashem proudly added his name, the first American ever, to the list of the Righteous.[13]

Sempo Sugihara, the Japanese consul general in Kaunas, Lithuania, flouted his government's orders in granting transit visas to thousands of Jews who were eager to leave the country in anticipation of a German invasion, and who wished to be allowed to pass through Japan on their way to other destinations. In July 1940 Sugihara was approached by a delegation of Jewish refugees headed by Dr. Z. Warhaftig (years later, a minister in the Israeli government). Sugihara told Warhaftig that he needed his government's approval and thus asked for a delay of several days. Cabling Tokyo several times for permission to grant the visas, he was repeatedly rebuffed. Time was running short, for Sugihara had been instructed to close the consulate and leave the country within a month. "I really had a hard time, being unable to sleep for two nights," he later recounted:

> I thought as follows: I can issue transit visas. . .by virtue of my authority as consul. I cannot allow these people to die, people who have come to me for help with death staring them in the eyes. Whatever punishment may be imposed upon me [for disobeying government instructions], I know I should follow my conscience.... I decided there was no further point to continue negotiating with Tokyo.... I began, on my own accord and with full responsibility on my part, to issue Japanese transit visas to the refugees without regard whether so-and-so had the necessary documents or not.

Several thousand persons owe their lives to this fearless Japanese diplomat, who was summarily dismissed from his post. In 1992, a memorial in Sugihara's name was dedicated in his hometown in Japan, in the presence of government and local officials. Attending from Israel was Dr. Warhaftig, the man who had negotiated the visa arrangement with him 52 years earlier. The Japanese government, however, has yet to officially recant and make amends to Sugihara's family.

In Budapest, Hungary, Giorgio Perlasca, a representative of an Italian agricultural firm, decided not to return to his country as directed after the Germans had installed a pro-Nazi regime there in September 1943. Instead he managed to have himself hired as a secretary in the Spanish legation. When the Spanish ambassador was instructed to vacate the city upon the approach of the Soviet armies in December 1944, Perlasca decided on a gambit of his own. He would pose as the official representative of the Spain's Francisco Franco regime, and in that capacity force the pro-Nazi Hungarian regime to adhere to previous agreements contracted whereby Jews claiming Spanish antecedents (whether real or fictitious) had been granted the protection of the Spanish government. Perlasca threatened reprisals against Hungarian interests in Spain if the Hungarian government failed to live up to its commitment. The bluff worked, and more than a thousand Jews were able to escape deportation to the death camps. The Spanish government in Madrid was unaware of the machinations of this upstart diplomat who claimed to speak in its name in the crucial months of December 1944 to February 1945, when Hungary was controlled by the fiercely anti-Semitic Arrow Cross movement and their German allies. "I only did what everyone else in my place would have done," the modest Perlasca told a journalist in a recent interview.

The name that comes foremost to mind when speaking of outstanding humanitarian diplomats is undoubtedly that of Raoul Wallenberg. He arrived in Budapest in July 1944 in the capacity of a first secretary in the Swedish embassy. In truth, he was dispatched there to represent the American War Refugee Board, set up by President Franklin Roosevelt in 1944 to aid Jewish refugees from Nazi persecution. His mission: to save as many Hungarian Jews as possible, who were then being decimated by the Nazis (headed by the archvillain Adolf Eichmann) and their Hungarian collaborators. On a cue from Carl Lutz, a colleague at the Swiss legation, Wallenberg decided to expand on the ruse of the "protective pass," a document purporting that the bearer was en route to Sweden and hence under the protection of the Swedish crown until travel arrangements could be worked out. The Hungarian authorities, eager for Swedish support in the international arena, played along with this game.

When the Arrow Cross movement grabbed power in October 1944, they at first canceled the "protective pass" and "protective home" scheme (whereby buildings flying a foreign flag were off-limits to others). Under intense pressure from Wallenberg and fellow diplomats in Budapest, they recanted and renewed the government pledge to honor these rights (although, in practice, the promise was not always kept). Thousands of Jews were to profit from this ploy. In November 1944, Eichmann organized a death march of more than seventy thousand Jews to the Austrian border (then a part of Germany), under the supervision of Hungarian gendarmes. Wallenberg followed this trail of misery in his car and, forcing himself on Hungarian commanders, was able to release hundreds of Jews by claiming they were under the protection of his government. As told by one survivor of this march:

> The conditions were frightful. We walked thirty to forty kilometers a day in freezing rain, driven all the time by the Hungarian gendarmes. We were all women and girls and I was 17 at the time. The gendarmes were brutal, beating those who could not keep up, leaving others to die in the ditches.... Suddenly I heard a great commotion among the women. "It's Wallenberg," they said. I didn't think he could really help me, and anyway I was too weak now to move, so I lay there on the floor as dozens of women clustered around him, crying "Save us, save us."
>
> I remember being struck by how handsome he looked and how clean—in his leather coat and fur hat, just like a being from another world, and I thought, "why does he bother with such wretched creatures as we?" As the women clustered around him, he said to them, "Please, you must forgive me, but I cannot help all of you. I can only provide certificates for a hundred of you." Then he said something which really surprised me. He said: "I feel I have a mission to save the Jewish nation, and so I must rescue the young ones first."... He looked around the room and began putting names down on a list and when he saw me lying on the floor he came over to me.

> He asked my name and added it to the list. After a day or two, the hundred of us whose names had been taken were moved out and put into a cattle truck on a train bound for Budapest. There were a lot more dangers and hardships for us, but we were alive—and it was thanks entirely to Wallenberg.

According to reliable estimates, the number of people who profited from Wallenberg's aid runs into the tens of thousands. He had a staff of 335 people, including doctors, who aided him (with funds funneled through the Swedish embassy) in this superhuman effort to rescue the remnants of Hungarian Jewry. To his aide, diplomat Per Anger, he confided, "I'd never be able to go back to Stockholm without knowing inside myself I'd done all a man could do to save as many Jews as possible."

By a tragic twist of fate, Wallenberg was arrested by the Russians when they captured parts of Budapest, on January 17, 1945. There were persistent rumors that Wallenberg had been seen in several Soviet prisons or camps, but the sightings could not be confirmed. The Soviet government has never been able to satisfactorily explain either the reasons for his arrest or the conditions of his imprisonment and his ultimate fate. In 1992, people from throughout the world celebrated Wallenberg's eightieth birthday. He remains a symbol of the best form of altruism and selfless devotion to the cause of others in distress.

Special Ingenuity

Also meriting special mention are individual rescuers of lesser renown, who devised ingenious ways and means to enlarge the scope of their rescue activities. Three such stories follow.

When the Germans overran Poland, Stanislaw Jackow (already alluded to earlier), a carriage maker, wondered what had happened to his school friend Max Saginur. On February 22, 1943, the remaining Jews in Stanislawow (who once had numbered close to 30,000) were marched off to the cemetery and shot. The city was now declared *judenrein,* clean of Jews. But the Germans had not counted on Jackow. Shortly before the final liquidation raid, on January 31, 1943, Jackow stole out of his house toward the ghetto wall where Max and his bride, Gitya, were waiting in an abandoned house. He took them to his home and hid them behind a wooden partition in the kitchen. When that proved unsatisfactory, Jackow enlarged his cellar and camouflaged it from the outside, making it possible to hide a larger group of people. For beds, Jackow brought in upholstered leather cushions from the factory where he worked. In all, 32 persons found themselves safely ensconced in that niche beneath Jackow's house. Most came penniless, in rags, after spending months hiding in the forest being hunted by Germans and enthusiastic anti-Semites from the local population. To further accommodate such a large group, Jackow and his wards drilled a well 25 feet deep to tap fresh water. They installed a hand pump as well as an indoor toilet. Upstairs, Jackow's family still had no plumbing.

The bunker came alive when Jackow tapped on the trapdoor and jumped down to visit them. He would stay for hours, joining them in chess and card games. He kidded about running "the biggest underground hotel in Stanislawow," deceiving not only the powerful Gestapo but even his own mother and sisters, who were unaware of the scope of Jackow's rescue operation. Friendly Poles helped him: a baker supplied fresh bread and at times cookies; a nurse at a local dispensary provided medicines; and several others ran vital errands to procure additional necessities and maintain contact with other potential hiders. Outside this hospitable nest, terror and death stalked the few Jews still living in the city. In Jackow's bunker, with ample food, warmth, and even laughter, normal life cycles were restored. Gitya and her sister-in-law, Wanda, both became pregnant. When, without advance notice, Jackow was conscripted for forced labor in Germany, he managed to elude his captors and detour through open fields and back streets until he reached his home. There he joined his charges in their hideout. The Germans rummaged through the home but never found the secret trapdoor leading to the elaborate underground hideout.

On July 29, 1944, the Russians liberated Stanislawow. Sixty-five Jews surfaced from hiding places, half of them from the single hideout of Stanislaw Jackow. "I never thought there would be 32," Jackow confided to his friend Max one evening. "I did it for you. . .to save you. I know, if it was the other way, if they were killing Poles, you would do the same for me." He then added an afterthought: "If they caught me saving only you, they would kill me. I might as well be killed for 32 as for one. But they won't catch us," he assured Max. "This house is blessed."

On November 30, 1941, Jan Lipke and his son witnessed a large-scale Nazi-instigated massacre of Jews in Riga, Latvia, claiming 10,000 victims. Turning to his son, Lipke said in an emotion-laden voice, "Look well, son, and never forget." Lipke was now resolved to dedicate himself to saving as many of the remaining Jews as possible. Leaving his job as a dockworker, he enlisted as an overseer in a German Air Force civilian outfit in which Jewish labor from the ghetto was employed. Thus he was able to enter the ghetto to fetch Jews for work duties, spiriting some away to hiding places. He then led them to his home, aided by a trustworthy Latvian truck driver who transported them on his lorry hidden beneath heaps of lumber, straw, and broken furniture, and taking along German military hitchhikers for good measure in order to pass spot-check controls on the road. At first, the Jews were sheltered in a specially constructed hideout in Lipke's home. Lipke also devised a plan to transfer Jews by boat across the Baltic Sea to Sweden. He began to construct a boat, but the plan had to be abandoned. Trying a variant approach, he sheltered Jews on a farm in Dobele and Miltini, which he purchased for this purpose.

David Fishkin, one of his beneficiaries, relates how he was saved by Lipke. At work for the Germans at a location outside Riga, he suddenly heard a whistle from the direction of a nearby field. "I turned my head in the direction of the noise and saw Lipke hiding in the tall grass. He asked me if I needed additional food and clothing and when I was prepared to come over to him." As David hesitatingly garbled words in response to this generous offer, Lipke suddenly threw him some jewelry, with which David was to bribe one of the guards when he had made up his mind to attempt an escape. When, in July 1944, David realized that the Germans were preparing to liquidate the remaining Jews on the work force, he decided to wait no longer. Bribing two Ukrainian guards, David jumped over the fence and met Lipke outside. They boarded a trolley filled with German soldiers and SS men. To distract their attention from the Semitic-looking David, Lipke had him face the window while Lipke harangued the passengers on the evils of communism and the need to help the Germans repel the advancing Russian army. When they dismounted they headed for the home of a Latvian woman, a collaborator of Lipke, who hid David as well as other Jews in a cellar. David and 41 other Jews owe their lives to this simple dockworker from Riga.

The person who single-handedly saved more Jews than any other rescuer was the German Oskar Schindler. He was a man of many shades and moods; to some he was a crass opportunist, riding the crest of German victories to his advantage; to many others he was a basically nice (though none too honest) person moved by the sufferings of others. Born in Zwittau (today Svitavy), in the formerly German-speaking Sudetenland region of Czechoslovakia, he arrived in Cracow in late 1939, in the wake of the German conquest of Poland. He immediately took over two previously Jewish-owned firms dealing with the manufacture and wholesale distribution of enamel kitchenware, over which he was appointed trustee by the occupation authorities. He then established his own enamel works, manufacturing mess kits and shell casings for the German army, in Zablocie, outside Cracow. There he employed mainly Jewish laborers, thereby protecting them from deportations.

At this early period, Schindler's main concern was in extracting pleasure for himself. He saw in this undertaking an opportunity to enrich himself and live it up. He would use the cheap but trustworthy Jewish labor in his enamel factory so as to maximize profits and siphon off as much as possible for himself, to allow him to squander money on racehorses, sports cars, choice liquor, and women—as well as to buy the goodwill of SS officers with whom he partied, to keep them at arm's length from his private shenanigans and his Jewish workers. He treated his Jewish workers humanely, barring the dreaded SS from his factory grounds, so that they would be further motivated to produce even more efficiently.

Then, in March 1943, Schindler witnessed the liquidation of the Cracow ghetto and was shocked by the brutality and inhuman methods of his own kinsmen. Something in him was kindled, a spark that grew larger with time and led him to a self-imposed commitment to do whatever was possible to save hundreds of Jewish laborers and their spouses. He cajoled, bribed, and courted SS and Gestapo officials and commanders, making them believe that "his" Jews were a valuable asset to a country at war. Although many of the 900 Jewish workers in Schindler's expanded factory were unqualified for the specialized labor of the enamel plant, the Germans grudgingly released to him some of the ghetto Jews who were being transferred to the newly created Plaszow labor camp, which was notorious for the brutality of its commander, Amon Goeth. Schindler had special barracks built for his workers on company grounds so that they did not have to spend nights in the dreaded Plaszow camp.

In October 1944 he was ordered to close his plant to prevent it from falling into the hands of the advancing Russians, and to release the Jewish workers to the SS. Instead, in an operation unique in the annals of Nazi-occupied Europe, he succeeded in transferring his Jewish workers and their wives—a total of 1,100 persons—to Zwittau in the Sudeten region, on the pretext of harnessing valuable labor for a new munitions plant that was to be set up. He was able to move his workers even after some had been dispatched to the Auschwitz killing camp—they were released on orders from Berlin. Reestablished in Brünnlitz (today in the Czech Republic), Schindler added a hundred other Jews who had been liberated from a stranded concentration camp convoy in a nearby train station and nursed back to life with the help of Schindler's wife, Emilie. When the war ended, he had to his credit some twelve hundred lives saved.

Schindler wound up penniless and miserable. He went back to drinking and womanizing, and despite the help of his many beneficiaries in his new business ventures (a mink farm in Argentina and a cement factory in Germany), he was not able to make ends meet and was reduced to almost total dependency. This jovial, happy-go-lucky, party-loving, and self-centered man, who initially was interested only in his own pleasure, whose private life was riddled with misbehaviors—this same man had exhausted his energies for a most noble cause, the saving of innocent lives, for which he derived no profit to himself. Had he not possessed the unsavory traits for which he was known, it is doubtful whether he could have orchestrated the rescue of so many Jews right under the nose of the Nazis.

Schindler's last request was to have his remains buried in Jerusalem. The pallbearers and cortege who carried the coffin to the Latin cemetery on Mount Zion in 1974 included several hundred of those he saved, including Moshe Bejski, a judge on Israel's Supreme Court bench. In a recent film, *Schindler's List,* the celebrated Hollywood producer Steven Spielberg has attempted to recapture the unique and bewildering character of this great humanitarian as an additional testament to future generations.

Other German rescuers of note include Gustav Schroeder, Albert Battel, and Max Liedtke. Gustav Schroeder was captain of the ill-fated *Saint Louis,* a boat that sailed from Hamburg to Cuba in May 1939 with more than nine hundred Jews on board. The Cuban authorities in Havana, under pressure from the United States government, refused to allow the refugees to disembark. Schroeder steered the boat off the coast of Miami to test America's sensitivity. Newspapers gave wide coverage to the ship's voyage and the plight of its human cargo, but the U.S. government proved adamant. Veering the boat back to Europe, Schroeder considered scuttling it off the southern coast of England, after disembarking all passengers, rather than returning the distraught Jews to Nazi Germany. The worldwide publicity that accompanied the *Saint Louis* drama finally produced a salutary outcome. Approaching the English Channel, Schroeder was instructed by telex to proceed to Antwerp, Belgium, where his refugees would be allowed to land. The deadlock had been broken; England, France, the Netherlands, and Belgium had agreed to split between themselves the Jewish refugees. Schroeder's weeks-long odyssey was over and his wards safe.

Major Max Liedtke was the commander of the German garrison in occupied Przemysl, Poland, and Lt. Albert Battel was his adjutant. In July 1942, the SS staged an "action" on the city's Jews, who were to be rounded up and killed. Several hundred of these people were at the time on assignment with the German military of the city. Forewarned of the SS operation, Liedtke and Battel told the SS command that they would not countenance any harm befalling the Jews under their supervision. When that demand proved ineffective, the two officers placed troops on a bridge spanning the San River that led to the Jewish quarter and gave orders to open fire on SS troops should they attempt to force their way into the Jewish quarter. The SS protested vehemently. The action of the two German officers led to recriminations up to the highest echelons of the SS command. Heinrich Himmler, head of the SS, in turn brought the matter before Hitler's adjutant, Martin Bormann. The decision was taken to remove Liedtke from his post and send him to combat duty on the Russian front. A note was made in Battel's personal file that punitive measures were to be taken against him immediately upon the end of the war. Battel and Liedtke survived the war, but Liedtke died in a Siberian prisoner-of-war camp.

Rescue from the Threshold of Death

Finally, there are those whose lives were saved at the eleventh hour, either on the threshold of death or of being enveloped by the Nazi infernal machine. The importance of these rescuers does not derive so much from the uniqueness of their persons as for the crucial role they played at the most critical juncture in the lives of those they saved.

Zofia Boczkowska was riding in her horse-driven buggy to town near Busk, Ukraine, when she saw from afar a young girl standing by a group of Jews digging their own graves before being shot. The girl was hopping, dancing, bowing, and carrying on a conversation with herself, or so it seemed. Her peculiar gesticulations drew Zofia's attention. Asking the coachman to draw near, Zofia saw her worst suspicions confirmed: the girl was to be shot, along with the adults.

These were the days of mass roundups of Jews by Nazi execution squads. Some nights, Zofia had seen naked, ghostlike creatures aimlessly wandering in the fields; they were those whom the bullets had missed but who had fallen into the large ditches alongside the others. Covered by the naked bodies of the dead, they remained still until late in the evening, when they crawled out of the pits and knocked at doors of surrounding farmhouses, begging for a morsel of bread, some water, and a minimum of clothing to cover their nakedness.

For some unexplainable reason, Zofia was resolved to save the girl. She told the commander of the execution squad that she knew the girl to be the orphan of a Christian family who had died in a recent bombing, and she was willing to prove it with proper credentials. She knew instinctively that this ploy alone would not work. She decided to whet the appetite of the commander by promising a suitable bribe, if only the girl's execution could be stayed for several days. The commander consented.

Hurrying home, Zofia told her puzzled husband, Stanislaw, of her encounter with the doomed Jews. He at first demurred, unwilling to become entangled with the German military, but late that night he consented to his wife's pleadings. After a few days, she returned with the necessary (false) credentials, a hefty bribe, and some delicacies for the commander's guards—the killing squad. The girl was released to her.

After Zofia had gained the child's confidence, the little girl told her story. She had been turned over by her parents to a Ukrainian woman. When her parents were shot, the woman realized she would no longer be able to exact payments for the girl's upkeep. She and a male friend took the girl to a bridge and threw her into a river. She hung on to a twig, and the current washed her ashore, where Ukrainian farmers dutifully turned her over to the Germans.

Years later, Zofia recalled her thoughts when she first saw the girl. "I was stunned and frightened, not knowing what to do, although I had to do something to save this little creature. I realized I must save her, otherwise I would never know peace and tranquillity again." Zofia later saved another Jewish girl who had lost her parents to the Nazis. Both girls grew up in the Boczkowska household, and later moved to Israel.

Helen Szturm and her father were similarly saved by strangers as they were on the point of passing out in a heavy snowstorm. They had escaped a Nazi execution raid in Debica, Poland, and had wandered the country-side in the direction of Tarnow. En route, a stranger had robbed them of their last belongings. It was a Sunday morning, and the road was covered with a thick layer of snow. "My legs were swollen and I could hardly drag myself along behind my father," Helen recalls. "Suddenly a Polish girl passed by me. When she saw the condition I was in, she whispered: 'Don't be afraid. I know you are Jewish but I won't harm you.... Let's walk together.'" The young girl, Stefania Job, then left to fetch her father, who picked up the girl and carried her home. Father and daughter's frozen boots were removed (not an easy task). The pair were then hidden in the attic in a nearby, as-yet-unfinished home during the winter of 1942-43.

They were sheltered in different locations thereafter, until the area's liberation. On the point of giving up on life, they had been saved by strangers.

Three-year-old Jack's parents had turned him over to a lady friend before they were dispatched to a concen-tration camp. This woman cared for him until one day she saw a poster on a bulletin board in Cracow warning the population against sheltering Jews, upon pain of death. Hurrying home, she decided that the safety of her own two children overrode concern for the Jewish child in her care. On her way out to turn him over to the

Gestapo, she ran into her mother-in-law in the lobby. The elderly Maria Maciarz asked her daughter-in-law where she was taking the boy. Upon learning the truth, the woman barred her daughter-in-law's way, snatched the boy, and took him to her own home. She cared for the child for two years, supporting herself by selling old clothes in the market. Jack's parents survived several concentration camps and returned home to profusely thank the woman who had saved their son. When they decided to reward Maria by turning over their previous home to her, they learned she could not sign her name. "Illiterate, but with a heart of gold," the boy's mother comments in her testimony.

Alexander Bronowski, a Jewish attorney from Lublin, Poland, had been lucky. He and his wife had eluded the Nazis and local anti-Semites and had found a safe niche in Warsaw. Bronowski's facial features appeared Aryan, and he confidently wandered the streets of Warsaw with a set of false credentials. One day in April 1943, however, he was nabbed on the street by two German military policemen, who insisted that in spite of his impeccable looks and bona fide credentials, he was a Jew. As it was late in the day, the two agents dropped him off at a nearby police station, promising to return the following morning to take him to Gestapo headquarters for a thorough cross-examination.

Late at night, Bronowski pondered his fate in his damp cell. The thought of the grueling investigation by Gestapo agents inside the notorious Pawiak prison, which awaited him the following morning, tormented him. He decided he was not going to allow himself to be reduced to a complete human wreck. Standing up in his cell, Bronowski asked to be allowed to warm himself in the warden's office. He struck up a conversation with Waclaw Nowinski, the warden of the night shift. He asked the officer for a favor: permission to step out in the courtyard and be shot in the back by the warden for ostensibly trying to escape. He explained that he preferred to end his life this way rather than be tortured to death by the Gestapo. Nowinski replied that it was out of the question for him to take a man's life innocently.

It was 2 A.M., just five hours before the arrival of the

German guards, when Nowinski called a halt to the conversation and left the jail. He returned four hours later and handed the startled Bronowski an envelope containing 5,000 zloty (Polish currency). Nowinski told Bronowski that when he was fetched in an hour's time, he was to step outside with the two Germans, hand them the envelope, and walk off. Nowinski had alerted his comrades in the underground and they had arranged to bribe the two German gendarmes. When Bronowski walked away from the jail courtyard, he felt a reborn person—saved at the last moment, not only by a total stranger, but by his own jailer. The friendship between the two dates from that moment.

In Cologne, Germany, Karola Metzger and her parents were picked up by the Gestapo in January 1944 and taken to a nearby detention camp en route to the Theresienstadt concentration camp. Assigned to tend the sick, Karola was permitted to leave the camp to fetch medicine. She took advantage of this liberal oversight by camp officials, and fled to the home of her friend Katharina Overath, asking for help. The following morning, Katharina approached the camp, which was guarded by the SS, and struck up a conversation with the guards. This was not difficult, she says, for she was "blond and 18 years old." Karola had told Katharina that her parents were assigned work in the camp kitchen. Katharina told the guards that her parents were non-Jewish paid day laborers from outside the camp, and she asked permission to personally deliver a food package to them.

Then, returning to the checkpost, Katharina kept the guards busy with small talk, assuring them that her "parents" would soon join them at the end of the day's shift. When her "parents" were late in leaving the camp, she went to fetch them. Katharina gave her overcoat to the elderly Mrs. Metzger and her chale to Mr. Metzger to hide the Jewish star emblem on their clothing. Hinting to the guards that she would soon be back to continue the flirting session, Katharina left the camp with the Metzgers. She brought them to her parents' home, where the three fugitive Jews were hidden for four months; then they were moved to a friendly farming family in the region. Karola Metzger and her parents survived, snatched from the captor lion's den moments before being deported to a concentration camp.

In Paris, Simon Dankowitz had counseled his sister, Claire Deutscher, to seek out his former non-Jewish business partner in the event she feared deportation to the camps. Claire's husband was a French prisoner of war being held in Germany, but the fact that he had fought for France was no guarantee that his wife would be spared deportation by the French police. When Claire's fears mounted, she went to see the former business associate, who had promised to help. But now he told the distraught woman that fear of retribution by the authorities had caused him to have second thoughts. As she left the man's office with her little son, his secretary nodded to her to step into a side room and wait.

When the day's work was over, the secretary, Hélène Bindel, fetched the frightened woman and told her she had eavesdropped on the conversation between the woman and her boss, and decided she would help. That night, mother and son slept in the secretary's home. The following morning, Hélène took the two to her aunt's home, where Claire stayed hidden for a full two years. Little Guy was enrolled in a boarding school under a different name. Both survived the war, to greet the returning husband and father from the prisoner-of-war camp and tell him of their rescue by a stranger. Claire showed her husband the note written by his brother, thrown from the train taking him to the death camps, reminding her to seek out this former business associate in the event of emergency. Luckily for the Deutschers, Hélène Bindel more than made up for her boss's lack of courage. The years after the war have cemented the close relationship between Hélène and the Deutscher family.

Eyewitness to Horror

The final story in this chapter is about a person who tried to alert the free world to what was happening to the Jews of Europe, and largely failed through no fault of his own. Jan Karski was an operative in the Polish underground. In October 1942, on the eve of a secret mission to the Polish government-in-exile in London, he was asked to meet with two Jewish leaders of the Warsaw ghetto to relay an important message to the outside world. That momentous meeting changed Karski's life.

Karski met the two leaders in a secluded place in a bombed-out building on the Aryan side of Warsaw. The two leaders, representing a Zionist and a Jewish-Socialist organization, gave the startled young man a detailed account of the systematic liquidation of the Warsaw ghetto's Jews, which had already claimed the lives of 300,000 persons and was still continuing unabated. During a second meeting with the two men, Karski asked what precise message they wanted him to relay to the outside world. They responded that since only force could sway Nazi Germany from its murderous course, German cities should be bombed, and accompanying leaflets should inform the German public that the attacks were in retaliation against the mass murder of Jews, for which the whole German nation was to be held accountable. The German people would be asked to exert pressure on their government to cease and desist or else the bombings would continue.[14]

They also asked that some German prisoners held by the Allies should be executed, and that such executions continue until the Nazis stopped the killing of Jews. "But that is utterly fantastic," Karski shot back. "A demand like that will only confuse and horrify all those who are sympathetic with you." "Do you think I don't know it?" replied one of the leaders. "We ask it because it is the only rebuttal to what is being done to us.... We demand it so people will know how we feel about what is being done to us, how helpless we are, how desperate our plight is."[15] The Allied nations should also explicitly state that the further prevention of the physical extermination of the Jews was part and parcel of the overall Allied war strategy. In addition, an appeal should go out to the pope to take up the cause of Jews who had converted to the Catholic faith, and to threaten excommunication of those who persecuted them. Such measures "might even make Hitler, a baptized Catholic, reflect," they added.[16] Finally, they urged the Polish government-in-exile to take strong measures against blackmailers within the Polish population.

Listening to both men, Karski felt like a thunderbolt had struck him. "It seemed to me that I was listening to an earthquake, that I was hearing cracking, tearing sounds of the earth opening to swallow a portion of humanity. One could hear the cries and shouts of the frantic people falling into the chasm."[17] The Jewish socialist leader gripped Karski's hand and in a frantic voice asked him to tell Jewish leaders in the free world "that the earth must be shaken to its foundations, the world must be aroused. Perhaps then it will wake up, understand, perceive.... German aims and methods are without precedent in history. The democracies must react in a way that is also without precedent.... If not, their victory will be only partial, only a military victory."[18]

Karski thought to himself that simply listening to the two distraught men was not enough; he foresaw that he would not be believed. He would have to see for himself what was happening inside the ghetto, in spite of the danger to himself. A few days later, Karski was smuggled inside the doomed ghetto through a secret passage. "I wore an old, shabby suit and a cap pulled down over my eyes. I tried to make myself look very small and thin."[19] He was shocked by the appearance of the ghetto. "A cemetery?" he asks. Not really, for the dying bodies still held some life. But, "apart from their skin, eyes, and voice there was nothing human left in these palpitating figures. Everywhere there was hunger, misery, the atrocious stench of decomposing bodies, the pitiful moans of dying children, the desperate cries and gasps of a people struggling for life against impossible odds."[20] Around him, he saw only death and despair. "I shuddered. A phrase came to my mind which I had heard often and thought I had never fully comprehended till that moment: Ecce homo—behold the man."[21] From a concealed window, he watched as two uniformed Hitler Youth boys picked off targets by shooting randomly at people in the ghetto. Two days later, Karski returned for a second visit to the ghetto, to make sure the scenes he had witnessed would register in his mind.

A short while later, it was arranged for Karski to witness a roundup of Jews. Karski believes that the camp he visited was Belzec. Estonian or Lithuanian guards were bribed to make it possible for him to enter in a guard's uniform. There he saw "starved, stinking, gesticulating, insane human beings in constant, agitated motion." Some waved their hands, shouted, and quarreled among themselves. "Hunger, thirst, fear, and exhaustion had driven them all insane." Karski was appalled at this ghastly sight, the memory of which would cause him recurrent nausea.[22]

Safely arriving in London in November 1942, he began a series of meetings with civic, religious, and political leaders, both in England and in the United States. These included Cardinal Spellman, Rabbi Stephen Wise, Nahum Goldman, authors Arthur Koestler and H. G. Wells, British Foreign Secretary Anthony Eden (who, on behalf of his government, rejected all demands for direct intervention), President Franklin Roosevelt, Secretary of State Cordell Hull and Secretary of War Henry Stimson, journalists Walter Lippmann and Dorothy Thompson, and many others.[23] In the United States he delivered some two hundred lectures. "In all of them I spoke about the Jewish tragedy." He contributed articles to *Collier's,* the *New York Times, Herald Tribune,* and *Harper's Bazaar* on what he saw and what needed to be done. He also published a book, *Story of a Secret State,* wherein his visit to the Warsaw ghetto and the concentration camp were central themes. He raised the voice of alarm. Most people listened to him attentively but doubted his description of the harrowing events. In the meantime, the slaughter of Jews continued unabated in German-dominated Europe.

Speaking at a gathering of survivors in 1981, Karski said: "The Lord assigned me a role to speak and write during the war, when—as it seemed to me—it might help. It did not."[24] He saw in himself merely a recording machine. The Holocaust he views as mankind's second original sin. "This sin will haunt humanity to the end of time. It does haunt me. And I want it to be so."[25] For his efforts and personal risks in witnessing, then alerting the world to the Holocaust in Europe, Jan Karski was honored by Yad Vashem as a "Righteous among the Nations."

Chapter 7

Dangers of Detection

Testimony of Rev. Hubert Celis (Belgium)

Being a priest of the Liège diocese, I was parson of the small parish of Halmaal, near St. Trond, Limbourg province. In September 1942, Monsignor Kerkhofs, Bishop of Liège, convoked several priests at the dean of Hasselt, to talk to them of the persecution of the Jewish people and ask for volunteers to help the Jews. I was one of those invited. The bishop did not want to impose this on anyone, because of the risks for those involved, but he wanted his priests to know how proud he would be of those prepared to risk their lives to save others.

As I was returning to my presbytery from this meeting in Hasselt, on the same day, for the first time in my life a Jewish woman came to see me, accompanied by one of my parishioners. She was the mother of the Rosenberg children, and had arrived with her family in my parish after leaving Brussels, where life for Jews had become more and more unbearable. Mrs. Rosenberg wept profusely as she explained that she was about to be arrested at any moment, and wanted to be reunited with her children after the war, in the hope she would survive.

I gave her my word of honor and promised her to save her children and give my life, if necessary, in that endeavor. Thank God, I remained faithful to my promise, and when I now see the children's happiness and their respective families, I give thanks to God for having given me the necessary strength. Following this promise, I placed the two girls, Régine (16) and Sonia (2), with my brother at St. Trond, and the two boys, Wolfgang (13) and Sigmund (9), with my other brother, a priest in Gotem, some 12 kilometers from Halmaal.

On October 29, 1942, the children's parents, betrayed to the authorities by an unknown informer, were arrested: the father in my presbytery, and the mother in another parish home. During the months of September and October, I had frequently met with the Rosenberg parents. Father Rosenberg was a pious person who had only one wish: to follow God's command. His wife was a tender mother, the symbol of honesty and goodness, and very religious. Hence, I am certain that these two good and faithful people, who had no evil in them, went straight up to heaven.

The same October 29, I was arrested for the first time, accused of helping the underground and Allied pilots, and of having hidden the Rosenberg children. While they were reading out the charges, I said to myself, "They are going to search for the children at my family, and will find them. . . . I must therefore confess to this last charge, in order to be able to deny, in full sincerity, all the other charges." So I calmly confessed to having placed the children and denied the other charges. I was then asked to disclose the children's whereabouts. I refused. They began to insult me and threatened to have me shot. This went on for about an hour and a half. I continued to respond calmly, "I am in your hands; I know I will be shot but I will never speak. A priest is not a traitor." The interrogator answered, "I too am Catholic!"

...At this point, I began to berate him as a Catholic for his behavior, saying, "You are a Catholic, and have forgotten that the Virgin was a Jewess, that Christ was Jewish, that he commanded us to love and help one another. . .that he told us: 'I have given you an example so that you do as I have done'. . .You are a Catholic, and you do not understand what a priest is! You do not understand that a priest does not betray!" The officer began to mumble, and made the excuse that he had received orders to do the interrogation, and if he did not do it he would be punished. I responded that I respect every person who does his duty, so he must do his duty, but that it was useless to insist, for I would not talk! I was then freed, and hurried to disperse the Rosenberg children, who were taken to other places.

On May 3, 1944, Régine was denounced by an informer and arrested in my father's home. This old man of about 80 years defended her like a lion, but was no match against the forces arrayed against him. The same day, I was arrested for the second time. By a fortuitous set of circumstances, I learned of the questions put to Régine and her answers, and this made it possible for me to defend myself efficaciously. Regine was sent to the Auschwitz extermination camp, from where, thanks to God, she returned to us in 1945.

I consider myself as having only done my duty. We are, after all, irrespective of our religion or our religious and political opinions, the children of the Good God; hence brothers who should help one another! This is precisely what Christ wanted to tell us when he asked us to help fellow man. I never thought of trying to convert the Rosenberg children to the Catholic faith. I always respected their religious beliefs: (1) because I did not want to take advantage of their unhappy situation to influence their minds; (2) because Mrs. Rosenberg had placed her full trust in me, and I had given her my word of honor as a priest. I had no right to betray this trust, but had the duty to remain faithful to the word given, so as to be able to restore these children to their parents or their family in the same way they had confided them to me; (3) because I foresaw that the children would, after the war, be returned to their family and to a Jewish ambiance. So I prefer a good Jew to a bad Christian.

Threats from the Germans

The reader of these rescue stories cannot help but be impressed by the dangers that all the rescuers faced—not only from the Germans, whose forces occupied most of Europe in the early 1940s, but also from collaborators and anti-Semitic elements within the local populations. These factors were more pronounced in Eastern European countries than elsewhere on the German-dominated continent.

In Poland, the Nazis treated the population with a cruelty unmatched elsewhere. The Nazi master plan called for the dissolution of the Polish state and the exile of the majority of its population to distant lands, so as to make room for the country's colonization by Germanic and kindred peoples, and its transformation into a "pure German" province. Hence Hitler instructed Hans Frank, his governor in occupied Poland, to treat the fiercely nationalistic Polish population with an iron fist and mete out harsh punishment for the slightest infraction of German laws. Almost a third of the prewar Polish territory was annexed to the Reich, and its native population expelled to the remaining part of the occupied countries, renamed *Generalgouvernement.* Close to two million Poles were conscripted for forced labor to replace manpower shortages in Germany.

The German authorities made it crystal clear that any infraction of the prohibition against helping fleeing Jews would be punishable with death. Warnings were posted on bulletin boards in major cities spelling out the nature of these capital "offenses." An example is the following warning issued by Dr. Ludwig Fischer, the German district governor of Warsaw, in November 1941: "Any Jew who illegally leaves the designated residential district will be punished by death. Anyone who deliberately offers refuge to such Jews or who aids them in any other manner (i.e., a night's lodging, food, or by taking them into vehicles of any kind, etc.) will be subject to the same punishment.... I forcefully draw the attention of the entire population of the Warsaw District to this new decree, as henceforth it will be applied with the utmost severity."[1]

A similar warning was issued in three languages in the occupied city of Przemysl: "(1) Any Pole or Ukrainian, who admits a Jew in his home or provides him with shelter, feeds him, or shelters him, will be shot. (2) Any Pole or Ukrainian, who in any form whatsoever extends aid to a Jew outside the Jewish residential area, will be shot. (3) Any Pole or Ukrainian who even attempts to act in the manners described in (1) and (2) will be shot."[2]

One may wonder how prestigious German universities were able to produce doctoral laureates who applied their academic knowledge and skills toward the perfection of the science of death, toward making more efficient the slaughter of innocent populations, without so much as batting an eye. After the war, those questioned on this point felt no moral compunction for their wartime crimes. They were simply carrying out orders, they stated in their defense.

Fear of German retribution is exemplified in many rescue stories. In Poland, all rescuers faced the likelihood of immediate death if discovered, or at best confinement to a concentration camp with slight chance of survival. When Wojciech Kalwinski heard that the Germans had publicly hanged a neighboring Pole who had sheltered a large group of Jews (the fugitives were shot on the spot), he reassured the 22 terrified Jews he was hiding in a cellar in Lwow that he would not ask them to leave to save himself and his family a similar fate. "Whatever your fate will be, children, it shall also be mine, and I trust that God will help us."[3]

In a village in the northeast part of the country, Waclaw and Maria Mickiewicz were burned to death in their farmhouse by the Germans after it was discovered that they had previously sheltered Jews. Kazimiera Marendowska, who had aided Jews in the Warsaw region in various ways, committed suicide in Pawiak prison rather than face prolonged Gestapo interrogation. Anna Bogdanowicz, who aided a young Jewish woman in the Kielce region, was apprehended and dispatched to Auschwitz camp, where she succumbed from typhus and her body was consumed by the camp's crematorium. (Her sons consider their mother's tree at Yad Vashem her last resting place.) Irena Sendler, who headed a network in the Warsaw region for helping Jewish children on the Aryan side, was betrayed to the authorities and grilled by the Gestapo. She too was condemned to death, but gained her freedom at the last moment thanks to the bribing of her jailers by the Jewish underground.

Those suspected of aiding Jews, but without incontrovertible proof, underwent brutal interrogation at the hands of the Germans (Gestapo, police, and other security arms of the occupying forces). Jerzy Kozminsky, whose family was hiding 14 Jews in the Wawer section of Warsaw, lost all his front teeth during a Gestapo interrogation at Pawiak prison. Kazimierz Korkurcz, a farmer in Ejszyszki, northeast Poland, had his face smashed, six teeth knocked out, his lip gashed leaving a permanent scar, and his ribs cracked with blows from a pistol. He was sent to a hospital to patch up his wounds so that the interrogation could continue. He managed to escape, without his captors' learning the precise location of the 16 persons he was hiding.

There was no consistency in Nazi retaliatory methods. Some victims were shot or burned to death; others were dispatched to concentration camps. Feliks and Romualda Ciesielski were caught helping Jews in Cracow. At first, they underwent a brutal interrogation in Montpeluc prison. Then Feliks was dispatched to Mauthausen camp, where he died; Romualda was taken to Auschwitz, where she was forced to undergo medical experiments on her body. She survived the war, broken in body, and was treated by a Jewish doctor, one of her previous beneficiaries. Igor Newerly, an aide to the renowned educator Janusz Korczak (a Jew who was killed in Treblinka together with the children of the orphanage under his supervision), was arrested in 1943 and survived two notorious concentration camps, Majdanek and Bergen-Belsen.

Natalia Abramowicz escaped immediate death but not harsh treatment at the hands of her captors. She was arrested in Radomsko for sheltering Jews in her home. At her trial in June 1943, she admitted to the charge and was sentenced to death. But due to her German ancestry (Poles claiming Germanic roots, known as *Volksdeutsche*, received somewhat more lenient treatment for violations of Nazi regulations than the native conquered populations), her sentence was commuted to life imprisonment. She was moved from one prison to another and was liberated by advancing British troops near Lübeck in May 1945. For many years she continued to bear the physical and mental scars of her ordeal under the Nazis.

The case of Zofia and Jakub Gargasz illustrates the German tendency to methodical neatness, and a meticulous clinging to written law and regulations without regard to their moral implications. They were discovered sheltering an aged Jewish woman in Brzezow, Poland, after she fled from a nearby ghetto. Let us follow the logic of the verdict by the learned court judges (two of whom sported Ph.D. titles), as it appears in official court minutes:

> The defendant woman claims that as an Adventist, her religion forbids expelling a sick person from one's home. This compelled her to keep the Jewess until she had recovered.... [However], according to paragraph 1 of police regulations..., it was forbidden for the Jewess Katz to be found in Brzezow after December 1, 1942.... Therefore, the moment the defendant woman decided, in spite of this, to keep the Jewess in her home, she is guilty as charged (in accordance with paragraph 3/2 of above).... It is therefore necessary to impose on the defendant woman the only penalty which the law provides—the death penalty. As for the defendant's husband, he too must bear this penalty, for the moment he discovered the Jewess in his home and did not expel her immediately but, on the contrary, together with his wife nursed the Jewess back to health, he too is an accomplice to the act of sheltering her.... As the law allows only for the death penalty for extending aid to Jews, this too must be imposed on the husband. In accordance with paragraph 465 (St. Po.), the defendants must bear the court costs.

So much for due process of law in the Third Reich. One may also sadly reflect on the fact that judges who imposed such sentences in the Nazi state continued to preside over defendants in the postwar democratic West German republic. In this particular case, Nazi governor Hans Frank commuted the death penalty to life imprisonment, and the two defendants survived the concentration camps.

The situation was no rosier for rescuers in other Eastern European countries. In Lithuania, Ona Simaite, a librarian at Vilnius University, was discovered sheltering a young girl in her home. At first she claimed that the girl had been orphaned in another city, but a quick check of the map and official records failed to produce any such town. She then underwent torture in an effort to make her reveal her accomplices. "I prayed that I would not speak during these tortures. I would purposely confuse names and addresses in order to forget them. I am not a believer, but at that moment I prayed with all my heart." Her interrogators broke her back, but she still refused to speak. She was sentenced to death, but through the intercession of friends and colleagues from academic circles, her sentence was commuted to imprisonment. She survived to witness liberation. Her back healed only incompletely, and she suffered extreme pain until her death in Paris.

Bronius Gotautas, the wandering monk mentioned earlier, who arranged hiding places for many Jews who had fled the Kaunas ghetto, at first proved elusive to the Germans because of his habit of passing the evening at different places. They finally caught up with him and dispatched him to the Stutthof concentration camp, where he survived. Jakob Suchenko, a Ukrainian from Rovno, helped several Jews escape from the Wolyn region into the interior of Ukraine with the help of false credentials that he prepared for them. He was eventually apprehended by the Nazis in 1943 and shot, together with a group of Jews he had tried to move to Kiev.

In Western Europe, the conquered populations were treated less brutally than those in the other half of the continent, but punishment for any infraction of Nazi laws was harsh.

In a previous chapter we noted how Adelaide Hautval was dispatched from France to Auschwitz camp in distant Poland, merely for protesting the inhumane treatment of Jews by the Germans. Similarly, Josèphe Cardin was arrested and sent to Drancy camp for merely showing her solidarity with Jews by pinning a yellow star on her vest. No non-Jew was permitted to wear the Jewish sign, so Miss Cardin had to be punished. She was lucky to be released after only several months of imprisonment.

When Pastor Roland de Pury was apprehended in his home in Lyon, France, for the graver offense of sheltering Jews and helping them flee to Switzerland, his life was indeed in danger. He was spared thanks to his Swiss citizenship, and after a long stay in jail he was turned over to Swiss authorities in exchange for Switzerland's release of German agents.

In Marseille, Pastor Jean Lemaire was arrested for allowing a conference room on church grounds to be used as a meeting place by a clandestine Jewish organization that helped Jews flee to safer places. While in prison awaiting Nazi judgment, Lemaire was placed in a cell where Jews were incarcerated. His long and prophetic-looking beard made the Jews believe he was a rabbi, and he was asked to lead them in Friday evening services. He was then dispatched to Dachau camp. He survived, with his zest and commitment to altruism and charitable deeds not the least impaired.

Others were less fortunate. The already-mentioned Father Jacques (Lucien Bunel), head of a Catholic private school in Avon, sheltered several Jewish boys, unknown to everyone but a few trusted aides. He was nevertheless betrayed to the authorities and dispatched to the Mauthausen-Gusen camp. He survived to witness liberation in May 1945, but his health was beyond repair, and he succumbed in a hospital in Germany several weeks later. His emaciated body was brought back to Avon and buried in a ceremony attended by a Jewish rabbi.

Father Louis Favre in Villa la Grand, on the Franco-Swiss border, was arrested, then brutally shot on July 14, 1944, for helping Jews flee to Switzerland from his seminary Juvenat, located on the border. Father Jean-Joseph Rosay, a priest in Douvaine, helped the OSE, a clandestine Jewish children's welfare organization, spirit children across the Swiss border after giving them temporary refuge in his village. In the words of an eyewitness: "He gathered the Jewish children in his church and instructed them in the Old Testament. He would say that it was unthinkable that these children ignore their past and the history of their people." He too was arrested by the Germans and deported to Auschwitz, thence to Bergen-Belsen, where he died in April 1945. After several Jewish boys were found sheltered in the children's home under his supervision, Daniel Trocmé, a distant cousin of Pastor André Trocmé of the Protestant Le Chambon-sur-Lignon community in central France, was dispatched to Buchenwald camp, where he died.

Others listed in the Scroll of Agony of French rescuers include Suzanne Spaak, who was shot by the Germans days before the liberation of Paris, in August 1944, after she had been imprisoned for a year for her clandestine activities in helping Jewish children. Elizaveta Skobtzova, better known as Mother Marie, a nun in the Russian Orthodox Church in Paris, and her aide, Father Dimitri Klepinin, were arrested by the Gestapo in March 1943 and charged with giving shelter to Jews in distress. They were dispatched to the camps after they declined to commit themselves to cease aiding Jews. Mother Marie died in Ravensbrück camp in March 1945; Father Klepinin died in Dora camp.

In Belgium, rescuers faced similar jeopardy to their lives and freedom. Fathers André and Bruno, who organized safe places for hundreds of Jewish children, had to live as fugitives until the country's liberation, after the Gestapo had discovered the magnitude of their rescue activities. In the Ardennes region of the country, Hendrik Mans was arrested in his home in April 1944, after being denounced for sheltering a Jewish mother and her infant son. Deported to Buchenwald, Mans survived the war and returned home, but he died soon afterward from physical exhaustion.

Farther north, in the Netherlands (Nazi race "experts" considered the Dutch a pure but lost Germanic tribe), the fate of those caught helping Jews was no less harsh than in other occupied countries. A German report gives the figure of 1,997 persons arrested by April 15, 1944, for helping Jews.[4] Joop Westerweel and Arnold Douwes, each responsible for the rescue of many Jews, were sentenced to death. Westerweel was executed on Dutch soil; Douwes's life was spared thanks to a last-minute raid by the Dutch underground on the jail where he was being held. The Germans also claimed the lives of Jaap Musch and Joop Woortman, organizers of the giant child-rescue operation code-named the NV Group. Victor Kugler, one of the rescuers of the Anne Frank family in Amsterdam (known as "Mr. Kraler" in the young girl's diary), was dispatched for forced labor in September 1944. He managed to escape during an air raid, and remained in hiding for the duration of the war. Rev. Gerardus Pontier, in whose home a Jewish family was sheltered, spent many months in prison. His jailers used force to try to elicit information on his connection with the NV group; they did not know that a Jewish family was at the same time being sheltered in his home. They finally relented and released him.

Corrie Ten Boom and her family sheltered many Jews in their Haarlem home. In early 1943 they were betrayed to the Germans and all were carted off to various camps. Corrie's 84-year-old father Willem died after 10 days in jail. He is reported to have stated, "If I am liberated tomorrow, I will save Jews the following day." Other members of the family were released after a short stay in jail. Corrie and her sister Betsy were moved to the notorious women's concentration camp Ravensbrück. Through the intercession of friends in Holland, Corrie was released in December 1944; her sister died inside the camp. "I learned later that after my release, they began to gas in Ravensbrück the sick, those with walking difficulties, and those above 50. I belonged to all these three categories" (Corrie was born in 1892). Corrie gives a stirring rendering of these sufferings, suffused with religious devotion, in her book *The Hiding Place.* Her deep faith in Christian tenets is proverbial. "No pit is so deep that He is not deeper still," is one of her better-known statements.

Chardon Kees, a Dutch attorney in Delft and an underground operative, helped find hiding places for Jews. Arrested by the Germans, he was sent to several camps, in the last of which he died from physical exhaustion soon after the camp's liberation. Elkje Lentink-de Boer's fate was only slightly less tragic. Caught sheltering 12 Jews (two of them children), she was dispatched to Ravensbrück, where she underwent medical experiments on her body. Released months before the end of the war as part of a Swedish-German arrangement (worked out by Count Folke Bernadotte representing the Swedish Red Cross), she was declared a 90 percent invalid.

Hetty Voute and Gisela Sohnlein, as mentioned earlier, worked for a student clandestine organization in Utrecht that helped Jewish persons find safe niches in various parts of the country (children as well as adults). They were arrested at a train station in 1943 as they returned from one of their errands, and were dispatched to Ravensbrück. Both survived and were released as part of the Bernadotte arrangement. We earlier mentioned Rev. Bastiaan Ader's involvement in moving persons from one place to another, and his eventual arrest and execution by the Germans in November 1944. The execution was justified as a retaliation for the death of a German soldier by the Dutch underground.

In another episode, a Dutch rescuer named Sietze Romkes was suspected of sheltering Jews. His home was raided by the German police ("Green Police"). From his hiding place in a cupboard, the youthful Abraham Hartog could hear the police shout and threaten Romkes's 16-year-old son, Jan. A gun was placed against Jan's temple, and he was warned that the trigger would be pulled unless he disclosed the whereabouts of the wanted Jew. Jan replied that the fugitive had already left for another undisclosed location. In desperation the Germans grabbed Jan's father and hauled him to the station, where he underwent a grueling investigation. Despairing of exacting information from him, they threw him out on the street.

Albertus Zefat, from the village of Valthe in northern Holland, was less fortunate. Someone had told the police that Zefat was sheltering 13 Jews in a nearby grove. The police thereupon raided his farmhouse in July 1944 and bluntly told Zefat to disclose to them the Jews' whereabouts. When he demurred, a policeman pulled out a pistol and shot Zefat point-blank in the head. Then they left. His wife Aaltje immediately ran to the place where the Jews were hidden, told them the tragic news, and made arrangements for them to be hidden elsewhere.

Throughout Europe, would-be rescuers were fully cognizant of the risks to themselves in the event of apprehension. They could count on no mercy from the Germans, only various degrees of pain and misery.

In Germany itself, the homeland of the Nazi movement, punishment for sheltering Jews was also severe. Dr. Karl Hermann, a physics chemist in Mannheim who worked for the I. G. Farben company, was charged with giving temporary refuge to a Jewish couple in his home. Due to his work at the Farben firm, which was important to the war effort, he received a relatively minor sentence of eight years in jail; he was required to appear at work every day, then return to jail after working hours to spend the evening.

Heinrich List was a farmer in Ernsbach, Hessen province. In March 1942 a foreign worker on the farm informed the authorities that List was sheltering a Jew in his home. List was promptly arrested by the Gestapo and grilled. The following transcript is from the Darmstadt police blotter:

> *Question:* For what reasons did you admit the Jew Ferdinand Strauss and give him shelter?
> *Answer:* Because we knew each other well since childhood, and he was now all alone.
> *Question:* Why did you not report him to the police?
> *Answer:* I was not aware that I had to report him to the police. It is quite out of the question that I hid him because of any possible hatred toward the regime. Only because we knew each other well, and previously we entertained good business relations. I took pity on him and gave him shelter.

List's answers did not satisfy his interrogators. Showing compassion to a Jew was a serious crime in Nazi Germany. In the words of a police investigator: "He must without any doubt be considered a friend of the Jews. I arrive at this conclusion, based on the fact that it was otherwise impossible to hide a Jew in a village of 298 inhabitants [without the others knowing of it]. I therefore take the position that he knew perfectly well what he was doing and what this implied. In my opinion, he kept [the Jew] from official apprehension and detention in full conscience and foreknowledge of the deed's implications." The 60-year-old defendant was sent to Dachau camp, where he died (or was murdered) a few months later.

In Prague, Bohemia (which during the Nazi period was part of the Greater German Reich), the former Viennese stage actress Marianne Goltz-Goldlust was beheaded in 1944 for helping Jews and others escape and elude Nazi control.

In summary, rescuers had no illusions as to the fate awaiting them from Nazi justice in the event they were apprehended for sheltering or otherwise aiding Jews. It was a justice system unparalleled in Europe since the days of the sixteenth-century Spanish Inquisition for its immorality, extreme brutality, and utter lack of compassion. But the rescuers also faced dangers from another direction—from their own kinsmen.

Threats from Local Collaborators and Anti-Semites

Although in countries dominated by the Germans the Germans constituted the principal threat, rescuers had to be no less wary of danger from their own countrymen—from political and military collaborators with the enemy; from local anti-Semites anxious to help the Germans be rid of the Jews; and from greedy collaborators, ready to turn in a hiding Jew for a pittance.

The Netherlands, for instance, produced its own version of a fascist movement, the NSB, with a self-styled "Leader," Anton Mussert, who called for collaboration with Hitler's Germany. The movement was held in contempt by the majority of the Dutch population, but with the Germans in full control of the Netherlands, NSB members filled important posts and were even allowed to have their own gendarme-style police units. These presented a constant threat for would-be rescuers, who feared being denounced to the Nazis by NSB vigilantes.

In Belgium, the pro-Nazi Rexist movement was somewhat less influential than its NSB counterpart, but it was no less feared by the majority of the population, whose dislike of the Nazis was no secret. In France, the situation was a bit more complicated. The southern third of the country was ruled by a semi-independent pro-German regime, with its seat in Vichy. Elements within this regime (especially Prime Minister Pierre Laval) clamored for a closer collaboration with the Germans. The most outspokenly pro-Nazi and viciously anti-Semitic group created its own paramilitary unit, the Milice, which aped the Nazis and the SS in their persecution of persons suspected of anti-German activities and in zealously hunting down Jews and their rescuers. One of their victims was the previously mentioned Renée Gaudefroy, an OSE operative active in finding hiding places for children. She was apprehended by the Milice and shot in July 1944, on the eve of France's liberation.

In eastern and southeastern Europe, the danger for would-be rescuers was even greater, given the region's long history of ethnic strife and strident anti-Semitism. In Croatia (formerly part of Yugoslavia), Father Dragutin Jesih was dragged out of his home by Ustase guards and beaten to death for having sheltered Jews in his home. The Ustase was a paramilitary organization at the service of the pro-Nazi regime (headed by Pavelic) that ruled the country during the war years. Slovakia, a breakaway country from a larger Czechoslovakia, also sealed an alliance with Hitler's Germany, and its Hlinka guards zealously rounded up Jews and turned them over to the Nazi overlords. The country was headed by a Roman Catholic priest, Father Josef Tiso, who was hanged after the war as a pro-Nazi collaborator.

One brush with danger involving the Hlinka guards in Slovakia took place when they rampaged the farmhouse of Michal Vitus in Mesto-nad-Vahom and failed by a hair's breadth to discover the seven Jews hidden in a haystack. This close encounter with danger frayed the nerves of Mrs. Vitus, who now wished the Jews to leave. Her daughter Viera intervened, in the following interchange:

> Mrs. Vitus: I don't want to die because of them. I have unmarried daughters and am responsible for them as well.
> Viera: You cannot chase them away, for their lives are in danger. You admitted them here; you shall keep them until the war's end.
> Mrs. Vitus: But if the Germans find them, they will kill me as well.
> Viera: At least you shall know you were killed trying to protect honest persons who did not sin nor commit any crime.

In response to Viera's courageous stance, Mrs. Vitus agreed to stay with relatives in a different city long enough to allow her fears to subside.

In Lithuania, to the north of Poland, the danger for would-be rescuers was equally serious. Many factions within the country had allied themselves with the Germans in the hope of removing the Soviet yoke from their shoulders. This alliance went hand in hand with the killing of Jews by Lithuanian "battalions," a paramilitary force under German supervision, at such a fast rate that the majority of the country's 150,000 Jews (not counting the 80,000 in Vilnius) were killed by the Lithuanians themselves, with the Germans looking on. Some Lithuanian clandestine groups harassed Jews. When Lithuanian partisans discovered that Mykolas Juskevicius was sheltering five Jews in his barn loft, they torched the home and were about to shoot the inhabitants when German troops, alerted by the fire, appeared on the scene and battled the partisans. Juskevicius, his wife, and the Jewish fugitives managed to flee during this exchange of fire and reach the forest, where they were temporarily safe.

Many of the pro-fascist irregulars continued to operate against rescuers in the immediate postwar period. Mykolas Simelis, a forester in Veyvis, gave refuge during the war years to a former business associate (who manufactured turpentine from trees sold to him by Simelis) and his family, a total of 14 persons. He saw them safely through the war period (including one particularly tense German house search for partisans and Jews), only to fall victim to Lithuanian anti-Semitic partisans immediately after the war. Lured into the forest, ostensibly to discuss a business proposition, Simelis was brutally knifed to death. The assassins proceeded to ransack his home, telling the housekeeper, "This is what happens to someone who saves Jews."

Equally tragic is the story of Jonas Paulavicius, a carpenter in Panemune, referred to in an earlier chapter. He made no secret of his role in saving 12 Jews in his home and nearby underground shelters; in fact, he prided himself on this. He too fell victim to several pro-fascist persons a year after the war. His beneficiaries learned the sad news while on their way to Israel.

Father Bronius Paukshtys, whose story is also mentioned in a previous chapter, told one of his beneficiaries that the Catholic hierarchy in Lithuania did not look kindly on his help to Jews. They feared that Paukshtys's rescuing of Jews could create doubts in the minds of the Germans about the church's loyalty to the German cause.

The Ukrainians, a large ethnic group that for decades had yearned for independence from their Russian overlords, similar to the Lithuanians, also chose to ally themselves with Hitler's Germany. In addition, Ukrainian nationalists in lands that had been part of Poland, which they now wished to annex to a future independent Ukraine, lashed out at both Poles and Jews in an attempt at ethnic cleansing under the cover of the war years. Jews bore the brunt of pogroms and massacres at the hands of the Ukrainians. Ukrainians also served as guards in Nazi concentration camps on Polish soil, and were co-opted in violent roundups of Jews in Polish cities. Ukrainian vigilantes wreaked vengeance on rescuers of Jews, and they were feared as much as if not more than the Germans. In Buczacz, Manko Szwierszczak was violently beaten by Ukrainian guards to make him disclose the whereabouts of the Jews he was rumored to be hiding (in an unused tomb). In Sokal, Poland, Franciszka Halamajowa was hiding 14 Jews in her barn loft. In 1944, strife erupted in that area between Ukrainian and Polish partisans. In order to protect her wards, Halamajowa even occasionally invited German security men to stay in her home.

Fear of Ukrainian militiamen or of hostile Ukrainian civilians was constantly in the back of the mind of many rescuers. Ivan and Domke Semeniuk, a farming couple in the Dubno region, gave shelter to two Jews they found hiding behind their house, in spite of the fact that their village of Studinka was known for the intense anti-Semitism of its inhabitants, many of whom served in the Ukrainian militia. In another case, the irate wife of a Ukrainian farmer in the Rovno region threatened to betray her husband and the Jewish family he was sheltering to the Ukrainian Bandera militiamen known to be operating in the region. Her husband withstood these pressures and kept the Jews until the area's liberation.[5] Isaac Emmet, his wife, and daughter were hidden by the Ukrainian farmer Pavlo Girasymchuk (mentioned in an earlier chapter), near Tuczyn. At first they were sheltered in the granary. Then, in fear of a search by the Ukrainian militia, the three fugitives were moved to a haystack. Finally, a hole was dug in the granary. Danger loomed continuously, not only from the Germans and the Ukrainian militia, but also from the anti-German Bandera partisans, who killed Jews with a vengeance at least equal to that of the Germans. After the area's liberation in July 1944, the Emmets fled the region, fearing further attacks by roving Ukrainian armed men (Jews were being killed so they could not testify against war-crime perpetrators).

Kalman Katz lost his family to Ukrainian militiamen in the Premyshlany region. At first, he was hidden on the farm of Ivan Kaczerovski in the village of Kosteniw. One day, Kaczerovski was warned by the village mayor that rumor had it he was keeping a Jew in his house, and if so it would be better for him to send the Jew away, for the Ukrainians were about to stage a raid. Katz was one of the lucky few who eluded the Ukrainian militia and survived.

Another rescuer threatened with punitive measures by Ukrainian militiamen was Anton Suchinski from Zborow, in the Tarnopol region. He was hiding six Jews in an underground bunker when he came under intense pressure by blackmailers. The Jews fled in panic, only to return later. Suchinski welcomed them with open arms, "and profusely weeping from joy, he kissed us with emotion," according to one of the survivors. On that occasion he told them: "My precious ones, I am so happy you have come to me. From now on I shall not allow for you to be persecuted again. Henceforth, no one will notice you." He built for them a new underground shelter, where they remained hidden for nine months. SS troops and Ukrainians raided his home and interrogated him, placing a pistol against his chest. He denied keeping fugitive Jews. To throw the troops' hounds off the scent, Suchinski spread waste from the outhouse and pepper over the fields near his home. At the end of the war, Suchinski was derided by his fellow Ukrainians for his help to Jews; but, dismissed as a naive fool, he was not harmed.

By a tragic twist of history, the majority of Jews in

Europe on the eve of the war were concentrated in Poland; some 3.2 million, constituting 10 percent of the general population. Close to three million of these were exterminated by the Germans in death camps set up on Polish soil: Auschwitz-Birkenau, Treblinka, Sobibor, Belzec, and Chelmno were the most notorious of these camps. The historical record shows conclusively that the majority of the Polish population saw the Jews as an irritating factor and were not unhappy to see them disappear under the brutal hands of the hated German occupiers. While the killing of Jews went on, most Poles continued to manifest the aged-old anti-Semitism traditional to the country. This atmosphere severely hampered Polish rescuers of Jews.

Moreover, as the war drew to a close, many elements within the powerful Polish underground (the AK, or Home Army) organized killing raids on the remaining Jews, in the forests or in open fields, as well as punitive raids against Poles who were sheltering Jews. This anti-Jewish killing spree increased in ferocity as German armies retreated from Polish soil, and reached a pitch in the immediate postwar period in mass riots in many cities and towns. Most of the remaining 200,000 Jews left Poland for neighboring countries in the West. In 1968, the Polish government launched another anti-Semitic campaign that led the remaining 80,000 Jews to flee the country. Today, there is hardly any Jewish community, even in the capital city of Warsaw, in a country that in the Middle Ages was a haven for Jews (persecuted elsewhere on the continent) and that was once the pride of Jewish culture and creativity. The sons and daughters of Polish Jews created the influential Jewish community in the United States and laid the foundations of the renascent Jewish state of Israel.

In contrast to other Nazi-controlled countries, Poland did not produce a political collaborationist movement, for the simple reason that German plans called for the obliteration of the Polish state in toto and its incorporation into a Greater Germany. According to Nazi designs, most of the population was eventually to be exiled to distant newly conquered lands, to be replaced with ethnic Germanic colonists. This left no room for even a minor form of collaboration. Immediately after the Nazi takeover of Poland, hundreds of thousands of Poles were evicted from lands adjacent to the prewar German border and pushed into the interior of the country. An unrestricted reign of terror was waged against the Polish population; no leniency was shown for the slightest infraction of Nazi laws and regulations.

The Poles responded by producing several underground factions, the most dominant of which, the Home Army (AK), became the largest underground organization in Nazi-occupied Europe (perhaps with the exception of Tito's partisans in Yugoslavia). The Home Army constantly gained in strength and gave the Germans a hard time; it also made life difficult for rescuers of Jews. No Jew could trust this powerful clandestine organization—there were too many incidents of forays by AK units into forests where Jews were reported to be hidden, in order to finish them off, and of physical harm to Polish rescuers sheltering Jews. It was safer to keep one's distance from them, or to keep one's Jewish identity a secret from AK operatives. There are records of help by AK members; in one notable instance in Hanaczow, eastern Poland (today part of Ukraine), an AK unit under the command of the three Wojtowicz brothers (Alojzy, Kazimierz, and Antoni) was involved in the rescue of more than two hundred Jews. These proved isolated cases, however, exceptions to the rule.

The Polish underground (9 of whose 13 political factions adopted platforms demanding the removal of Jews in a postwar Poland) made only halfhearted efforts to limit the scope of the professional blackmailers who roamed the streets of Warsaw. Tadeusz Seweryn was one of the few Poles affiliated with the underground who was responsible for bringing these malefactors to justice. But the plague of denunciations was so widespread that many Jews preferred the discomforts of the ghetto to the tense atmosphere of being constantly hounded by professional blackmailers outside ghetto boundaries.[6]

Christopher Browning, in his study of a German police battalion's participation in the killing of Jews in Poland, cites the surprise shown by the Germans at the widespread satisfaction of Poles over the killing of Jews, while themselves at the same time committing outrages both against Jews and Poles. Many Germans reported how their work was facilitated through the collaboration of Poles in spiriting Jews out of their hiding places, and how on occasion the Poles participated in the beating and shooting of Jews. Browning's study also confirms the brutal retaliations practiced by the Germans against Poles found sheltering Jews, such as shooting them on the spot and burning down their farms.[7] One wonders how many of these Polish martyrs of humanity fell victim as a result of betrayal by fellow Poles.

Nechama Tec, who undertook a special study of Polish rescuers of Jews, was struck by the prevalent anti-Semitism in most strata of the Polish population. Polish rescuers questioned by her confirmed this widespread feeling. One Pole stated that there exists in the country "some wild animal-like response" toward Jews. One woman rescuer spoke of her husband's deep hatred of Jews, adding: "Many Poles feel the way he did. I had to be careful of Poles." Tec notes that the cultural climate of Poland was "antagonistic" toward Jews, and those willing to help had to be wary of this prevailing tendency. "Poles were reminded at every turn that Jews were unworthy, low creatures, that helping them was not only dangerous but also reprehensible."[8]

The Catholic church played a large role in creating this hostile climate, accusing the Jews of deicide and keeping alive the charge of the supposed use of Christian blood for Jewish ritual purposes. Jewish children hidden in Christian homes were often reminded of the supposed unfaithfulness and filthiness of Jews, and many of those released after the war still feared being sacrificed for ritual purposes.[9] In *The Holocaust Kingdom,* Alexander Donat tells of his and his wife's miraculous survival from several German concentration camps. Returning to Poland to fetch their little son, who was hidden in a Catholic orphanage, they discovered that he had been turned into a rabid anti-Semite. "He hated everything Jewish," his mother relates. He continuously ranted against them: "All Jews are thieves and swindlers.... They killed the Lord Jesus and now they kill Christian children to mix their blood in the matzos."

Only with great effort and much pain were they able to slowly erode the anti-Semitism of their own son. "All Jews can't be bad," little Wlodek told his mother. "You're Jewish and you're not bad at all."[10]

This latent anti-Semitism, even among intellectuals and rescuers, is a phenomenon quite hard to understand. Zofia Kossak-Szczucka, a noted prewar Catholic writer, was also known for her anti-Jewish feelings, of which she made no secret. She maintained this prejudice during the war years, even as she became involved in the rescue of Jews. She was sent by the Germans to Auschwitz for political offenses, and released before the end of the war. Her position vis-à-vis the Jews did not change. Her paradoxical stance is stated in the following words: "Today the Jews face extermination. They are victims of unjust murderous persecution. I must save them.... To be sure, after the war the situation will be different.... I will tell the Jews: `I had saved you, sheltered you when you were persecuted. To keep you alive I risked my own life.... Now I am depriving you of my home. Go and settle somewhere else.'" She considered the Jews "political, economic, and ideological enemies of Poland," for reasons not fully explained.[11]

Miriam Peleg, a Jewish woman working for a Polish clandestine organization in the Cracow region, who was able to mask her Jewish identity, states: "If only the Poles would have preferred not to notice us—the few Jews who managed to live on the Aryan side—then many, quite many of us, would have remained alive."[12]

This situation in Poland—of a people who were ruled more harshly by the Nazis than any other occupied country, yet did not rise to the occasion to temper their own anti-Semitic fervor—places Polish rescuers in a special category. Since they faced more risks than their contemporaries in other occupied areas, both from the Germans and from many of their own kinsmen, their deeds are the more laudatory and meritorious. The following are but a few examples of the special concerns of Polish rescuers.

In 1942, Esther Goldenberg's family of eight persons found shelter on the farm of Andrzej and Anna Dajtrowski. One day they overheard a visiting farmer boast before Dajtrowski how he had met some Jews wandering in the open, and after taking their belongings and promising to return with food, he instead alerted the Gestapo. He was proud to have outsmarted the Jews. On another occasion, Anna visited the market and was told how the Gestapo, acting on a tip from a neighbor, had raided a nearby farm. They had netted seven Jews, who were promptly shot in broad daylight together with their Polish rescuers. The fear instilled by this event caused other farmers to turn out their Jews—but not the Dajtrowskis.

After surviving the Germans, the Goldenbergs ran into a frenzied mob in Rzeszow, out for vengeance against Jews for the supposed killing of a Christian boy in order to use his blood for the Passover feast. They were saved by Russian soldiers. Continuing to Tarnow, they were again beset by an anti-Semitic mob, and were again extricated by passing Russians. In the words of Esther Goldenberg: "In the schools as on the streets, the anti-Semitism was felt everywhere. The same insults we had heard before the Holocaust were again being shouted at us. `Dirty Jews, what Hitler didn't accomplish, we will.'" The Goldenbergs eventually moved to Canada, where they continued to maintain close links with their Polish rescuers, the Dajtrowskis.

The Ogonowski and Duda families sheltered 10 persons in Szydlowice, northeast of Kielce. Yitzhak Mintz, one of the beneficiaries, describes the generosity of the Ogonowski family in the following words: "How we were welcomed. God Almighty! Natural parents do not welcome [their children] with greater love. I shall never forget the words of Franciszka, may she rest in peace: `Either we all reach the shore safely or we all perish. . . .' At that time, with hatred surrounding us, they knew what hiding Jews implied." In May 1943, an NSZ unit (a faction within the Polish underground) raided the home, demanding the hidden Jews. When the rescuers demurred, they shot dead the 30-year-old Wladyslaw and wounded his 32-year-old brother Stefan in the legs. After the raiders left, Franciszka Ogonowski, the victims' mother, rushed to the secret hideout and told her charges the harrowing news. Then, instead of allowing herself to be consoled by her frightened wards, she consoled them. In the words of Mintz: "She said it was God's will. She then reassured us. Imagine, for 27 months they shared their food with us, even cigarettes, and they were only hard laborers."

Even more frightening is the story of Stefan Sawa, who was sheltering several Jews in a village outside Kielce. In early 1944, a Home Army unit warned Sawa to be rid of the Jews. Several weeks passed, and as it became clear that Sawa would not heed this request, the Sawa home was torched by the AK unit, consuming all those inside, the hidden Jews and their Polish rescuers as well. After the war, the police undertook an investigation of the incident, and the culprits were punished with a slap on the wrist. Zevi Zelinger, whose sister was among those consumed in the flames, and who had himself previously stayed in that home but left to join his father in Warsaw before the AK raid, is still determined to bring the culprits (those still alive) to justice.

The fear of retribution by fellow Poles for helping Jews is further illustrated in the story of Kazimierz Oczynski from Raszyn, who hid Avraham Erder in the attic of his farm for 22 months. After the war, Oczynski thought it better not to accept Erder's home as a gift, for this would be an admission to neighbors that he had helped a Jew. As recently as 1987, during a visit by Erder to his benefactor, the Oczynski family kept the story a secret from neighbors.

Wojciech Kalwinski, the good Pole who hid 22 Jews in a house on the outskirts of Lwow, likewise kept his actions secret. During the long period of hiding, they had heard of Poles shot by Germans after having been betrayed by fellow Poles. For instance, in May 1944, it was learned that 12 Jews were discovered a block away. "A daughter informed on her own mother.... The mother was hanged and the Jews were killed."[13] After the war, Kalwinski asked his charges to leave quietly in the early hours of the day and not come back to visit him, for "it would go hard for him if it were known that he had hidden Jews." "How sad was the situation in Poland," survivor Leon Wells sadly comments, "that when a man proved he possessed high, idealistic qualities, he should be ashamed and unpopular for doing such a great deed!. . . Why? We didn't expect them to help us, but why did they so enthusiastically help to murder us?" When Wells accosted the woman who had betrayed his mother to the Germans, and asked her the reason, she responded: "It wasn't Hitler who killed the Jews; it was God's will, and Hitler was his tool. How could I stand by and be against the will of God?"[14]

Estelle Nadel's mother was betrayed to the Germans by a man she knew from before the war. The mother had left her hiding place at the home of a Polish woman to forage for food, when she was accosted by a group of four men who filched her few possessions, then turned her over to the Nazis, who shot her. In 1992, Estelle returned to the site of her mother's betrayal and confronted one of the informers, who refused to recant; he even justified his deed to her face. Luckily for Estelle, she and other members of her family were sheltered by kindhearted Poles for close to two years.[15]

In the house where Janina Pawlicka sheltered 11 Jews in one of its apartments, the doorkeeper tried to extort money from her and threatened to denounce her to the Gestapo. The courageous Janina went to the police to complain that she was being blackmailed by the doorkeeper, who needed the money to support his drinking habit. The ruse worked and the man was warned to desist or face imprisonment. Stories such as these, of blackmail, extortion, and betrayal by fellow kinsmen, were more common in Eastern Europe than elsewhere on the conquered continent.[16]

As the Germans withdrew from Poland, attacks on Jews and their protectors by local vigilante groups affiliated with the underground increased. A group of partisans raided the Suchodolski farmstead in Krzynowloga Wielski, after it was learned that the family had sheltered a Jew for more than two years. The farm was ransacked, and shots were fired. Michael, the fugitive Jew, managed to flee through a window.

Stanislaw Sobczak, a farmer in Frampol in the Lublin region, had hidden 12 Jews in the attic of his granary. As the front moved closer to Sobczak's village, shells exploded and the Sobczak farm caught fire. The hidden

Jews fled to a nearby forest. Six of them were caught and shot dead by Polish partisans. When the Germans had been evicted from the village, the partisans returned and ransacked Sobczak's home, mercilessly beating the farmer for having helped Jews.

Szczepan Bradlo, a farmer in Lubcza, in the Tarnow region, was threatened with punishment after the war for having sheltered 13 Jews in an underground shaft for 26 months, unless he paid 10,000 zloty to a secret underground organization committed to fighting communists and Jews. Bradlo preferred to move elsewhere.

Krzysztof Dabowski hid nine persons in his farmhouse in the Bialystok region. At first, he agreed to keep them for a week; the hospitality was continuously extended. His wife pleaded with him to let the Jews go, for fear of retribution by the Germans, but he held his ground. He kept his wards for over a year, until the area's liberation. His home was then raided by vigilantes, who demanded the gold the Jews had supposedly paid him. They did not accept his pleading that he had no gold. Losing patience, they killed him in front of his wife.

This great animosity toward Polish Jews by their own countrymen was a factor that Polish rescuers had to keep constantly in mind. Esther Miller lost her father, sister, and brother, hiding in the forests near Jozefowa in the Zamosc region, to peasants who turned them over to the Germans. She and the remainder of her family fled to a different corner of the forest. One day, they saw a man standing in front of them: "I am not a German but Polish and you have no reason to be afraid of me," said the stranger. At first they suspected a trap, since "we did not yet know it that God had sent us a guardian angel; his name was Jan Tadra." They told him they were on the way to a certain farm. He told him to drop the plan, for it was a trap. He came back with food, then arranged shelter for them in an unused barn. There they stayed for two years, with Tadra visiting them twice a day. "In return, we had nothing to give him but our profound gratitude," Esther recalls.

Wanda Shamir and Margaret Asher are two of the many Jewish children who were sheltered during the war in the children's home in Pludy, supervised by Franciscan nuns and headed by Sister Matylda Getter (who operated a larger charitable network). In these homes, many Jewish children (especially girls) found a secure nest from Nazi ravages. In 1945, soon after the country's liberation, Wanda Shamir left Warsaw to join a group preparing to emigrate to Palestine. Passing through Cracow, she ran into a frenzied anti-Semitic mob. The young girl managed to escape with only bruises on her body. The psychological scars of being mercilessly beaten by Poles after surviving the Nazis, however, have not completely healed. At the same time, she is thankful to Mother Matylda Getter and her aides for their selfless devotion in saving her and many others. A tree in the name of this courageous woman stands at Yad Vashem opposite the Hall of Remembrance, which recalls those who perished during this terrible conflagration. The trees recall the courage of these non-Jewish rescuers who braved threats to themselves from the Germans and, in many instances, also from their own countrymen.

Chapter 8

The Significance of the "Righteous" Deeds

Testimony of Margaretha Van Dijk (Holland)

In 1938 I started working at the Nieuwe Handelsschool in The Hague as a teacher of typing and shorthand. I also taught languages and performed bookkeeping assignments. It was a private school, founded by Jacob Moses and his wife Ro Kolthoff. I was then 18 years old, happy at my job, and I became close to the Moses family. They had four children. The youngest, Dikki, was born in 1939. When war came upon Holland, my parents insisted I live with them in a distant city. One day, Mrs. Moses called me on the phone and informed me that according to a new regulation, Jews were forbidden to teach non-Jews. She asked me whether I was prepared to return to my job, and I naturally agreed. It was 1941.

One evening, a year later, Mrs. Moses and myself were preparing the Sabbath eve meal, when she suddenly said: "When the order will come for Poland, I will go with the small boy. I don't know what my husband will do with the other children." But how could I allow a sweet three-year-old boy, whom I had known since his birth, to go to Poland? So, I spontaneously responded, without understanding the implications of my words: "That's impossible: I'll take care of Dikki." Mrs. Moses did not say a word. She suddenly left the kitchen. It seemed to me a long time until she returned, while I continued to cut the spinach. It's strange how these things remain stuck in one's memory. She said: "If you look after Dikki, none of us will go to Poland." Well, that was that! Mr. Moses, through his many connections, was able to find hiding places for his three older children, and separately for himself and his wife. In the summer of 1942, I took Dikki with me to Den Bosch, where I found for him a secure hiding place. I returned to manage the school as though nothing had happened.

Days passed, and anti-Jewish decrees increased. The Jewish students of the school sensed that I had a hand in the disappearance of the Moses family, so some of them asked me to help them too. Until then, I was not aware that, other than the Moses family, there were other Jews needing shelter. During one of my searches for hiding places (the Moses' original place had proved unsafe), I met a woman clandestine associate, which proved a turning point for me. She was surprised that I was doing this work all by myself. She gave me the address of someone who, with others, was involved in finding hiding places. This too was a revelation for me! There were, indeed, others who were helping persecuted people.

Then tragedy struck the Moses couple. A person who was hiding with them was moved to another place. On the way there, he was arrested and through him the others were arrested too. Why them? They were the only people that I cared for who did not make it safely through the war.

Soon thereafter, I closed the school and, upon the recommendation of a friend, found a job in a government office. As most of the workers there were anti-Nazi, this gave me much time to continue my illegal work. I had to move Dikki Moses frequently from place to place, for he stood out with his Jewish-looking face. On weekends, I accompanied Jews and non-Jews to various hiding places in the country, visited them to bring them food ration cards and false credentials. I also arranged for them new hiding places when danger threatened.

I dealt with many children, such as a 10-year-old boy whose name I have forgotten. One day, I was told that the boy had run off. When I got to his house, he had already returned, and his adoptive mother, frightened and angry, locked him in his room. The boy told me that he was concerned about his parents' fate. When his yearnings grew, he boarded a train, without buying a ticket. He returned the same way. A Jewish boy without a ticket on a train, and no one stopped him!

In another episode, one weekday evening, I was sitting with a cup in my hand but could not concentrate on anything. I was somehow ill at ease. It was as though an inner voice was telling me, "go visit Dikki." I said to myself this was pure nonsense, for only this past Friday I had visited him and everything seemed fine. But I could not get rid of this uneasy feeling, so I took my bike and drove over to Dikki. The moment the adoptive mother saw me, she said: "What luck that you came!" It turned out that a woman neighbor, a member of the Dutch Nazi party, had dropped in for a visit and started asking questions about the boy. The adoptive mother took fright and asked me to take the boy elsewhere. The next morning, I came to fetch his things and learned what had happened. The previous evening, the inquisitive woman returned with another woman and insisted on seeing the boy. Luckily he was not home.

Now I want to explain why I did not maintain contact with all those people that I knew and worked with during the war. When the war ended, I was completely exhausted—perhaps not as much physically as mentally. We had devoted all our energies to them, but did not have time to "recharge our own batteries." I thought to myself: The war is over, the children are back in their places, the adults have blended anew in their social environment and need me no longer. Why maintain contact and arouse unpleasant memories of those unhappy years? That's why I left all this behind and started a new page in my life. What I did seemed plain and simple to me. I helped as much as I could, where there was a need. It was nothing extraordinary, just a natural thing, and a way of resisting the cruelty of the Nazis.

This short overview of the role of Gentile rescuers in the saving of Jewish lives necessitates the drawing of some conclusions on the significance of their deeds. Any attempt to provide convincing explanations of this particular phenomenon, however, forces us to explore human nature at a deep level; to explore the depths of the human mind is fraught with pitfalls and misinterpretations. There are, moreover, no antecedents from which we may draw lessons as to what constitutes proper human behavior in a situation of unparalleled cruelties and inhumanities by otherwise civilized nations and peoples. Bearing these precautions in mind, I offer a few observations on some common behavioral traits of the rescuers.

Decision making. Rescuers made decisions of potentially

grave consequence to themselves: to become personally involved in an undertaking that, at any moment, could backfire and land them in great danger; to face the prospect of immediate death or, at best, incarceration in a Nazi concentration camp. They decided to save the lives of persons toward whom they owed no unalterable obligation or personal responsibility.

Most rescuers, in spite of all recent studies, do not seem to have previously displayed any greater individualism than the many others who stayed aloof and did not help. They had not been prepared for such drastic and crucial decision making, from which, once the first step was taken, they could backtrack only with great difficulty. The decision to help was, in many cases, made spontaneously, especially when a destitute Jew stood in front of the rescuer, asking for help. The rescuer knew that his or her response could very well spell the difference between life and death. Many rescuers were prompted into action, especially in Eastern Europe, as a result of such tense confrontations; they found themselves challenged with becoming principal actors in a real and highly charged human drama of life and death. Others made the fateful decision to become involved after witnessing the cruelties accompanying anti-Jewish measures. Such confrontations with Nazi brutality triggered persons of diverse backgrounds into significant rescue actions; examples include the student nurse Marion Van Binsbergen (Pritchard) and the businessmen John Weidner and Oskar Schindler. The decision to risk one's life in the cause of others was undoubtedly one of the most grave decisions ever made by these persons.

Breaking with standard norms. To get involved, many had to break rank with their kinsmen who either held to traditional views that led them to oppose helping Jews, or who rationalized that the potential risks to themselves and their loved ones ruled out any readiness to help Jews (in some countries, the Germans threatened collective punishment as reprisal for helping "enemies" of the state). They also had to distance themselves from their own inbred opinions and seriously reexamine their inherited prejudices and stereotypes and neutralize these. This required great moral courage.

Taking responsibility. Rescuers knew they were incurring a great personal responsibility in helping Jews, in flagrant violation of current laws. In case of apprehension, they would not be able to fall back on any excuses; no alibis would save them; there was no passing the buck. They would bear the full penalty. In the Nazi system of orderly lawlessness, there was no just legal recourse and no appeal to a higher authority.

Moral action. The rescuers decided to obey no one but their own conscience and the call of a higher ethic. Subordinating their behavior to a moral code that lay dormant in their subconscious mind, they were able to tap a great moral strength.

Taming fear. Rescuers had to contend with ever-present fears of apprehension and punishment at the hands of the authorities. Most were surprised to learn that, with time, they could master these fears for the greater duration of the rescue operation.

Most rescuers of Jews possessed some or most of the previously enumerated qualities in various degrees. In otherwise ordinary times, such attributes are the preserve of unique morally gifted individuals. The persons in this study, however, were mostly not known for their great individualism or exceeding moral behavior, and yet for reasons still largely unknown they decided to set themselves apart from the norms of their society (especially in Eastern Europe) with regard to helping Jews. They did all this in order to uphold a cause that for many was not clearly defined in their minds.

To stray from the commonplace and go against the stream is never an easy task, given social pressures and our psychological disposition to stay within the confines of the greater group into which we are born and bred, which give meaning and direction to our lives. Add to that the self-imposed discomforts and risks concomitant with helping Jews during the Holocaust, and the riddle of human behavior, especially during times of great stress, seems even more perplexing.

Students of social behavior have noted that people are not born in a void as solitary beings functioning on their own, but as part of larger social groups. There is, perhaps, no such thing as human behavior except within specific social frameworks. From childhood onward, the individual is trained to adapt to the norms of his or her immediate larger group and to internalize social axioms by which life is regulated and given meaning. One of society's chief axioms, subtly drummed into our minds, is to obey and be guided by the counsel and wisdom of those above us, especially those in high authority. Throughout life—whether at home, in school, in the army, or at work—people turn toward authority for confirmation of their personal worth. A whole array of rewards and punishment within society reinforces a tendency in the individual toward obedience and conformity.[1]

As a result of this social programming, by adulthood, individuals have been conditioned to evaluate themselves in light of the standards and norms of their immediate larger group, whose moral standards they unwittingly assimilate as their own. Subverting their own selves to the demands of those in authority, they are in what Stanley Milgram terms the "Agentic state," under the agency of an authority. The danger in such conditioning is that when acting as part of the larger group, the individual may no longer see himself or herself as responsible for his or her own actions, attributing all initiative to a higher authority. The greater the stratified nature of the society, the more the individual suspends moral judgments over deeds performed as part of his or her official capacity.[2] When fully integrated into this higher organizational structure, as in totalitarian systems, the individual conscience merges with the organizational one, and a new creature replaces the autonomous person, unhindered by the limitations of individual morality, freed of humane inhibition, and mindful only of the sanctions of authority.[3]

The view of society as the sole arbiter of morality has been advocated by many students of human behavior. In Émile Durkheim's view, morality, in all its forms, is never met with except in society; there is no moral life outside it.[4] The alternative to society is the rule of animal passions. The sixteenth-century political philosopher Thomas Hobbes and the more recent psychoanalyst Sigmund Freud propounded similar views of society as the sole arbiter of human behavior. They expressed the fear that individuals, left to their own devices, would be their own undoing; they would bring havoc to themselves and to everybody else, since they were incapable of controlling their inherently wild passions and aggressive drives. Societies were specifically created for this very purpose: to reduce internal violence caused by humankind's aggressive nature, and to enhance our ability to deal with our environment.

All this may be true when society upholds universally accepted principles of moral behavior in the biblical sense, as espoused by the prophets. When society's prescription of law and order is at variance with fundamental humanitarian principles of moral conduct, however, the individual's subservience to country may be exploited and cunningly utilized for inhumanities of unprecedented scale—as the case of Nazi Germany amply demonstrates. Obedience, a basic element in the structure of social life, the cement that binds people to systems of authority, may at times be ennobling and educative and lead to acts of charity and kindness, but it can also lead to monumental criminal deeds.[5]

As shown by Christopher Browning, the men in Police Reserve Battalion 101 were not necessarily trained in brutality and Nazi thinking; yet, when ordered to kill indiscriminately, they stopped short of refusing, of stepping out and breaking rank. To refuse to shoot meant admitting to one's weakness, leaving one's buddies in the lurch, refusing one's share of an unpleasant collective obligation. To elect such a course meant facing the ostracism, isolation, derision, and rejection of fellow members in uniform and even being considered asocial.[6] According to Milgram's conclusions, only a few people will have the needed strength to disobey orders that are incompatible with fundamental standards of morality, given society's pressure to subordinate the individual will to that of the greater group and to respond to abstract rank, to insignias, uniforms, or titles.[7]

This digression on human behavior in various social contexts, and on individual synchronicity with the powers that be, makes us appreciate better the uniqueness of the righteous, those who threw conformity and social obedience to the wind when confronted with a moral challenge of the first degree. They are proof that there is another, not yet fully explored, dimension of human behavior that can come to the fore and manifest itself during periods of crisis. The stories of the Righteous Gentiles demonstrate that when society backslides and fails in its most fundamental moral duty, then, like running waters dammed in one place and surfacing in another, the moral breakthrough takes place at the individual level. At such times, the Righteous rescuer typifies the opposite of the fully socially subservient and simultaneously morally lacking person.

In contrast to the free-floating responsibility of the perpetrator, passing the buck elsewhere, and the nonchalant evasiveness of the bystander, the rescuer takes on the full moral responsibility for his or her deeds in caring for those in desperate need. It is a relationship whose gist is aptly expressed in the motto: "My responsibility is the one and only form in which the other exists for me."[8] It is a responsibility that arises out of the proximity of the other. Many rescuers initiated action when faced by fugitive Jews desperately in need of help, usually after they had escaped from ghettos, concentration camps, or Nazi roundups. Samuel Oliner terms such relationships an "ethics of care," which he defines as a concern with the welfare of others without the expectation of reciprocity, "a willingness to give more than is received," of "benevolence and kindness."[9]

If, as Oliner notes, bystanders were overcome with fear and a sense of hopelessness,[10] rescuers by contrast learned, through a process of trial and error, to master their fear, coupled with a gradually evolving self-confidence in themselves and their capacity to find the proper ways and means to help their wards survive the Nazi attempts to destroy them. Nechama Tec, in her study of Polish rescuers, emphasizes the individuality of most rescuers, their high level of independence and self-reliance. She makes the additional important observation that with individuality "come fewer social constraints and more freedom. More freedom in turn means more independence.... If rescuers are less controlled by their environment and more independent, they are more likely guided by their own moral imperatives, whether or not these imperatives conform to social demands."[11]

Whether, as Tec suggests, rescuers were unable to blend into their society, or, as is more probable, they were able to extricate themselves from social constraints the moment they felt that the humanitarian "sleeper" within them stood at variance with social norms, she makes the point that rescuers "were propelled by moral standards and values not necessarily shared by others, standards that did not depend on the support and approval of others but rather on self-approval. Again and again they repeated that they had to be at peace with themselves and with their own idea of what was right or wrong."[12] They saw in front of them, if only for one moment, not necessarily a distraught Jew, but a persecuted human being in desperate need of help. Tec concludes that the less the person is integrated into a community, the less constrained and controlled by the community's norms and values, the more likely the person is to resist the pressures of the community and act independently. This she terms autonomous behavior, in contrast to normative (community-sanctioned) behavior.[13]

My own study of the rescuers does not cause me to draw the somewhat far-reaching conclusion that these people stood at the margins of their societies. The evidence seems to point in the opposite direction—that most were well-integrated into their society. Still, Tec's point is a salient one; for during the whole period of the rescue operation, rescuers (especially those in Eastern Europe), whether they were conscious of it or not, were indeed removed from the mainstream of their society's thoughts and norms when these conflicted with the need to extend help to distraught Jews. But only on this point did they stand apart from their immediate larger group, particularly where anti-Semitism was part of the social cultural web.

Seen from a different perspective, if the Holocaust shows that violence is a latent predisposition in human beings, which can be triggered into action and turn into a frenzy of slaughter, it also demonstrates that there is a humanitarian "sleeper" instinct that may spark the individual to altruistic deeds under inordinately difficult conditions.[14] Who is to tell what sort of human behavior would derive in conditions of minimum social constraints? Would then a reckless and chaotic free-for-all prevail, or would more people be able to evolve into more autonomous beings and cultivate the altruistic drive at the expense of the aggressive instinct? This, of course, is a hypothetical and simplistic question. But is the proposition that men are by nature aggressive and self-destructive no less an a priori simplistic statement on the true nature of homo sapiens? Responsibility toward others may be the original and fundamental structure of human relations,[15] a responsibility that is not colored by premeditated calculations of tangible reciprocal benefits, but is rather a nonsymmetrical relationship. Zygmunt Bauman terms this a true "social," as opposed to "societal," relationship. In his words, moral behavior is conceivable only in the context of coexistence, of "being with others," not where supraindividual agencies are the arbiters of individual moral conduct.[16] The possibility of such a type of human behavior should not be discounted, especially in light of the example of the Righteous.

We do not submit that societal and bureaucratic structures are ipso facto incapable of articulating moral precepts. The Judeo-Christian ethos, rooted in the biblical message, espouses a just society, and this hope gave impetus to many messianic movements, religious as well as secular. During the eclipse of humanity represented by the Holocaust, however, humanity came into its own principally at the individual level; during that awesome period, "when the individual is working on his own, conscience is brought into play."[17] This was personified by the Righteous Gentiles of the European nations—heroes of a special kind, responsible human beings when all others had abdicated their moral responsibility.

Such persons were, relatively speaking, few (although they numbered in the tens of thousands) and represented the exception to the rule. No dry statistical comparison between the numbers of those killed and those saved, however, will do justice to the phenomenon of the Righteous. We all know that it is easier to destroy than to build, to snuff out many lives than to bring into fruition a single new life. Death comes suddenly, life is brought about slowly. Nazi Germany was one of the most powerful states in the world and had at its command sophisticated weapons, technological skills, and an obedient civil service that scrupulously obeyed orders handed down from above. This largely explains the high death toll of Jewish and other victims, by a country simultaneously at war with three other major powers (the United States, Soviet Union, and Great Britain).

In contrast to the killers, who were supported and backed by persons at the highest level of their government, the rescuers mostly stood alone. They had nowhere to turn but to themselves, to their conscience and heart. The killers could dispense with individual responsibility and claim that they were required to carry out orders, even if it meant to kill and destroy. The rescuers had to make personal decisions and abide by them. If apprehended, they could not claim constraint by others; it was the individual rescuer's choice, his or her own alone, for which the individual was fully responsible.

The killer could snuff out at will dozens, hundreds, and even thousands of lives. In Treblinka camp, a staff of some 150 Germans and Ukrainians murdered 780,000 Jews, who were brought there in cattle wagons at prescheduled intervals. No rescuer alone could save more than a handful. The more dexterous might save a dozen or slightly more. To save hundreds, one had to be extremely manipulative and use the most unorthodox methods, including lying, cheating, conniving, and bribing—and be above reproach as an ostensibly bona fide Nazi, and then still need much luck. Only one person, Oskar Schindler, was able to marshal all these talents and doubtful qualities and rescue 1,200 Jews. (In contrast to Raoul Wallenberg, Schindler could not fall back on diplomatic immunity in case of trouble.) To save more than a handful of lives, the rescuer had to make temporary alliances and rely on others—who could also betray the rescuer. The perpetrators had no such fears. They killed indiscriminately and with impunity, and went home to their buddies, wives, and children after a "hard" day's work.

The Holocaust is a terrible legacy to pass on to future generations. This unspeakable and monstrous crime, this senseless destruction of the lives of a whole people, by an ostensibly civilized nation, will forever remain an indelible stain in the human record and a stumbling block to our self-confidence and self-perception as sensible human beings. In a subtle and pernicious way, the Nazi phenomenon gives credence, not merely to the pseudo-teaching of superior and inferior races, but also to Social Darwinistic theories and related philosophies that preceded the Nazis. This world outlook can be summarized as follows: Life is a constant struggle for the survival of the fittest, or of the best and the brightest, accompanied by little mercy or compassion. In a relentless struggle, the strong prevail and the weak submit or go under. The human, as Hobbes and Freud professed, is essentially an aggressive and destructive being, bent on the fulfillment of neurotic pleasures. In order to achieve these aims, the individual retains few qualms about the feelings and needs of others. The only law that prevails in human affairs, to put it bluntly, is that of the jungle, tempered somewhat by the laws of society and religion. Society and religion came into being solely to restrain humans from wreaking havoc on others, and by derivation on themselves. For humans, given free rein, would be their own undoing; and in those instances where they act charitably toward others, they do so only to derive tangible profits and hedonistic pleasures. All this, the Holocaust abundantly confirms.

But this represents only part of a larger picture. It portrays human behavior in its worst aspects, without consideration of the other more salutary manifestations of behavior. We must, therefore, ask ourselves in all candor whether this is the kind of legacy we wish to bequeath to our children—a teaching that would encourage them to reject the fundamental premises on which Western civilization resides, the Judeo-Christian ethos of the human as a morally responsible being. Would we not be cutting away the very roots of our society?

The example of the Righteous Gentiles shows us that this somber outlook does not encompass the whole gamut of human behavior; that people can and indeed often do act in the worst ways imaginable, but that there is also another dimension to human behavior, as intrinsically human as the aggressive side. This other side is altruism and love of fellow human beings, concretized in edifying deeds, even at great discomfort and risk to oneself. If Hobbes and Freud laid bare the unpleasant, even ugly, aspects in our nature, this is only part of the picture. Let us not be mesmerized into hopeless indifference by a negative, reductionist viewpoint of human behavior; let us not embrace without qualification the view of humanity as fallen beings and born sinners, at the price of overlooking the other more positive facets in human behavior. Human backsliding need not blind us to manifestations of humanitarian behavior of a most edifying kind, which are as intrinsically human as the other less pleasant manifestations.

The human being has the capacity for doing both good and evil. This is no mere philosophical statement, but is borne out by facts. So far, over thirteen thousand persons have been awarded the Righteous title by Yad Vashem, and these constitute only a fraction of a larger population of rescuers of whom we may never know for lack of sufficient documentation. These men and women risked their lives, day in and day out, to save Jews from death, not from any expectation of future reward but simply because it had to be done. They are ample proof that there is another dimension to human behavior—goodness, kindness, and charitableness. Humans, left to themselves, need not necessarily turn into beasts. The Righteous Gentiles, in spite of pressures from the outside, from the forces of "law and order," chose to turn inward, unto themselves, and act on their own understanding of what constituted right and wrong behavior. They made personal decisions and took personal risks. Some paid with their lives. No one forced them to do so.

What about those who killed? Were they not more numerous than those who saved? There are two answers to this rhetorical question. The killers were not really the gigantic group they are made out to be. They numbered in the thousands and tens of thousands, but not in the hundreds of thousands. They were simply well organized, trained, and armed, and had the backing of a highly skilled and technologically efficient modern state and of additional tens of thousands of obedient and morally drained civil servants. The overwhelming majority of the conquered populations either cowered in silence or, egged on by their own blind anti-Semitism and love of the Nazis, applauded the perpetrators and helped them to nab the Jews, or simply stood by and did nothing. The killing of innocent Jews was not their immediate concern, especially if protesting implied high risks for themselves.

But there is an even more compelling argument to the numbers game, of comparing statistics between killers and rescuers. It has to do with the way Jewish and Christian traditions relate to historical events and place them in a meaningful context; with the ways in which persons and events are selected as role models to encourage similar behavior. The righteous Noah is the only person known to us of the whole Deluge generation. Had Abraham been able to produce 10 righteous persons in sinful Sodom, those few would have occupied a more significant place in religious history than the thousands of wicked persons who inhabited the city. In Christianity, the parable of the Good Samaritan has had a greater impact on behavior than the wicked deeds of hundreds of others.

The molding of human responsiveness over generations is rooted in positive premises and represented by symbolic acts and role models of a select few, not the many. Herein lies the uniqueness of the Righteous Gentiles. Persons like Father Jacques, who preferred imprisonment rather than betray three innocent Jewish children in his care, or Raoul Wallenberg, who left the security of his home in Sweden in order to rescue Hungarian Jewry—heroes like these are capable of firing our imagination and inspiring our behavior to a much greater degree than the more numerous perpetrators and bystanders.

The immediate lessons to be drawn from the deeds of the Righteous may then be summed up as follows:

1. The Holocaust was a true and horrifying event, notwithstanding recent attempts by some to trivialize its demonic character and historical uniqueness—or else Jews everywhere in Europe would have had no need to go into hiding, and Gentile rescuers would not have had to fear for their lives, and sometimes even pay with their lives in the attempt to save innocent Jewish men, women, and children from destruction.

2. The Holocaust raises many troubling questions about human behavior. Nazi Germany demonstrated how well-educated and law-abiding citizens can be transformed, in the words of Franklin Littell, into "technically competent barbarians."[18] At the same time, the examples of the Righteous among the Nations show us that the riddle of human behavior is more complex and not a hopeless exercise, as the crimes committed during the Holocaust would lead us to believe.

Many questions still remain unresolved, such as: Can altruism and prosocial behavior stand on the same side, or only on opposite sides of the fence? Does society encourage or discourage individual altruistic acts that, in some cases, are at odds with social norms and obligations or that have not previously been approved by the larger group? Can true altruism come to light only a certain distance from society, from its demands and pressures? The examples of the Righteous among the Nations would lead us to speculate that a greater and more authentic individuality, one in which a person feels at home with his or her true self, goes hand in hand with a greater awareness of the common human chain that binds all people, of a common belonging to what Kristen Monroe terms "John Donne's people," in the idea professed by this sixteenth-century poet: "No man is an island, entire of itself.... Any man's death diminishes me, because I am involved in mankind."[19]

3. The rescuers were a much larger phenomenon than many people are prepared to admit. But because of the forces arrayed against them, they could save only a fraction, relative to the millions murdered. Their presence and deeds do not diminish by one iota the immensity of the Holocaust, but add a ray of hope and a reaffirmation of the Judeo-Christian ethos of the primacy of the human spirit.

4. The Righteous were not saints, but ordinary people doing their bit, when everyone else either cowed under for fear of retribution, placed blinders on their eyes, or hailed the perpetrators or joined them. Herein lies the significance of their deeds.

5. The Righteous phenomenon is ample proof that it was indeed possible to help. Fear has a paralyzing effect but need not bring us to a complete standstill. When society fails, the individual can assert humanity's undying moral principles, even under the most trying circumstances, as thousands have demonstrated. True heroism is of the spirit, not of crude matter. The human being is (or at least can be) a responsible being. Caring for the helpless other represents a most elevated form of self-fulfillment.

6. The rescuers saved Jews not necessarily because of their love of Jews, but because they felt that every human being, whatever his or her worth and merit, has a right to life and a minimum decent existence; that this most precious gift ought not be arbitrarily trampled upon. They believed that destroying the Jews, simply because they were born, constituted a threat to non-Jews as well; that when confronted with the challenge to save, they had no choice but to help. There is a bottom line that no one dare trespass, or else life loses its ultimate meaning and becomes indeed what the Nazis professed it to be—a brutal struggle for the survival of the fittest.

7. The example of the Righteous can serve as a potent palliative against depressive and hopeless feelings pro-

duced in us by a confrontation with the hellish world of the Holocaust. It represents a barrier against the psychologically battering effect of the Nazi legacy. The Righteous provide us with true heroes, versus the villains of whom we hear so much. The Righteous show us that the individual person does have an intrinsic wisdom of what constitutes good and evil behavior, and that the individual's decision to act does make a difference; that even when one is living under totalitarian conditions, social pressure can be overcome. By identifying with the Righteous, we lay claim to the goodness in us, which is as inherently human as the other less pleasant manifestations in our behavior.

The fact that there were not many more such persons ought not distract us from the significance of those who acted in the best interest of humanity. Most people were inhibited from acting likewise by fear of the Nazis, a centuries-bred anti-Semitism, and social disapproval of such acts. At the same time, in every country that felt the frightening stomp of the Nazi boot, the Righteous were to be found. This a comforting sign that the search for the ultimate better society of human beings, which is the goal of all of the world's major religions, is not an empty quest. The deeds of the Righteous Gentiles are a reminder that this quest is still filled with much energy, drive, and hope.

Appendix

The Righteous among the Nations at Yad Vashem

In 1953, Israel's parliament enacted a law establishing in Jerusalem a memorial by the name of Yad Vashem to commemorate the six million Jewish victims of the Holocaust who perished at the hands of the Nazis and their collaborators. An important stipulation in the law required that Yad Vashem also honor "the Righteous among the Nations who risked their lives to save Jews." Consequently, the Righteous program is endowed with the official backing of the State of Israel.

Since 1962, a special commission made up of independent members of various professions has studied applications for the Righteous title. Named the Commission for the Designation of the Righteous, it is headed by a Supreme Court justice and is charged with the task of deciding on whom to award the title of "Righteous among the Nations." To guide it in its work, the commission follows certain criteria in examining all pertinent documentation. Testimonies are solicited, principally from survivors and rescuers, but also from other eyewitnesses and, when necessary, from reputable archival institutions.

In order to arrive at a fair and proper evaluation of the rescuer's deeds and motivations, the commission takes into consideration the following factors:

1. How was the original contact made between the rescuer and the rescued?

2. What was the nature of the aid extended?

3. Was any material compensation paid in return for the aid, and if so, in what amount?

4. What dangers and risks faced the rescuer?

5. What were the rescuer's motivations, insofar as this is ascertainable: friendship, altruism, religious belief, humanitarian considerations, or other?

6. What evidence is available from the side of the rescued persons? (This is an almost indispensable precondition for the purpose of this program.)

7. Do any other relevant data and pertinent documentation shed light on the authenticity and uniqueness of the story?

In general, when the data on hand clearly demonstrate that a non-Jewish person risked his or her life, freedom, and safety in order to rescue one or several Jews from the threat of death or deportation to death camps, without exacting in advance monetary compensation, the rescuer is qualified for serious consideration of the Righteous title. This applies equally to rescuers who have since passed away.

A person recognized as a "Righteous among the Nations" is awarded a specially minted medal bearing his or her name, a certificate of honor, and the privilege of having his or her name added to the Righteous Wall of Honor at Yad Vashem. (This last is in lieu of tree planting, which was discontinued for lack of space.)

The Medal of the Righteous, designed by Nathan Karp of Jerusalem, gives both artistic and symbolic expression to the talmudic saying: "He who saves a single life is as though he has saved the whole world." Two hands grasping a lifeline of twisted barbed wire seem to reach out from a void, while the lifeline circling the globe and giving it impetus proclaims that deeds such as those of the Righteous justify the world's existence and our faith in humanity.

The Certificate of Honor reads:

> This is to certify that on its session of _____ the Commission for the Designation of the Righteous, established by Yad Vashem, the Holocaust Heroes' and Martyrs' Remembrance Authority, on the basis of evidence presented before it, has decided to honor _____,

> who during the Holocaust period in Europe, risked ___ life to save persecuted Jews. The Commission, therefore, has accorded _____ the Medal of the Righteous among the Nations and has authorized _____ to have ___ name inscribed on the Righteous Wall of Honor, at Yad Vashem, Jerusalem Vashem, Jerusalem.

The awards are distributed to the rescuers, or next of kin, in moving ceremonies during their visit to Israel. Those not able to make the trip are similarly honored in their countries of residence through the good offices of Israeli diplomatic representatives, in public ceremonies attended by government representatives and with wide media coverage.

To date, more than 13,000 men and women have been recognized as Righteous among the Nations. This figure, which includes family members who shared in the rescue of Jews, represents more than 5,000 authenticated rescue stories. These numbers do not present a realistic portrait of the numbers of persons saved. For instance, of those recognized, over 4,000 are from Poland, and some 3,600 are from the Netherlands. The two figures combined make up 69 percent of all rescuers but, paradoxically, represent countries where the fraction of survivors was among the lowest in Europe. These figures, in truth, represent the flow of information reaching Yad Vashem, not the actual rescue figures for each Nazi-dominated country.

Yad Vashem's current policy is to continue the Righteous program for as long as necessary, for as long as requests for the Righteous title are received and are supported by solid evidence meeting the criteria for this honor.

Righteous among the Nations per Country and Ethnic Origin (as of 1995)[1]

Poland	4,478
Netherlands	3,774
France	1,249
Belgium	685
Ukraine	431
Germany	294
Czech Rep. and Slovakia	301

Hungary	283
Lithuania	266
Italy	177
Greece	178
Yugoslavia (all regions)	135
Russia	139
Austria	78
Albania	48
Romania	46
Latvia	35
Switzerland	19
Bulgaria	13
Denmark (2)	12
England	9
Sweden	7
Moldova	5
Norway (2)	6
Armenia	3
Spain	3
Luxembourg	1
Brazil	1
Estonia	1
Japan	1
Portugal	1
Turkey	1
U.S.A.	1
Total Persons	12,681

1. These figures are based solely on material made available to Yad Vashem and are in no way to be construed as reflecting the actual number of Jews saved in each country. For instance, more Jews were rescued in Belgium than in Holland, yet we have six times as many persons for Holland as we do for Belgium; the same for Italy with relation to Poland. On the other hand, although fewer Jews were saved in Poland and the Netherlands than in other countries, rescue possibilities were more difficult in these two countries than elsewhere in Europe.

2. The underground movements in Denmark and Norway played a major role in the rescue of the Jews in their communities. These two organizations have asked that no individual names be divulged.

Notes

File references pertain to files at Yad Vashem, Department of the Righteous among the Nations.

Chapter 1

1. See David Wyman, *The Abandonment of the Jews* (New York: Pantheon, 1984).

Chapter 2

1. Rozalia Paszkiewicz, file 44; also Wiktoria Pokrywka, file 1061.
2. See Viktor Kugler, file 706.
3. Hendrina Taselaar-Ponsen, file 3443.
4. Valenti Beck, file 2687.
5. See Leon Weliczker-Wells, *The Janowska Road* (New York: Macmillan, 1963), 224–31.
6. Hubert Pentrop and others, file 463.
7. Weliczker-Wells, *The Janowska Road,* 227–54.
8. Richard Gutteridge, *Open Thy Mouth for the Dumb* (Oxford, England: Basil Blackwell, 1976), 103.
9. Ibid., 104.
10. Ibid., 273–74.
11. Ibid., 141, 232.
12. Some estimates place the figure higher; see ibid., 132.
13. Ibid., 185.
14. Ibid., 251–52.
15. Ibid., 312.
16. See also Valdemar and Nina Langlet, file 101.
17. See Ivan Yatsyuk, file 2656.
18. See the similar Pieter Linschoten story (file 2734), in chapter 5.
19. This story appears in the case of Andreas Szeptycki, file 421.
20. Herta Mueller, file 678.

Chapter 3

1. Waclaw Nowinski, file 611.
2. Zofia Kubar, *Double Identity* (New York: Hill & Wang, 1989), 159–61.
3. Ibid., 10–11.
4. Ibid., 17.
5. Franciszka Kotowicz, file 4178.
6. Miriam Peleg, *Outside the Ghetto Walls* (in Hebrew) (Jerusalem: Yad Vashem, 1987), 43.
7. Ibid., 139.
8. See also literature on Monsignor Angelo Rotta, in Randolph L. Braham, *The Politics of Genocide,* 2 vols. (New York: Columbia Univ. Press, 1981); see index under Rotta for source references. Levai Jeno, *Black Book on the Martyrdom of Hungarian Jewry* (Zurich: Central European Times, 1948), 197–201.
9. Janina Zemian, manuscript, Department of the Righteous, Yad Vashem.
10. For example, Kazimiera Marendowska, file 3555.

Chapter 4

1. See Rev. Georges Cazalis's description of such a crossing, in Jeanne Merle d'Aubigne et al., *Les Clandestins de Dieu* (Paris: Fayard, 1968), 189–201.
2. Teofilius Zarnauskas, file 4764. The processing of this case was terminated on the request of the rescued person.
3. Erwin and Gertruda Moldrzyk, file 4023.
4. See, for instance, Rev. Otto Moerike and Rev. Alfred Dilger, files 412 and 4882.
5. See Valerie and Andrea Wolffenstein, *Erinnerungen,* in file 3010a (Rev. Carl J. Strecker).
6. Elie Wiesel, *Night* (New York: Hill & Wang, 1960).
7. See note 5 above on the Wolffenstein sisters.
8. See note 4 above for source reference.
9. On Zegota-connected persons, see Helena Wojcik, Jozefa Kaliczynska, Stanilawa Cebulakowa, and Lucia Kobylinska, files 1832, 1833, 1773, 1897.
10. See Georgos Peanas and Georgos Kaloyeromitros, files 3699, 3670.
11. The stories of Attila Szombathy (file 3898) and of Kalman Horvath (file 5012) further illustrate the crucial role of Hungarian commanders of labor battalions in facilitating the flight of their workers, at a time when persecution of Jews had become the official policy of the Hungarian government.

Chapter 5

1. See the special edition by Johannes Blum, *Pére Bruno*

Reynders, Héros de la Résistance (Brussels: Les Carrefours de la Cité, 1991), 75.

2. See also Carol Rittner and Sondra Meyers, eds., *The Courage to Care* (New York: New York Univ. Press, 1986), 31–32.

3. John and Juliette Charrière, file 4100.

4. See also the file on Nicholas Winton (5109); he was not awarded the Righteous title because of lack of risk by the rescuer (he operated out of England).

Chapter 6

1. This contrasts sharply with the weak statement issued by the head of the Hungarian Catholic Church, Cardinal Seredi, in 1944, in which he condoned the government's anti-Jewish policy but cautioned against excessive measures. Even this diluted pastoral letter was withdrawn at the last moment after the government guaranteed the cardinal that Jewish converts to Christianity would be granted special care and not be abused in the same fashion as full Jews. See R. L. Braham, *The Politics of Genocide: The Holocaust in Hungary*, 2 vols. (New York: Columbia Univ. Press, 1981), 1034–40.

2. Under Article 19 of the Franco-German armistice of June 1940, the French were obligated to surrender to the Germans, on demand, any German national, or national of any country under German control. These persons were sought by the Gestapo because of their known previous anti-Nazi stance.

3. On Roosevelt's halfhearted consent to this operation, see Mary Jayne Gold, *Crossroads Marseilles, 1940* (Garden City, N.Y.: Doubleday, 1980). Gold relates that, exasperated after trying for twenty minutes to persuade her husband (on the phone) "with reasonable arguments" and getting nowhere, Mrs. Roosevelt (in the presence of the founding members of the committee who had come to solicit her help) threatened that her friends, with her encouragement, would rent a ship to bring the refugees over the Atlantic. "If necessary, the ship will cruise up and down the East Coast until the American people, out of shame and anger, force the President and the Congress to permit these victims of political persecution to land!" Hearing this, the president relented and agreed to instruct the State Department to issue the extra 200 visas; see Gold, pp. xiii–xiv.

4. Varian Fry, *Surrender on Demand* (New York: Random House, 1945), 12–13.

5. Ibid., 31.

6. Ibid., 107, 216, 218.

7. Ibid., 128. During one of his visits to the U.S. embassy in Vichy, Fry was shown a cable from the State Department, which read: "This government cannot countenance the activities as reported of Dr. Bohn [a colleague of Fry's] and Dr. Fry and other persons in their efforts in evading the laws of coun-

tries with which the United States maintains friendly relations" (ibid., 81).

8. Ibid., 86, 125, 219.

9. Ibid., 80.

10. Ibid., 219, 221–22, 224.

11. Fry (p. 229) notes that he was told that "my expulsion had been ordered by the Ministry of the Interior, with the approval of the American embassy, and neither the Embassy nor the Interior had any intention of reversing the verdict."

12. Gold, *Crossroads Marseilles*, 151.

13. By May 1941, 15,000 persons had been handled by Fry's organization, of whom 1,800 were found to be within the organization's scope of aid; these represented a total of 4,000 persons, out whom 1,000 were sent out of the country.

14. Jan Karski, *Story of a Secret State* (Boston: Houghton Mifflin, 1944), 325. See also Brewster Chamberlain, ed., *The Liberation of the Nazi Concentration Camps 1945* (Washington, D.C.: U.S. Holocaust Memorial Council, 1987), 177.

15. Karski, *Story of a Secret State*, 326.

16. Ibid., 177.

17. Ibid., 327.

18. Ibid., 327–28.

19. Ibid., 329.

20. Ibid., 330.

21. Ibid., 332.

22. Ibid., 344–45, 352.

23. See ibid., 180, for the list of influential public figures whom Karski met.

24. Ibid., 181.

25. Ibid.

Chapter 7

1. Yad Vashem Archives.

2. Yad Vashem Archives.

3. Leon Weliczker-Wells, *The Janowska Road* (New York: Macmillan, 1963), 322.

4. Raul Hilberg, *Perpetrators, Victims, Bystanders* (New York: HarperCollins, 1992), 314, note 50.

5. Fiodor Kalenczuk, file 346.

6. See Emanuel Ringelblum, *Polish-Jewish Relations* (Jerusalem: Yad Vashem, 1974), 123–28, 184–85, 224–25, 303–4, and elsewhere.

7. Christopher Browning, *Ordinary Men* (New York: Harper Collins, 1992), 156–57.

8. Nechama Tec, *When Light Pierced the Darkness* (New York: Oxford Univ. Press, 1986), 54, 55, 58.

9. Ibid., 138, 143.

10. Alexander Donat, *The Holocaust Kingdom* (New York: Holt, Rinehart & Winston, 1985), 355–60.

11. Tec, *When Light Pierced the Darkness,* 198, 111–12.

12. Miriam Peleg, *Outside the Ghetto Walls* (in Hebrew) (Jerusalem: Yad Vashem, 1987), 5.

13. Weliczker-Wells, *The Janowska Road,* 238.

14. Ibid., 256–57.

15. Jan and Maria Kurowski, file 5822.

16. Of the 308 survivors studied by Tec, some 85 percent experienced close calls with arrest due to denouncement; 71 percent experienced blackmail (p. 47).

Chapter 8

1. Stanley Milgram, *Obedience to Authority* (New York: Harper & Row, 1974), 147, 371.

2. Ibid., 8, 134, 143, 147, 155.

3. Ibid., 124, 131, 188.

4. Zygmunt Bauman, *Modernity and the Holocaust* (Ithaca, N.Y.: Cornell Univ. Press, 1989), 173.

5. Milgram, *Obedience to Authority,* 371.

6. Christopher Browning, *Ordinary Men* (New York: HarperCollins, 1992), 72, 87, 125, 129, 185.

7. Milgram, *Obedience to Authority,* 6, 137.

8. Bauman, *Modernity and the Holocaust,* 182.

9. Samuel and Pearl Oliner, *The Altruistic Personality* (New York: Macmillan, 1988), 163.

10. Ibid., 146.

11. Nechama Tec, *When Light Pierced the Darkness* (New York: Oxford Univ. Press, 1986), 154, 160, 180.

12. Ibid., 160, 164.

13. Ibid., 152, 176–77, 190.

14. Bauman, *Modernity and the Holocaust,* 168.

15. Ibid., 183.

16. Ibid., 177, 179.

17. Milgram, *Obedience to Authority,* 129.

18. Franklin L. Littell, *The Crucifixion of the Jews* (New York: Harper & Row, 1975), 14.

19. Kristen Monroe, M. Karbon, and U. Klingemann, "Altruism and the Theory of Rational Action: Rescuers of Jews in Nazi Europe," *Ethics 101* (October 1990): 117.

Bibliography

Anger, P. *With Raoul Wallenberg in Budapest: Memories of the War Years in Hungary.* Translated by D. M. Paul and M. Paul. New York: Holocaust Library, 1981.

Arad, Y., Y. Gutman, and A. Margaliot, eds. *Documents on the Holocaust.* Jerusalem: Yad Vashem, 1981.

Barnouw, D., and G. Van der Stroom. *The Diary of Anne Frank: The Critical Edition.* New York: Doubleday, 1969.

Bartoszewski, W., and Z. Lewin. *The Righteous among the Nations: How Poles Saved Jews.* London: Earls Court, 1969.

Bauminger, A. *The Righteous.* Jerusalem: Yad Vashem, 1983.

Bejski, M. "The `Righteous among the Nations' and Their Part in the Rescue of Jews." In *Rescue Attempts during the Holocaust,* Proceedings of the Second Yad Vashem International Historical Conference, Jerusalem, 8–11 April 1974: 627–47. New York: Ktav, 1978.

Bierman, J. *Righteous Gentile: The Story of Raoul Wallenberg.* New York: Viking, 1981.

Boehm, E. H. *We Survived: The Stories of Fourteen of the Hidden and the Hunted of Nazi Germany.* New Haven, Conn.: Yale Univ. Press, 1949.

Borwicz, M. *Les Vies Interdites* (Fobidden lives). Paris: Casterman, 1969.

Braham, R. L. *The Politics of Genocide: The Holocaust in Hungary.* 2 vols. New York: Columbia Univ. Press, 1981.

Carpi, D. "The Rescue of Jews in the Italian Zone of Occupied Croatia." In *Rescue Attempts during the Holocaust,* 465–525.

Chary, F. B. *Bulgarian Jewry and the Final Solution, 1940-1944.* Pittsburgh: Univ. of Pittsburgh Press, 1972.

Dawidowicz, L. S. *The War Against the Jews 1933-1945.* New York: Holt, Rinehart & Winston, 1975.

De Jong, L. "Help to People in Hiding." *Delta: A Review of Arts, Life and Thought in the Netherlands* 8, no. 19 (Spring 1965): 37–79.

Deutschkron, I. *Ich Trug den Gelben Stern* (I wore the yellow star). Koeln: Wissenshcaft und Politik, 1978.

Donat, A. *The Holocaust Kingdom: A Memoir.* New York: Holt, Rinehart & Winston. 1965.

Fabre, E. *Les Clandestins de Dieu: CIMADE 1939-1945.* Paris: Fayard, 1968.

Fleischner, E., ed. *Auschwitz: Beginning of a New Era?* Hoboken, N.J.: Ktav, 1977.

Fogelman, E. *Conscience and Courage: Rescuers of Jews During the Holocaust.* New York: Doubleday, 1994.

Ford, H. *Flee the Captor.* Nashville: Southern Publishing Assoc., 1966.

Frank, A. *The Diary of a Young Girl.* Garden City, N.Y.: Doubleday, 1967.

Friedman, P. "Righteous Gentiles in the Nazi Era." In *Roads to Extinction: Essays on the Holocaust.* Edited by A. J. Friedman. Philadelphia: Jewish Publication Society, 1980, 409–21.

________. *Roads to Extinction: Essays on the Holocaust.* Edited by A. J. Friedman. Philadelphia: Jewish Publication Society, 1980.

________. *Their Brothers' Keepers.* New York: Holocaust Library, 1978.

Garfinkels, B. *Les Belges face à la Persécution Raciale, 1940-1944.* Brussels: Université Libre, 1965.

Gilbert, M. *The Holocaust: The Jewish Tragedy.* London: Fontana, 1986.

________. *The Macmillan Atlas of the Holocaust.* New York: Macmillan, 1982.

Goldstein, B. *Five Years in the Warsaw Ghetto.* Garden City, N.Y.: Doubleday, 1961.

Gross, L. *The Last Jews in Berlin.* New York: Simon & Schuster, 1982.

Grossman, K. *Die Unbesungenen Helden* (The unknown heroes). Berlin Grúnewald: Arani Verlag, 1961.

Gutman, I., ed. *Encyclopedia of the Holocaust.* 4 vols. New York: Macmillan, 1990.

Gutman, Y., and S. Krakowski. *Unequal Victims: Poles and Jews during World War II.* New York: Holocaust Library, 1986.

Gutman, Y., and L. Rothkirchen, eds. *The Catastrophe of European Jewry.* Jerusalem: Yad Vashem, 1976.

Gutman, Y., and E. Zuroff, eds. *Rescue Attempts during the Holocaust.* Proceedings of the Second Yad Vashem International Historical Conference, Jerusalem, 8–11 April 1974. New York: Ktav 1978.

Hackel, S. *Pearl of Great Price: The Life of Mother Maria Skobtsova 1891-1945.* London: Darton, Longman & Todd, 1981.

Haesler, A. *The Lifeboat Is Full: Switzerland and the Refugees, 1933-1945.* New York: Funk & Wagnalls, 1969.

Hallie, P. *Lest Innocent Blood Be Shed: The Story of Le Chambon and How Goodness Happened There.* New York: Harper & Row, 1979.

Heller, C. S. *On the Edge of Destruction: Jews of Poland Between the*

Two World Wars. New York: Schocken Books, 1980.

Hellman, P. *Avenue of the Righteous*. New York: Bantam Books, 1981.

Herzer, I. "How Italians Rescued Jews." *Midstream* (June/July 1983): 35–38.

Hilberg, R. *The Destruction of the European Jews*, vols. 1–3. New York: Holmes & Meier, 1985.

Horbach, M. *Out of the Night*. New York: Frederick Fell, 1967.

Huneke, D. *The Moses of Rovno*. New York: Dodd, Mead & Co., 1985.

———. "A Study of Christians Who Rescued Jews during the Nazi Era." *Humboldt Journal of Social Relations* 9, no. 1 (1981/82): 144–50.

Im Hof-Piguet, *A.-M. La Filiere: En France Occupee 1942-1944* (The network: in occupied France). Yverdon-les-Bains, Switzerland: Edition de la Thiele, 1985.

Joutard, C., C. Poujol, and P. Cabanel. *Cevennes: Terre de Refuge (1940-1944)* (Cevennes: land of refuge). Club Cevenol: Presses du Languedoc, 1987.

Karski, J. *Story of a Secret State*. Boston: Houghton Mifflin, 1944.

Keneally, T. *Schindler's List*. New York: Simon & Schuster, 1982.

Kermish, J. "The Activities of the Council of Aid to Jews ('Zegota') in Occupied Poland." In *Rescue Attempts during the Holocaust*, 367–98.

Krakauer, M. *Lichter im Dunkel*. Stuttgart: Quellverlag, 1980.

Kubar, Z. *Double Identity: A Memoir*. New York: Hill & Wang, 1989.

Kugler, V. "The Reminiscences of Victor Kugler, the `Mr. Kraler' of Anne Frank's Diary." *Yad Vashem Studies* 13 (1979): 353–85.

Laqueur W., and R. Breitman. *Breaking the Silence: The Secret Mission of Eduard Schulte Who Brought the World News of the Final Solution*. London: Bodley Head, 1986.

Latour, A. *The Jewish Resistance in France 1940-1944*. Translated by I. R. Ilton. New York: Holocaust Library, 1981.

Lazare, L. *Le Livre des Justes*. Paris: J. C. Lattes, 1993.

Leboucher, F. *The Incredible Mission of Father Benoit*. Translated by J. F. Bernard. Garden City, N.Y.: Doubleday, 1969.

Leuner, H. D. *When Compassion Was a Crime: Germany's Silent Heroes 1933-1945*. London: Oswald Wolf, 1966.

Levin, N. *The Holocaust: The Destruction of European Jewry, 1933-1945*. New York: Schocken Books, 1973.

Littell, F. H. *The Crucifixion of the Jews*. New York: Harper & Row, 1974.

Littell, F. H., and H. G. Locke, eds. *The German Church Struggle and the Holocaust*. Detroit: Wayne State Univ. Press, 1974.

London, P. "The Rescuers: Motivational Hypotheses about Christians Who Saved Jews from the Nazis." In *Altruism and Helping Behavior*, edited by J. R. Macaulay and L. Berkowitz. New

York: Academic Press, 1970, 241–50.

Lowrie, D. A. *The Hunted Children: The Dramatic Story of the Heroic Men and Women Who Outwitted the Nazis to Save Thousands of Helpless Refugees in Southern France During World War II.* New York: W. W. Norton, 1963.

Marrus, M. R., and R. O. Paxton. *Vichy France and the Jews.* New York: Schocken Books, 1981.

Midlarsky, M. I. "Helping During the Holocaust: The Role of Political, Theological and Socioeconomic Identifications." *Humboldt Journal of Social Relations* 13, no. 1–2 (1985/86): 285–305.

Midlarsky, E., and L. Baron, eds. *Altruism and Prosocial Behavior: A Special Issue. Humboldt Journal of Social Relations* 13, nos. 1–2. Arcata, Calif.: Humboldt State Univ. Reproduction Center, 1986.

Monroe, K., M. Karbon, and U. Klingemann. "Altruism and the Theory of Rational Action: Rescuers of Jews in Nazi–Europe." *Ethics 101* (October 1990): 117.

Morley, J. F. *Vatican Diplomacy and the Jews during the Holocaust, 1933-1943.* New York: Ktav, 1980.

Morse, A. D. *While Six Million Died: A Chronicle of American Apathy.* New York: Random House, 1967.

Neshamit, S. "Rescue in Lithuania During the Nazi Occupation." In *Rescue Attempts during the Holocaust,* 289–331.

Oliner, S. P., and P. M. Oliner. *The Altruistic Personality: Rescuers of Jews in Nazi Europe.* New York: Free Press, 1988.

Paldiel, M. "The Altruism of the Righteous Gentiles." In *Holocaust and Genocide Studies* 3, no. 2 (1988): 187–96.

________. "Fear and Comfort: The Plight of Hidden Jewish Children in Wartime Poland." In *Holocaust and Genocide Studies* 6, no. 4 (1991): 397–413.

________. "Hesed and the Holocaust." *Journal of Ecumenical Studies* 23, no. 1 (Winter 1986): 90–106.

________. *The Path of the Righteous: Gentile Rescuers of Jews during the Holocaust.* Hoboken, N.J.: Ktav, 1993.

________. "Radical Altruism: Three Case Studies." *Midstream* 33 (April 1987): 35–39.

________. "Sparks of Light." In Libowitz, ed., *Faith and Freedom: A Tribute to Franklin H. Littell.* Oxford: Pergamon Press, 1987, 45–69.

________. "To the Righteous among the Nations Who Risked Their Lives to Rescue Jews." *Yad Vashem Studies* 19. Edited by A. Weiss. Jerusalem: Yad Vashem, 1968, 403–25.

________. Articles on: Abegg, E.; Andre, J.; Baublys, P.; Beccari, A.; Benoit, M.; Binkiene, S.; Bogaard, F.; Borkowska, A.; Choms, W.; Deffaugt, J.; Douwes, A.; Evert, A.; Getter, M.; Grüninger, P.; Hautval, A.; Helmrich, E.; Kowalski, W.; Le Chambon sur Lignon; Lipke, J.; Lutz, C.; NV Group; Nevejean, Y.; Nicolini, G.; Overduijn, L.; Schindler, O.; Schmid, A.; Sendler, I., Simaite, O., Skobtsova, E., Sousa Mendes, A., Sugihara, S., Sztehlo, G.; Van der Voort, H.; Zabinski, J. In I. Gutman, ed.,

Encyclopedia of the Holocaust. 4 vols. New York: Macmillan, 1990.

Poliakov, L. *Harvest of Hate.* New York: Holocaust Library, 1979.

Poliakov, L., and J. Sabille. *Jews under the Italian Occupation.* New York: Howard Fertig, 1983.

Presser, J. *The Destruction of the Dutch Jews.* New York: E. P. Dutton, 1969.

Ramati, A. *The Assissi Underground: The Priests Who Rescued Jews.* New York: Stein & Day, 1978.

Ringelblum, E. *Polish-Jewish Relations During the Second World War.* Edited by J. Kermish and S. Krakowski. New York: Howard Fertig, 1976.

Rittner, C., and S. Myers, eds. *The Courage to Care.* New York: New York Univ. Press, 1986.

Rorty, J. "Father Benoit." *Commentary* 2/6 (December 1946): 507–13.

Rosen, D. *The Forest My Friend.* Translated by M. S. Chertoff. New York: World Federation of Bergen–Belsen Association, 1971.

Rothkirchen, L. "Czech Attitudes Towards the Jews During the Nazi Regime." *Yad Vashem Studies* 13 (1979): 287–320.

Silver, E. *The Book of the Just.* London: Weidenfeld & Nicolson, 1992.

Steinberg, L. *Le Comité de Défense des Juifs en Belgique 1942-1944* (The Jewish Defense Committee in Belgium). Brussels: 1973.

Szonyi, D. M. *The Holocaust: An Annotated Bibliography and Resource Guide.* New York: National Jewish Resource Center, 1985.

Tec, N. *Dry Tears: The Story of a Lost Childhood.* New York: Oxford Univ. Press, 1984.

________. *When Light Pierced the Darkness: Christian Rescue of Jews in Nazi-Occupied Poland.* New York: Oxford Univ. Press, 1986.

Ten Boom, C. *The Hiding Place.* London: Hodder & Stoughton, 1971.

Thomas, G., and M. Witts. *Voyage of the Damned.* New York: Stein & Day, 1974.

Warmbrunn, W. *The Dutch under German Occupation 1940-1945.* Stanford, Calif.: Stanford Univ. Press, 1979.

Wells, L. *The Janowska Road.* New York: Macmillan, 1963.

Wiesel, E. *Night.* New York: Hill & Wang, 1960.

Wundheiler, L. N. "Oskar Schindler's Moral Development During the Holocaust." *Humboldt Journal of Social Relations* 13, nos. 1 & 2, 333–56. Arcata, Calif.: Humboldt State Univ. Reproduction Center, 1986.

Yahil, L. *The Rescue of Danish Jewry: Test of a Democracy.* Translated by M. Gradel. Philadelphia: Jewish Publication Society, 1969.

Zuccotti, S. *The Holocaust, the French and the Jews.* New York: Basic Books, 1993.

________. *The Italians and the Holocaust: Persecution, Rescue, and Survival.* New York: Basic Books, 1987.

Index

Number in brackets indicates file number in the Dept. of the Righteous, Yad Vashem, for a person awarded the title of "Righteous among the Nations" by Yad Vashem. An asterisk sign after this number indicates file number for person not awarded the Righteous title.

Abbeloos, Antoine, 18, [944]
Abraham, Ruth, 119
Abramowicz, Natalia, 164, [533]
Adamowicz, Irena, 97, [3075]
Ader, Reverend Bastiaan, 36, 90, 170, [423]
Adrien, Father Jean, 38, [1033]
AK (Armja Krajowa = Home Army), Poland, 95–6, 177–78
Alekseyev, Serafin, 98, [5375]*
Alfonsa, Sister. *See* Wasowska, Eugenia
Alice, Princess, 72, [5643]
Althaus, Paul, 31
Anagnostopoulos, Dr. Kostas, 72, [4204]
Andre, Abbe Joseph, 39, 107, 168, [486]
Anger, Per, 144, [1915]
Anhalt, Istvan, 58–59
Antal, Father Janos, 58, [5463]
Armann, Hugo, 100, [3254]
Aschoff, Heinrich, 81, [463]
Asher, Margaret, 184–85
Assanowicz, Halina, 114–15, [2376]
Assisi, Italy, 34

Babilinska, Gertruda, 114, [11]
Baptists in Ukraine, 37, 132–33
Barak, Aaron, 76–77
Baratz, Miriam, 83
Barazetti, Bill, 123–24, [5904]
Barot, Madeleine, 95, [3830]
Barouch, Abraham, 97
Bartulovic, Olga, 81, 97, [185]
Battel, Albert, 149–50, [1979]
Bauman, Zygmunt, 195
Beccari, Father (Don) Aldo, 40, 69, 89, [35]
Bechar, Betty, 118
Beck, Valenti, 207, [2687]
Bejski, Moshe, 125–27, 149
Benoit-Marie, Father (Peteul, Pierre), 55, 88–89, [201]
Bereska, Helena, 120, [321]
Berger, Sylvia, 55–56
Bernadotte, Count Folke, 169–70
Bielski, Tuvia, 98–99
Billieres, Marcel, 44, [44]
Bindel, Helene, 155, [2203]
Binkiene, Sofija, 76, [383]
Birgy, Rolande, 68, [2613]
Blaauw, Cornelia, 122, [233]
Boccard, Father Raymond, 89, [3601]
Bockma Harmen & Sara, 109, [374]
Boclet, Suzanne, 45, [4747]
Boczkowska, Zofia, 151–52, [239]
Bogaard, Johannes, 25, [28]
Bogdanowicz, Anna, 75, 163, [2685]

Bondzic, Grozdana, 83, [1810]
Boratynski, Boleslaw, 21, [5134]
Borkowska, Anna, 35, [2862]
Born, Friedrich, 57, [3560]
Bouwman, Sophia, 121
Bradlo, Szczepan, 22, 184, [3351]
Bredoux, Sister Marie-Gonzague, 16, 41, [5380]
Breton, Dr. Rita, 197, [2290]
Brillenburg-Wurth, Reverend Gerrit, 47, 74, [48]
Bronowski, Dr. Alexander, 53, 153–54
Browning, Christopher, 178–79, 192
Brunacci, Father (Don) Aldo, 34, [1236]
Bruniany, Wawrzyniec, 45, [1020]
Brunin, Lucien, 112, [1108]
Bruno, Father. *See* Reynders, Father Bruno
Bunel, Lucien (Father Jacques), 42, 55, 167, [3099]
Burlingis, Wiktoria, 117–18, [5510]*

Canova, Alfonso, 69, [310]
Caraj, Jan, 29, [204]
Cardin, Josephe, 166, [5535]
Cattaneo, Lydia, 69, [873]
Cavilio, Josef, 72
Cazalis, Reverend Georges, 208
Cazals, Marcelin, 99, [5805]
CDJ (Jewish Defense Committee), Belgium, 43, 95, 107
Ceglewska, Celina, 76, [4930]
Celis, Father Louis, 38–39, 159–61, [1777]
Chacze, Edward, 100, [213]
Chambon-sur-Lignon, France, 25, 36, 66, 73, 130–31
Charriere, John & Juliette, 44, [4100]
Chodor, Jan, 28–29, [5761]
Choms, Wladyslawa, 51, [6]
Chrysostomos, Bishop, 130, [130]
Ciesielski, Feliks & Romualda, 164, [214]
CIMADE (Protestant welfare organization), France, 95
Cohen, Felicia, 112–13
Confessing Church, Germany, 80, 90
Couvret-Damevin, Pierre, 51, [4163]
Creuzberg, Reverend Jelis; daughter Pieta, 120–21, [967]
Czismadia, Olga & Malvina, 81, [111, 3619]
Czubak, Genowefa (Sister Dolorosa), 55, 82–83, [1851]

Dabowski, Krzysztof, 184, [5436]
Dajc, Julija, 83
Dajtrowski, Andrzej, 27, 180–81, [4471]
Daman, Jeanne, 95, [560]
Damaskinos, Monsignor Theophilos, 129–30, [547]
Danzig, Nina, 114–15
David, Konrad, 79–80, [1818]
De Pury, Reverend Roland, 66, 90, 166, [1066]
De Simione, Father (Don) Giovanni, 36, 47, [174]
De Zoete family, 74
Delord, Reverend Albert, 37, [3134]
Demosthenes, Pouris, 72, [5643]
Deutscher, Claire, 155
Diamant, Lea, 112
Dilger, Reverend Alfred, 208, [4882]
Diller, Sara, 74–75
Dohmen, Nico, 109–10, [2878]
Dolorosa, Sister. *See* Czubak, Genowefa

Donat, Alexander, 179–80
Donnier, Andre, 19, [5065]
Douwes, Arnold, 25, 94, 134–35, 168, [56, 1148]
Driessen, Bert, 74, [2489]
Drzewecka, Sister Aleksandra, 117–18, [5510]
Dubois, Maurice, 68, [3195]
Dubuis, Pierre, 44, [466]
Duda, Antoni & Helena, 181, [141a]
Dumas, Abbe Antoine, 35, [4905]
Durand, Helene, 73, [1484]
Durkheim, Emil, 191
Dzywulski, Wasyl, 28, [265]

Engel, Julien, 103–04
Elzas, Carolien, 111
Emmet, Isaac, 175–76
Erben, Eva, 86
Erder, Avraham, 182
Etingin, Max, 21
Evert, Angelos, 51, 130, [553]

Favre, Father Louis, 89, 167, [193]
Ferrari, Sister Maria-Angelica, 41, [5533]
Filozof, Janina, 17–18, [952]
Finkelbrand, Sarah, 77
Finkelstein, Geertruida, 93
Fischbach, Jonas, 19
Fischer, Dr. Ludwig, 162
Fishkin, David, 146–47
Fleury, Father Jean, 73, [57]
Fogelman, Simcha, 98
Fort, Alban & Germaine, 43, 104–05, [3133]
Frank, Anne, 19, 168
Freud, Sigmund, 191, 197–98
Friedman, David, 75
Fry, Varian, 70, 137–41, [6150]

Gans, Lou, 135
Gargasz, Zofia & Jakub, 164–65, [1622]
Gau, Father Albert, 55, [3444]
Gaudefroy, Renee, 73, 102, 172–73, [1038]
Getter, Sister Matylda, 39, 185, [3097]
Geulen, Andree, 95, [4323]
Gilad, Michael, 84–85
Gineste, Marie-Rose, 128, [3256]
Girasymczuk, Pavlo, 27, 175–76, [4577]
Gittelman, Lea, 117–18
Glagolev, Father Aleksey, 56, [4998]
Glinski, Leonard, 78, [2826]
Glowiak, Zofia, 76, [2264]
Gold, Mary Jane, 139–40, 209
Goldenberg, Esther, 180–81
Goldfein, Dr. Olga, 55, 82–83
Goldman, Julian, 76
Goltz-Goldlust, Marianne, 171, [3845]
Gommans, Reverend Engelbert, 74, [2490]
Gotautas, Brother Bronius, 77, 166, [780]
Grabowski, Henryk, 97, [2653]
Grueninger, Paul, 68–69, [680]
Guichard, Georges, 44, [4161]
Gut Op Dyke, Irena, 45, [2317]
Guy, Marinette, 74, 102, [518]

Haertel, Erna, 86, [243]
Halamajowa, Franciszka, 27, 175, [2804]
Hardaga, Mustafa, 72, [2811]
Harder, Loni & Albert, 87, [225]
Hartog, Abraham, 170
Hautval, Adelaide, 135–36, 166, [100]
Helmrich, Eberhard & Donata, 26, 79, [154]
Hendriks, Leonard (Brother Bernardinus), 40–41, [2607]
Hermann, Dr. Karl, 170–71, [970]

Hesse, Reverend Helmut, 32
Hirschman, Albert, 140
Hlinka Guards, Slovakia, 173
Hobbes, Thomas, 191, 197–98
Holbek, Helga, 67, [2142]
Home Army. *See* AK (Armja Krajowa = Home Army)
Horvath, Kalman, 208, [5012]
Hryhoryszyn, Olena, 46, 83, [144]

Im Hof-Piguet, Anne-Marie, 68, [3195b]
Iwanski, Henryk & Wiktoria, 96, [54]
Izmalkova, Vera & Nadezhda, 79, [5040]

Jackow, Stanislaw, 16, 21, 144–46, [277]
Jahn, Kristof, 86, [2428]
Jesih, Father Dragutin, 173, [5418]
Job, Jozef & Stefania, 18, 152, [1828]
Joseph, Sister, 41, [3579]
Jurytko, Bruno & Bronislawa, 85–86, [4947]
Juskevicius, Mykolas, 174, [1848]

Kaczerowski, Ivan, 28, 176, [2474]
Kahn, Irene, 38
Kalenczuk, Fiodor, 210, [346]
Kaloyeromitros, Georgos, 208, [3700]
Kalwinski, Wojciech, 23, 29–30, 163, 182–183, [322]
Kaminski, Zbigniew, 18, [2425]
Kanabus, Dr. Felix, 54, [87]
Karp, Nathan, 204
Karski, Jan, 96–97, 155–58, [934]
Katz, Kalman, 176
Kees, Chardon, 169, [64]
Kerkhofs, Monsignor Louis, 39, 159, [1361a]
Kiraly, Capt. Bela, 101, [5596]
Kleiman, Frieda, 86
Klepinin, Reverend Dimitri, 42–43, 168, [3078a]
Kmita, Karolina, 47, [301]
Knezevic, Slobodan, 83, [1810]
Kobylec, Piotr, 72, [86]
Kocun, Stefan, 72, [5428]
Koerner, Nusia, 80
Korczak, Janusz, 164
Korkucz, Kazimierz, 163–64, [786]
Korlenchik, Leah, 77
Korn, Ursula, 82
Kossak-Szczucka, Zofia, 180, [2377a]
Kostrz, Andrzej, 71, [809]
Kotowicz, Franciszka, 208, [4178]
Kovner, Abba, 35
Kowalski, Wladyslaw, 46, [4]
Kozlovsky, Kustyk, 98–99, [5927]
Kozminsky, Jerzy, 20, 163, [115]
Krakauer, Max, 80, 90–91
Kruger, Gertruud, 122, [748]
Kruger, Rabbi Haim, 137
Krygier, Esther, 107–08
Kubar, Zofia, 53–54
Kugler, Victor, 168, [706]
Kuna, Reverend Vladimir, 37, [721]
Kuperszmid, Zysla, 16, 23–24
Kurjanowicz, Ignacy, 19, [819]
Kurowski, Jan & Maria, 211, [5822]

Lada, Waclaw, 51, [3377]
Langlet, Valdemar & Nina, 34, 57, [101]
Legrand, Lucien, 45, [235]
Lemaire, Reverend Jean, 166, [1039]
Lentink-de Boer, Elkje, 169, [5]
Leons, Max, 25, 94, 134
Leruth, Mathilde (Sister

Marie), 40, [486]
Lesage, Gilbert, 100, [3012]
Levin, Rachel, 91–92
Lieberman, Samuel, 85
Liedtke, Max, 149–150, [1979a]
Linschoten, Pieter; daughter Elizabeth, 121, [2734]
Lipke, Jan, 146–47, [207]
List, Heinrich, 171, [5525]
Littell, Franklin, vii–viii, 200
Livne, Malka, 85
Lomnicki, Michal, 72, [5429]
Lozinska, Pelagia, 47, [216]
Lutz, Carl, 57, 142, [46]
Maciarz, Maria, 153, [2960]

Majercik, Dr. Michal, 17, [2086]
Makuch-Szymanska, Barbara, 51, [1654]
Mamen, Hans-Christian, 61–62, 70, [1248]
Mandelbaum, Avigdor & Feiga, 28
Manilewitz, Celina, 86–87
Mans, Hendrik, 168, [2971]
Marciniak, Edward, 75, [375]
Marendowska, Kazimiera, 163, [3555]
Marie, Pierre, 99–100, [2268]
Marom, Hugo, 124
Mathieu, Camille, 74, [1098]
Maurier, Jeanette, 55, [804]
Mazak, Father Stanislaw, 91, [2788a]
Meerburg, Piet, 94, [862]
Mendes, Aristides de Sousa, 49–50, 70, 136–37, [264]
Metzger, Karola, 154–55
Mickiewicz, Waclaw & Maria, 163, [1279]
Mieloo, Laurens, 17, [855]
Mikolajkow, Dr. Alexander, 23, [90]
Milgram, Stanley, 191–192
Milice (militia), France, 172
Milkowski, Bronislawa, 116, [4028]
Miller, Esther, 184
Mingat, Anne-Marie, 113, [2249]
Mintz, Yitzhak, 181–182
Modijetsky, Charles, 45
Moerike, Reverend Otto, 208, [412]
Moldrzyk, Erwin & Gertruda, 85, [4023]
Molmans, Franciscus, 18, [941]
Monroe, Kristen, 200
Moses, Jacob, 186–87
Moshinska, Sarah, 115–17
Mueller, Herta, 208, [678]
Muller, Alice, 67
Musch, Joop, 94, 108–09, 168, [2083]
Mussert, Anton, 172
Myrgren, Reverend Erik, 37, 71, [3546]

Nadel, Estelle, 183
Neff, Dorothea, 16, [1652]
Nevejean, Yvonne, 43, 95, [99]
Newerly, Igor, 164, [2090]
Niccaci, Father Rufino, 34, [876]
Nickel, Maria, 119, [474]
Nicolini, Monsignor Giuseppe, 34, [1235]
Niemoeller, Reverend Wilhelm, 30–31
Nieuwlande village, Netherlands, 134–35
Nodot, Rene, 67, [899]
Nowinski, Waclaw, 153–54, [611]
NSB movement, Netherlands, 172
NV Group, Netherlands, 94, 108–09, 168

Oczynski, Kazimierz, 182, [4757]
Ogniewski, Irena, 122, [2019]
Ogonowski, Franciszka, 181–82, [141]

Oldak, Apolonia, 119–20, [272]
Oliner, Samuel, 193
ONE (Oeuvre National de l'Enfant), Belgium, 43, 95
OSE (Oeuvre de Secours aux Enfants), 73, 107, 167, 172
Overath, Katharina, 154–55, [4365]
Overduin, Reverend Leendert, 36, [805]

Paszkiewicz, Rozalia, 24, 207, [44]
Paukshtys, Father Bronius, 91–93, 174–75, [1143]
Paulavicius, Jonas, 20, 174, [2472]
Pawlicka, Janina, 183, [76]
Peanas, Georgos, 208, [3699]
Peleg, Miriam, 180
Pentrop, Hubert, 207, [463]
Perlasca, Giorgio, 57, 142, [3911]
Pernoud, Father Gilbert, 67, [3558]
Petenyi, Dr. Geza, 44, [2543]
Petsche, Lt. Roman, 100, [2265]
Pfleger, Br. Albert, 34, [2008]
Philip, Mireille, 51, 66–67, [1026]
Piller, Capt. Jeno, 101, [5555]
Piotrowski, Zofia, 28, [217]
Poddebniak, Father Jan, 51, 78, [3386a]
Pokrywka, Wiktoria, 24, 207, [1061]
Pontier, Reverend Gerardus, 17, 168–69, [422]
Popstephanova, Anna, 72, [2551]
Post, Johannes, 134, [124]
Postuma, Siege, 74, [2488]
Potesil, Maria, 118–19, [1400]
Prital, David, 37, 132–33
Pritchard (Van Binsbergen), Marion, 110, [1993b]
Protective Passes, 57, 142–43
Przedborski, Zisla, 112
Puchalski, Jan, 11–13, 26, [3466]
Pulver, Jacques, 51, 68

Rabinowitz, Masha, 92
Rajszczak, Feliks, 75–76, [1456]
Rakevicius Jaroslavas, 76–77, [1072]
Regereau, Sister Clotilde, 35, [6270]
Reichelberg, Arieh, 44, 112
Reviczky, Col. Imre, 101, [72]
Rexist movement, Belgium, 172
Reynders, Father Bruno, 39, 107–108, 168, [84]
Rhodes island, 5–6
Righteous Among the Nations, 2, 203–06
Rigler, Hannah, 87
Riquet, Father, 54
Robert de St. Vincent, Gen. Louis, 131, [3547]
Rodziewicz, Wiktoria, 122–23, [1178]
Romkes, Sietze, 170, [1148]
Roosevelt, Eleanor, 137
Roosevelt, Franklin, 142, 158
Rosay, Father Jean, 89, 167, [3580]
Roslan, Alexander, 16, [427]
Rotta, Monsignor Angelo, 57, 101, [8333]*
Rowe, Catherine, 121, [2737]

Safonov, Gennady, 97–98, [5496]
Sagalowicz, Dora, 78–79
Sagan, Jan, 27, [2743]
Saginur, Max & Gitya, 144–46
Saliege, Monsignor Jules-Geraud, 38, 127–29, [197]
Salzberg, Anna, 85
Saperstein, Rabbi Marc, 107
Sawa, Stefan, 182, [5013]
Schiff, Lilli, 16
Schindler, Oskar & Emilie,

125–27, 147–49, [20]
Schivo, Don Beniamino, 38, 82, [3362]
Schmid, Anton, 100, [55]
Schroeder, Gustav, 149–50, [5353]
Sekreta, Anna, 56, [5299]
Semeniuk, Ivan & Domke, 175, [14]
Sendler, Irena, 96, 114, 163, [153]
Sendler, Zofia, 115, [2514]
Seredi, Cardinal Jusztinian, 209
Seweryn, Tadeusz, 178, [2230]
Shamir, Wanda, 184–85
Simaite, Ona, 76, 165–66, [383]
Simelis, Mykolas, 20, 174, [2550]
Skobtzova, Elizaveta (Mother Marie), 42–43, 131–32, 168, [3078]
Skowronek, Janina, 16, 23–24, [784]
Slachta, Sister Margit, 34–35, [495]
Sliwinski, Leon, 75, [5013a]
Smit, Arend, 93–94, [2816]
Sobczak, Stanislaw, 183–84, [589]
Socha, Leopold, 47–48, [1379]
Sohnlein, Gisela, 109, 169–70, [3853a]
Soroka, Tadeusz, 75, [2695]
Spaak, Suzanne, 102, 167–68, [62]
Spiegel, Siegmund & Marga, 80–81
Spielberg, Steven, 149
Spiliakos, Dimitris, 81–82, [3566]
Spira, Willi, 141
St. Louis boat, 6–7
St. Vincent, Louis. *See* Robert de St. Vincent, Gen. Louis
Stakauskas, Juozas, 44, [917]
Stein, Gertrude (Sister Bernarda), 7–8
Sterno, Ida, 95
Struik, Clazina, 46, [5030]
Szturm, Helena, 152
Suchenko, Jakob, 83, 166, [2540]
Suchinski, Anton, 20, 176, [910]
Suchodolski, Adam & Stanislawa, 183, [953]
Sugihara, Sempo, 71, 141, [2861]
Swital, Dr. Stanislaw, 77–78, [1968]
Sycz, Janina, 114, [2272]
Synnestvedt, Alice, 67, [2142]
Szandorowska, Janina, 78, [2509]
Szczecinska, Maria, 21, [2126]
Szeptycki, Andreas, 207, [421]*
Szombathy, Attila, 208, [3898]*
Sztehlo, Reverend Gabor, 40, [722]
Szumielewicz, Wiktoria, 106–07, [1998]
Szwierszczak, Manko, 47, 175, [2644]

Tadra, Jan, 184, [5436]
Taquet-Mertens, Marie, 108, [3773]
Taselaar-Ponsen, Hendrina, 3443, [3443]
Tec, Nechama, 179, 193–194
Ten Boom, Corrie, 169, [330]
Theas, Monsignor Pierre-Marie, 128–29, [197]
Tiso, Father Josef, 173
Todorov, Aleksander & Blaga, 118, [1766]
Tory, Abraham & Penina, 91–92
Trocme, Reverend Andre & Magda, 36–37, 130–31, 167, [612]
Trocme, Daniel, 167, [1037]
Trojanowski, Prof. Andrzej, 54, [190]
Tzaut, Paul, 44, [828]

Ujvary, Sandor, 57, [3110]

Ulens, Victor, 74, [2411]
Uris, Leon, 136
Ustase militia, Croatia, 173

Valendovitch, Jelena, 46, 120, [1620]
Van Binsbergen, Marion. *See* Pritchard, Marion
Van Dijk, Margaretha, 110–11, 186–88, [4626]
Van Lennep, Hester, 109, [2018]
Van Thijn, Ed, 109
Van Verschuer, Anne Marie, 108–09, [2083n]
Van den Berg, Alida, 111–12, [5292a]
Van der Voort, Hanna, 109, [2879]
Van, Sister Zsuzsanna, 35, [4879]
Vancourt, Father Raymond, 38, [909]
Verduijn, Arie, 74, [2487]
Verhaag, Piet, 74, [2491]
Vidal, Juliette, 74, 102, [518]
Vigneron, Edouard, 99–100, [2268a]
Vitus, Michal; daughter Viera, 173, [2935]
Von Galen, Bishop Klement, 32
Von Jan, Reverend Julius, 32
Voute, Hetty, 109, 169, [3853]

Wallenberg, Raoul, 142–45, [31]
Warhaftig, Dr. Zorah, 141
Wasowska, Eugenia (Sister Alfonsa), 39, [1929]
Weidner, John, 67–68, [1391]
Wells, Leon, 22–23, 29, 182–83
Wells, Stan, 87, [4042]
Westerweel, Joop, 69–70, 94, 133–34, 168, [32]
Wiejak, Alexander, 28, [5478]
Wiesel, Elie, 84
Winton, Nicholas, 123, [5109]*
Witkowski, Leo, 45
Wojtowicz brothers: Alojzy, Kazimierz, Antoni, 178, [5664]
Wolffenstein sisters, 90
Wolosianski, Izydor, 20–21, [290]
Woortman, Jaap, 94, 108–09, 168, [2083]
Wurm, Bishop Theophil, 31–32

Yad Vashem, Israel, 2–3, 203–05
Yatsyuk, Ivan, 207, [2555]

Zabinski, Dr. Jan, 45, [170]
Zalwowski, Franciszek, 26, [1151]
Zandman, Felix, 11–13
Zarnauskas, Teofilis, 208, [4764]*
Zefat, Albertus & Aaltje, 46, 170, [731]
Zegota organization, Poland, 96, 208
Zelinger, Zevi, 182
Zemian, Janina, 59–60
Zimmerman, Zevi, 71–72
Zimon, Stefania, 85, [4530]
Zwonarz, Jozef, 22, [331]